Bt 4.50

W9-CJN-803

THREE CRITICAL YEARS

THREE CRITICAL YEARS

is one of the
Makers of History Series
Other titles in the Series include:

Three Critical Years

(1904-05-06)

Maurice Paléologue

Makers of History Series

ROBERT SPELLER & SONS

New York 36   New York

© 1957 by Robert Speller & Sons, Publishers, Inc.
33 West 42nd Street
New York 36, New York

Library of Congress Catalog Card No. 57-11886

First Edition

PRINTED IN THE UNITED STATES OF AMERICA

THREE CRITICAL YEARS

Chapter I

JANUARY 1ST—FEBRUARY 5TH, 1904[1]

Friday, January 1, 1904.

YESTERDAY evening, Delcassé asked me to let him have a memorandum at the earliest possible moment on Russia's military preparations in the Far East. I took it to him first thing this morning, as I appreciate that he has been greatly worried for some days about the Russo-Japanese war and all the alarming possibilities it involves.

I arrived at the Ministry at the same time as he did. He was returning from the Elysée[2] where he had called with the other ministers for the official New Year's Day ceremonies.

He skimmed through my memorandum, asked me to indicate on a map the points where the Russians are concentrating for the offensive and then dismissed me. Before leaving, I remarked:

"What would you like me to wish you for the new year, Monsieur le Ministre?"

He did not hesitate over his answer:

"Number One; that Russia and Japan don't come to blows. That's much the most important! Number Two; wish me luck in my negotiations for agreements with England, Italy and Spain."

"Aren't you going to include Morocco?"

"I don't need to. If Russia keeps her hands free for Europe and I make my agreements with England, Italy and Spain, you'll see Morocco drop into our lap as simply and easily as a ripe apple from a tree."

Wednesday, January 6, 1904.

The negotiations for a Franco-British agreement have made good

[1] At this time I was Minister-Plenipotentiary and Deputy-Director of Political Affairs at the Ministry for Foreign Affairs. "Special business" was assigned to my department.

[2] Official residence of the French president.

1

progress.[1] Lord Lansdowne and Paul Cambon, both of them first-
class minds, have succeeded in reaching agreement on all the serious
matters at issue between the two countries—Egypt, Morocco, Siam,
the African coast, Newfoundland, etc.

A few difficulties remain to be solved in connection with the
Newfoundland question and the irritating and complicated problem of the French Shore. They are of such minor importance that
they cannot be allowed to compromise the success of the negotiations, but there is some chance that they may seriously delay the
final conclusion, as the refractory Newfoundland ministers have still
to be consulted.

Thursday, January 7, 1904.

Today I lunched with the financier X——, who is chairman of
one of our great credit institutions, one of those which are literally
stuffed up with Russian securities. Among the guests were Eugène-
Melchior de Vogüé, Paul Doumer and Gabriel Hanotaux.

Our host's face usually radiates intelligence, cynicism and resolution, but today I seemed to be looking at a somewhat lugubrious
mask.

The secret of his line of thought was betrayed by the very first
questions he asked in an anxious voice:

"Do you think there's going to be war between Russia and Japan?
Won't France and England intervene to avert such a catastrophe?"

But Vogüé, Doumer and Hanotaux were in no mood to prophesy;
or rather their usual prophetic talent found expression in such inten-
tionally guarded, vague, ambiguous and contradictory language that
their conclusions left everything to the imagination. We might have
been consulting Madame de Thèbes.

X—— turned a despairing, imploring eye on me:

"For Heaven's sake open up a bit, Paléologue . . . give us your
opinion!"

I decided on the following, non-committal, answer:

"Negotiations are in progress between St. Petersburg and Tokyo.
Whether they will succeed or fail is still in the lap of the gods, but
I think that the chances of a peaceful outcome are far from ex-
hausted."

---

[1] These negotiations, which opened on July 7th, 1903 with a personal interview
between Delcassé and Lord Lansdowne, were to lead up to the General Agreement
of April 8th, 1904.

X—— looked really frightened.

"So you don't regard a war as impossible?" he said.

"History shows that one must always allow for sheer lunacy in the affairs of nations."

The poor financier buried his face in his plate and said not a word until the meal ended. But Vogüé suddenly became oracular:

"If war breaks out, it will be a long and terrible business, because it will mean a clash between two civilisations. One of the belligerents, possibly the aggressor, would be the noble and warm-hearted Tsar, who, barely five years ago, was solemnly inviting the powers to reduce their standing armies and usher in the reign of eternal peace on the basis of international arbitration! If that's what we are going to see, and quite soon, what an irony of fate it will be! It makes me think Renan was right when he said that the Architect of the world, the *grand Démiurge*, revelled in unexpected ironies!"

Descending from these heights, Gabriel Hanotaux made the shrewd remark:

"How Berlin must be gloating over the prospect of this war!"

Our host's alarm at the very possibility of a war is only too natural: the splendid concern which he controls has for ten years been one of the principal dealers in Russian securities on the French market.

In 1892 the figure for Russian government securities quoted on the Paris exchange amounted approximately to 2,500,000,000 francs.

In 1894, a few months after the Franco-Russian alliance had been secretly signed, it rapidly rose to 8,752,000,000. In 1898 it was 11,017,000,000 and, in 1901, 11,809,000,000. Today, January 7, 1904, the figure is 12,200,000,000 (to say nothing of negotiations now in progress).

Wednesday, January 13, 1904.

At the Tsar's express request Delcassé is intervening in the Russo-Japanese negotiations with a view to inducing the Tokyo cabinet to show a more conciliatory spirit.

He has therefore invited the subtle, cunning Motono, Japanese minister in Paris, to an official discussion with him "to see what can be done to save the cause of peace." Their talk was satisfactory. Motono has wired to Tokyo for instructions.

Delcassé simultaneously informed the British government in confidence of his acceptance of the office of mediator. Discussing the matter with me, he remarked:

"This is a very ticklish job I've taken on: when I've finished calming down Japan I shall have to set about calming down Russia. I'm running the risk of quarreling with both. . . . In any event, I can't imagine my doing any good in these negotiations unless I have the support of England. If I have London behind me, I shall be all the stronger in dealing with Petersburg and Tokyo."

Tuesday, January 19, 1904.

From a secret and unimpeachable source in St. Petersburg we have learned that the Emperor William is assiduously pursuing his policy of flattering and inciting the Emperor Nicholas. He is perpetually feeding the flames of his wrath with talk about "dirty little Japan which has the impertinence to mock at great and holy Russia." He is not merely urging him to annex all the Manchu territories but trying to prove that the peninsula of Korea (220,000 square kilometres and eighteen million inhabitants) is a natural and inevitable extension of Russian domination in eastern Asia.

We are told that the weak-willed Tsar is falling more and more under the spell of the tempter.

Saturday, January 23, 1904.

Delcassé is skilfully continuing his efforts to bring St. Petersburg and Tokyo nearer together. He has hit upon certain ingenious formulæ which would simultaneously solve both the Manchu and Korean problems. He has been equally skilful in exploiting the support he has managed to get from London. Lansdowne, Komura and Lamsdorf have been showering thanks upon him.

"I think I'm going to bring it off," he said to me this morning. His face was radiant and his eyes positively sparkled.

Unfortunately, I had the painful duty of throwing a certain amount of cold water on his over-optimistic hopes; I had to tell him that if the Russo-Japanese tension was inclined to diminish in a *diplomatic* sense, the situation was getting worse from the *military* point of view.

I keep in daily touch with the Intelligence Department of our General Staff and it is a fact that since October I have been able to follow day by day the alarming expansion of Russian armaments in eastern Asia.

A few weeks ago, Colonel Moulin, our military attaché at St. Petersburg, managed to get hold of the Russian plan of concentration which has been prepared for the eventuality of a war with Japan. The broad features of the plan are as follows: one army at Vladivostok, one army at Port Arthur and Mukden, a general reserve between Harbin and Tsitsihai and a reserve army consisting of the Xth Corps (Kharkov), the XVIIth (Ryazan) and four divisions (Kazan). Since December 20th the Russians have been engaged in carrying out this plan with mathematical precision but in an atmosphere of deadly secrecy. Each day sees some fresh progress. It can thus be anticipated that somewhere about February 7th we shall witness some military *coup*, when the diplomatic veils will suddenly be torn asunder and the two adversaries will fly at each other's throats.

This fateful date, February 7th, is fixed by facts which there is no disputing; it is the automatic result of the series of steps which have been taken since October. Besides, it is of vital interest to the Russians that the commencement of hostilities shall not be deferred beyond February 7th. Lake Baikal has been completely frozen over since January 15th; the troops can cross it on the ice and the movement of transport required for the concentration would be facilitated to such an extent that the Russians could take the offensive in the valley of the Yalu before the thaw sets in.

I told the Minister of the latest revelations which make me feel certain that Russia wants war, or at any rate is putting herself in a position to send Japan a threatening ultimatum which will almost inevitably result in war.

Delcassé's face clouded over at once:

"You don't expect me to believe *that*, do you? I'm corresponding daily with the Tsar. Only yesterday he thanked me for comprehending his views so well and working so hard in the cause of peace. And, according to you, he means war all the time! What next!"

"Forgive my obstinacy, Monsieur le Ministre. But all our information from Petersburg goes to show that the war party, the Bezobrazov-Abaza-Vorontzov gang, is busier and more arrogant than ever. My opinion is that the negotiations in which you have been involved are nothing but a stratagem—a screen to hide the truth from the Japanese and the Emperor himself."

"My dear Paléologue, you're a pessimist and I don't blame you for it. Pessimism is a virtue in a subordinate. But the man at the top should always be an optimist. That's why I'm an optimist."

Sunday, January 24, 1904.

At five o'clock I had tea with the Grand Duke Paul and Madame Olga Valerianovna[1] at 10, Avenue d'Iéna.

I found my friends alone, quite absorbed in reading some letters which had just been brought by a former aide-de-camp of the Grand Duke who left St. Petersburg the day before yesterday. From these letters they had first-hand information about the course of the Russo-Japanese crisis.

After an enquiring glance at her husband, Olga Valerianovna translated one of the letters for me; it emanated, she said, "from someone high up . . . someone very high up."

The moment she began to read, I realized that the writer was someone at Court who was in close personal contact with the Emperor and Empress. This must be the Grand Duke Alexander Mikhailovich, I thought.

The letter fully confirmed the conclusion at which I had arrived as to the baffling attitude of the Emperor in the present crisis. Delcassé is right in thinking that Nicholas II is extremely anxious to settle the quarrel between Japan and Russia in the Far East by diplomatic means; he is still the warm-hearted sovereign who offered the world the noble chimæra of 1898—the reduction of standing armies, the Hague Tribunal and compulsory submission to arbitration of all international disputes. But at the same time he believes that Providence has called him to high destinies; he dreams of extending his frontiers still further and annexing Manchuria, Korea, Tibet, Persia and the Dardanelles! Moreover, he is not very intelligent, but timid, credulous, slack, vacillating, very superstitious and most susceptible to occult influences and what Chateaubriand called 'celestial sorceries.' And he lets himself be

[1] The Grand Duke Paul Alexandrovich, brother of Alexander III, had had to leave Russia some years before as the result of his morganatic marriage with Madame Olga Valerianovna Pistolkhors (subsequently Comtesse de Hohenfelsen and Princess Paley). His position at this time was very delicate, owing to his quarrel with the Emperor Nicholas II and the Empress Alexandra, and he was living in close retirement, to which I had the honour of being admitted. The Tsar pardoned him soon after.

led by a gang of visionaries, speculators and filibusters who are
absolutely set on war.

Wednesday, January 27, 1904.

Cardinal de Richelieu remarked once: 'To negotiate and keep
on negotiating is absolutely necessary for the welfare of states.'
The axiom might be Delcassé's motto.

Thursday, January 28, 1904.

I will give the precise origin of the serious dispute which may
very well kindle the fires of war between Russia and Japan.

Towards the close of the year 1900, an ex-captain of the *Cheva-
liers-gardes*, Alexander Mikhailovich Bezobrazov, a speculator and
adventurer of the first water, induced the Korean Government to
grant him a concession of immense timber areas on the banks of
the Yalu, on the frontiers of Manchuria. Tact and good manners
soon enabled him to get powerful backing from official circles in
St. Petersburg—including the imperial family, in particular,
Count Vorontzov-Dashkov, member of the Council of Empire, and the Grand Duke Alexander Mikhailovich, the Emperor's brother-in-law. The protection of these two carried with
it the friendly interest of the Tsar.

Henceforth he was the real director of Russian policy in the
Far East. His schemes, ostensibly industrial and commercial in
character, aimed at nothing less than the annexation of Manchuria
and Korea. As the result of a purely personal decision of the Emperor, two million roubles were put at his disposal to get the project
going. Japan became very excited, protested and complained to
London.

But the influence of the adventurer increased from day to day.
In May 1903, for instance, an imperial *ukase* conferred on him
the title of Secretary of State. The tone of the Japanese Government's protests became distinctly hostile and the clouds of armed
conflict began to gather on the horizon.

In July, Count Lamsdorf, the Foreign Minister, begged the
Emperor to cease backing Bezobrazov's mad adventure and accept
the latest Japanese proposals, which he regarded as conciliatory.
He was vigorously seconded in his efforts by his colleagues at the
ministries of War and Finance, General Kuropatkin and Witte.
The weak Nicholas II at first appeared to have yielded to their

persuasion; but, shifty and a dissembler—like all weak creatures—
he cunningly evaded the opposition of his ministers by issuing a
'Supreme Command' (of which they first heard through the press)
creating the office of Viceroy of the Far East. This new post
concentrated all administrative, military and diplomatic authority
in the hands of its holder. Henceforth the political affairs of Far-
Eastern Russia, including relations with China and Japan, were
to be handled by a 'lieutenant of His Majesty the Emperor,' stationed at Khabarovok, on the Amur. This 'lieutenant' was Admiral
Alexeiev, Bezobrazov's chief associate, creature and tool!

A few days later General Kuropatkin remarked to General Sakharov, his Chief of Staff:

"There'll be no avoiding a war with Japan *now!*"

Saturday, January 30, 1904.

An extraordinary council, the Grand Duke Alexis presiding,
was held the day before yesterday at St. Petersburg to discuss the
final reply of the Russian Government to the latest proposals of
the Japanese Government. It was attended by Count Lamsdorf,
Foreign Minister, General Kuropatkin, Minister of War, Admiral
Avellan, Minister of Marine, Admiral Abaza and several *tchinovniks*
of high rank.

Lamsdorf vigorously and persistently emphasized that the present
dispute in no way involves the vital interests of Russia and does
not therefore justify the enormous risks of a war which, in any
event, the Russian people would not understand. His conclusion
was that the Tsar's government should leave no stone unturned
to find some peaceful solution of the crisis.

With the exception of Admiral Abaza, the council endorsed
Lamsdorf's opinion. So everything would be for the best had it
not gone on to decide that the matter should again be referred to
Admiral Alexeiev! . . . Which is tantamount to saying that it
is the imperial lieutenant in the Far East who will have the last
word.

Monday, February 1, 1904.

Delcassé was inclined to be expansive today. We were talking
about the weighty negotiations which Paul Cambon is conducting
in London with the object of arriving at a general *entente* with
England.

"Our immediate concern," said the minister, "is the settlement of all our old quarrels. But I need hardly say that I shan't stop there. The settlement should lead us—and I mean it to lead us—to a political alliance with England! . . . What glorious prospects will open for us then, *cher ami!* If we had both Russia and England behind us, shouldn't we be strong against Germany!"

"You once told me that you had long ago conceived the idea of a Franco-British alliance . . ."

He interrupted me:

"Yes, indeed! Long, long ago! But the idea's not mine; I got it from Gambetta, and you know that great patriot is a hero of mine; my only ambition is to continue his work, so the dream of a Franco-British alliance has always haunted me—even during the Fashoda crisis. You surely remember that the trouble was hardly over before I proclaimed in the Chambers that France and England were equally interested, very deeply interested, in drawing closer together. Unfortunately, my words have had no echo. Public opinion here was still too inflamed against the English. . . . But look at the progress we've made these last few years. I believe I'm reaching harbour now."

After a moment's thought, he resumed:

"The part which will remain difficult will be to fit this Franco-British alliance into the Franco-Russian alliance. . . . Oh, well! Sufficient unto the day is the evil thereof."

Delcassé's remark about his being "haunted" long ago by the idea of a Franco-British alliance is strictly accurate. Two proofs:

On February 7th, 1898 (five months before he became Foreign Minister and nine months before the Fashoda incident) he wrote to his friend Ruiz, once secretary to Gambetta:

> *I had gone on a visit to Casimir-Périer when you came. . . . We must be blind if we cannot see that the clash of interest and ambitions—which will only become intensified—between England and Germany gives us our supreme opportunity. Our policy is to make ourselves strong, very strong, and keep our hands free.*

Eleven months later, on December 29th, 1898, I made an entry in my diary:

> *Delcassé has been talking about his negotiations with England, which are making good progress: "The evacuation of Fashoda*

*will soon be nothing but an evil memory . . . ." he said. He went
on to remark that he was delighted with his personal relations
with the Russian Foreign Minister, Muraviev.*

*Apropos of this, I told him that the Grand Duke Vladimir, the
Emperor's uncle, had recently remarked to me at dinner with the
Comtesse de Talleyrand: "I hope I shall live long enough to witness the death of the British lion: it is the subject of my daily
prayer to the Almighty! . . ." This prayer, in the mouth of the
impetuous Grand Duke, was no surprise whatever to me, but it
made Delcassé leap from his chair: "What a mistake! What
blindness! To Russia as to France, England is a rival, and a rival
whose behaviour is often very annoying; but she is not an enemy
and certainly not The Enemy! . . . If only Russia, England
and France could combine against Germany! . . ."*

Wednesday, February 3, 1904.

At seven o'clock this evening I was sent for by the minister, who
was in conference with the Political Secretary.[1] I found them both
looking very glum. They were extremely worried about the inexplicable delay in sending the Russian reply to the Japanese Government. More than six days have passed since Lamsdorf triumphed
over the intrigues of the war gang who have been trying to hang
things up! . . . Besides, the news from Tokyo is bad: the Government has reached the limit of its patience and is in danger of
soon having its hand forced by an outburst of national feeling.

In a harsh, jerky voice the minister asked me:

"Have you heard anything on the military side?"

"No, but I presume that tomorrow, or the day after tomorrow,
we shall hear of the mobilisation of the Russian Tenth Corps, the
Kharkov Corps. And then . . ."

"And then . . . ?" Delcassé flung at me.

"In all probability it will mean war."

The minister cast an anxious glance at Cogordan:

"Do you share Paléologue's opinion?"

"I think he's too cocksure; but I confess that the facts and
reasoning on which it's based have impressed me greatly during
the last two days."

---

[1] The Political Secretary at that time was my old and dear friend, Georges Cogordan, whom I accompanied on his mission to China and Korea (1885-1886).

Delcassé seemed dismayed for a moment, but quickly recovered himself:

"Speaking for myself, I want to remain optimistic. . . . You can go, gentlemen."

Thursday, February 4, 1904.

At eleven o'clock this morning Count von Gröben, Councillor of the German Embassy, paid me a call at the office. Of all the German diplomats I know I like him much the best: he is straight, reasonable and conciliatory—characteristics which have on several occasions enabled me to settle very ticklish affairs, in particular certain incidents connected with espionage. In private life he is a model of good breeding and his manners are charming. I meet him now and then at the house of a lovely foreign woman at which he is a constant visitor.

As I say, he came into my room this morning. Standing erect, he said in grave tones:

"I've come to pay you a farewell visit: I'm leaving the embassy. But I don't want to go without thanking you for the kind reception you've always given me."

"What! You're leaving Paris? Going to another post?"

"No, I'm only leaving the embassy. I intend to stay in Paris a few months longer. But I've had to send in my resignation as I don't get on with my chief."

"Oh! You don't get on with Prince von Radolin? . . . But I always thought he was most kind and courteous!"

"As regards kindness and courtesy, I've no fault whatever to find! . . . Our disagreement is over something else."

I did not pursue the matter—for obvious reasons. But I asked Gröben if he had said goodbye to the Political Secretary.

"No," he replied, "I thought I'd just leave a card on him . . . M. Cogordan is always so busy."

"I'm sure the Secretary wouldn't be satisfied with your card; he would be annoyed with me for letting you go without giving him a chance of shaking hands."

I took him straight to Cogordan whom he treated with the same discreet candour:

"I'm leaving the embassy for personal reasons; I'm not in agreement with my chief."

After making this mysterious remark he left the room with his usual affability.

As a matter of fact, the cause of dissension between Prince von Radolin and Count Gröben has been known to us for several days; our source of information is quite certain, authentic *and direct.*

The critical point on which they split is nothing less than the orientation of Franco-German relations. Gröben's views can be expressed thus: "Germany has no chance of getting the French Government to cooperate in her general policy so long as the question of Alsace-Lorraine continues to dominate public feeling in France. From a practical point of view, the most that can be hoped for between the two countries is correct relations and, occasionally, particular agreements on specific matters. Any other policy is doomed to spectacular failures which might easily react unfavourably on the peace of Europe."

But Prince Radolin, on the urgent inspiration of the Emperor William and with no aim in life but to please him, maintains that he is now in a position to bring pressure on the government of the Republic and, in particular, that the moment is favourable for detaching it from the Russian alliance. In a recent confidential letter to his impulsive sovereign, he wrote as follows:

> *If I have not made much progress with M. Delcassé, I have gained the entire confidence of the President of the Republic. After a long talk with M. Loubet the other day, he said to me: "When you have anything particularly private to say to the French Government, don't say it to M. Delcassé but come and tell me. I shall know what to do."*

The Emperor, delighted with the news, wrote in the margin: *Bravo, Radolin!*

The letter was sent to Paris so that the ambassador could see the marginal note. The document was then shown to Gröben who burst out: It's *untrue! The President of the Republic couldn't have said that!* The ambassador interrupted his subordinate: *Do you mean that I've told a lie!—Yes, Your Excellency has told a lie!*

Such is the whole explanation of Gröben's guarded farewell this morning.

We now have full confirmation of the secret and *direct* intelligence from which we have known for some time of the recent differences of opinion between the ambassador and his First Councillor. This evening Delcassé sent for me to discuss the matter with Cogordan:

"I could have guessed that Radolin, this Polish renegade, the Kaiser's lickspittle, was up to something against us . . . I've always told you that German policy, whether in the hands of William, Bülow or Holstein, has only one object, and it never varies— the disruption of the Franco-Russian alliance! . . ."

The minister did not breathe a word about the Russo-Japanese question. But there was no need for him to explain his reticence. The unhappy Lamsdorf is still struggling with the powerful camarilla and is reduced to begging Delcassé "to keep Motono quiet for four or five days longer."

Friday, February 5, 1904.

This year the Emperor William has celebrated his birthday (January 27, 1859) in special style. He went out of his way to issue an invitation to the King of the Belgians, Leopold II—a gentleman for whom, as a matter of fact, he professes no particular liking.

After spending a couple of days in Berlin, Leopold II returned to Brussels on January 29.

In the intervals between the various ceremonies the Kaiser and his guest had several long talks. What did they talk about? According to Gérard, our ambassador in Berlin, the royal visit is not supposed to have had any political importance. It is thought that, beyond official banalities, the only specific topic of conversation between William and Leopold was affairs in the Congo. "The King of the Belgians," writes Gérard, "has gained such a reputation for *finesse*, skill and smartness in negotiation that anyone discussing anything with him instinctively adopts a defensive attitude."

On the other hand, a secret service man in our Intelligence Department, in whom General Pendézec has complete confidence, has just reported his very different impressions of Leopold II's visit to Berlin. Far from adopting 'a defensive attitude' towards his guest, the Emperor is thought to have drawn him 'with brutal frankness' into the most delicate and dangerous topics; he even went so far as to say that 'the Franco-British policy is incompatible with the peace of Europe. . . . Any day I may be compelled to draw the sword. When that time comes, you will not be able to remain neutral. For Germany there will only be friends or enemies. You may rest assured that she will be victorious, and make your arrangements accordingly.' King Leopold, cunning old dog, is said to have slipped away, 'pleading a heavy cold,' like La Fontaine's fox at the court of the lion.

When I told Delcassé of this report, he remarked:

"That bit of news smacks of the truth."

General Pendézec did not think it proper for him to give me the name of the 'casual and most reliable informant' who revealed these startling pronouncements of William II. But he ended up with the remark:

"Between Leopold and my informant there's only one person —someone in the best position to know what was said at the tête-à-tête in Berlin between the Kaiser and his guest."

Delcassé, by way of hypothesis, has suggested an explanation which seems to me highly plausible. It is by the King's orders that we have been made aware of William's mad outburst. Leopold must have reported them to his Foreign Minister, the Baron de Favereau, and both must have thought that the French General Staff should be privately warned so that it should be on its guard. But Favereau, anxious not to compromise the King in the eyes of the Kaiser, has probably made use of some reliable intermediary who has pretended to be acting on his own initiative in revealing to us the dangers of the situation.[1]

---

[1] Prince Bulow's *Memoirs* (Vol. II, pp. 108 *et seq.*) edify us completely as to the impulsive statements of the Kaiser to the Belgian sovereign. After reminding his royal visitor of the glorious days of ancient Burgundy and the great figures of Philip the Good and Charles the Bold, he suggested nothing less than the idea of re-establishing their vast territories by recovering the sovereignty of French Flanders, Artois and the Ardennes. "At first Leopold's eyes opened wide in amazement; then he replied with a sneer that neither his ministers nor the Belgian Chambers would hear of such ambitious schemes. William, losing patience and roused to righteous anger, told the King that 'he thought nothing of a sovereign who considered himself responsible to Chambers or ministers and not to the Lord who reigns in the Heavens . . .' Then, drawing himself up to his full height, the *Imperator gloriosus* uttered these words: "I don't allow joking with me. In a European war, he who is not with me is against me. . . . As a soldier, I am of the school of Frederick the Great and Napoleon I. Just as the former began the Seven Years War with the invasion of Saxony and the latter fell upon his foes with the speed of lightning, in the same way, if Belgium does not take my side, I shall not allow anything but strategic considerations to guide me."

Chapter II

FEBRUARY 6TH—APRIL 7TH, 1904

Saturday, February 6, 1904.
THE Japanese Minister at St. Petersburg has handed Lamsdorf a
note, which concludes in the following terms:

> The Japanese Government can no longer tolerate the inex-
> plicable delays of the Russian Government over the pending
> negotiations, and the military preparations in which it is engaged
> in the Far East; nor, after all its efforts, can it see any prospect
> of inducing the Russian Government to cooperate in the estab-
> lishment of a lasting peace on the shores of the Pacific Ocean.
> It therefore finds itself compelled to terminate these vain nego-
> tiations. It further declares its intention of safeguarding the rights
> and interests of Japan in eastern Asia by such measures as it may
> deem necessary.

After handing this note, Kurino asked for his passports; he was
under orders to leave St. Petersburg at the earliest possible moment.

Though war has not been officially declared, it is now inevitable;
the state of uncertainty is over.

The blow to Delcassé is all the greater because only yesterday,
when pressed by anxious colleagues at the cabinet council, he told
them firmly: "I'll answer for peace myself." At the conclusion of
the meeting, Rouvier, the Finance Minister, repeated this assurance to the bankers. Hence the persistent rise on the exchange . . .
and, equally naturally, the rage of Rouvier!

The Japanese have commenced hostilities with amazing audacity.
Last night the Port Arthur squadron, comprising sixteen ships, was
careless enough to remain anchored in the outer harbour without
any sort of guard. Quite suddenly they were attacked by ten Japanese destroyers which had approached under cover of darkness. The
destroyers sank or completely disabled the battleships *Tsarevitch*

15

(13,000 tons) and *Retvisan* (12,800) and the cruiser *Pallada* (6,700).

The same day, February 9th, off Chemulpo on the western coast of Korea, the Japanese squadron cunningly destroyed the cruiser *Varyag* (6,750) and the gunboat *Korietz*.

In thus commencing hostilities without a declaration of war, the Japanese are repeating against their enemy the mean tactics which the Russians themselves employed against the Turks on November 30th, 1853, when they surprised and destroyed the Ottoman Black Sea squadron, at anchor off Sinope.

Saturday, February 13, 1904.

Our military attaché in London, Colonel d'Amade (he is an old friend of mine and I have often realized his sound judgment), has just dealt with the opening of hostilities in the Russo-Japanese war in a report which bodes ill for our ally. I will quote from the chief passages:

For more than thirty years the Japanese have devoted all their efforts to methodical and steady preparation—worthy of the highest admiration—for the event which has now occurred. Her army and navy have been created solely with a view to an armed conflict with Russia and the Sino-Japanese War of 1894-95 was merely an experiment with her military machine—a sort of grand manœuvre, or rehearsal of the complete stage-play which is about to be presented. There is thus no reason to be surprised by the opening of hostilities; they are the logical and rational outcome of long preparation.

The way in which hostilities have begun also reveals Japan's mighty and methodical concentration of all her forces, diplomatic, financial, naval and military. The very moment that the order to break off diplomatic relations was out, the army and navy got to work. It seems as if the Japanese had only to press a button to set in motion a skilfully adjusted machine: naval demonstrations, troop movements, the occupation of strategic points, etc. . . . All this has been done with a most masterly display of co-ordination and resolution.

There does not seem to have been the same clearness of vision on the Russian side. Even the intentions of the St. Petersburg

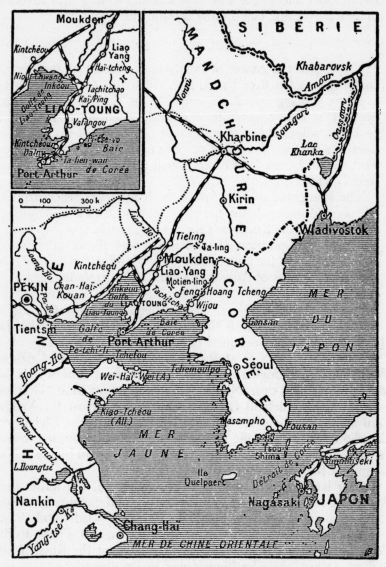

THE SCENE OF THE RUSSO-JAPANESE WAR, 1904-1905.

government fluctuated. The Tsar was said to be a firm advocate of peace. Nothing could more certainly lead to war.

.   .   .   .   .   .

Turning to the course of events in the future, it is probable that the Russian fleet has lost its chance of embarrassing the Japanese landing operations and that we shall soon hear what points they have selected for their bases. I am inclined to think that they will establish themselves at the mouth of the Yalu and near Niu-chwang, and then carry out a converging advance on Port Arthur by the land routes which they followed in the campaign of 1894-95.

The stronghold of Port Arthur, with the Japanese controlling the sea and commanding the approaches to the fortress by their occupation of the Kinchow-Talienwan peninsula, seems to be in a highly perilous position. If the Russian fleet allows, or is powerless to prevent, its investment, it may suffer the fate of the Spanish squadron of Admiral Cervera at Santiago de Cuba . . .

Tuesday, February 16, 1904.

The Emperor William is the tempter who has driven Nicholas II into designing the conquest of Manchuria and Korea.

As long ago as 1895, at the conclusion of the Sino-Japanese War[1] the Kaiser dangled the illusory prospects of eastern Asia before the eyes of his dear 'Nicky.' He kept on telling him: "God has ordained you to defend Christian civilisation against the Yellow Peril and bring about the triumph of the cross of the Saviour on the shores of the Pacific Ocean . . ." We have in our secret archives a document which reveals the intensive and highly skilful labours of the Emperor William.

A year later, it was again on the instigation of the Kaiser that Russia set foot in the northern provinces of Manchuria to secure the extension of the Trans-Siberian railway to Vladivostok.

It was William II again who took advantage of a visit to St. Petersburg in 1897 to persuade the Tsar to plant the Russian flag at Port Arthur while he himself was to be allowed to plant the German flag at Kiauchow.

[1] The Treaty of Shimonosaki, which ended the war, was signed on April 17th, 1895.

The treaty of March 27, 1898, by which China ceded (though ostensibly leased) the territory of Port Arthur to Russia contained the germs of the war which has just broken out.[1]

I am indebted to the Grand Duke Paul for some odd but accurate information about the private relations between William and Nicholas; he once said to me:

"Every time the two emperors have met, at Peterhof, Berlin or Darmstadt, William has made such a fool of himself and been so indiscreet, presumptuous and boastful that after their first talk my nephew, who is the soul of simplicity, could not bear him. . . . During one of their walks one day, William carried presumption to the point of having himself photographed with his hand on the shoulder of Nicholas, (who is much shorter than he) thus towering over him and seeming to be protecting him. At first our dear Emperor noticed nothing; but, when a proof of the snapshot was shown to him, he was extremely angry and had the negative immediately destroyed. . . . On another occasion, after a long talk with the Kaiser, he said to my brother Vladimir: 'I'd like to break something to relieve my feelings. Would you believe that I've just had a scene with William over my relations with France? . . . He entirely forgets the proprieties between sovereigns . . .'"

The Grand Duke Paul added this last tit-bit:

"My brother Alexander III has often said to me: 'William is as good a liar as his manners are bad.'"

Monday, February 22, 1904.

The Union Démocratique, one of the most important groups in the Chamber, has just taken a step which was necessitated by

---

[1] The private correspondence of the two monarchs has been published by the Bolsheviks; it confirms, and more than confirms, all that we know or thought we knew. In particular, it reveals the determined and prolonged efforts of William to drive Russia into a war with Japan. For three years he never stopped telling his cousin: "God has plainly called you to bring about the triumph of the law of Christ in the Far East. So Korea and Manchuria must belong to you. . . . The great conflict which it is your duty to wage with Japan will be the final struggle between the Christian and Buddhist religions . . ." One day in 1902 the two Emperors arranged to meet on their yachts off Reval. After a most effusive greeting, the Kaiser once again dangled the tempting mirage of the Far East before the dazed eyes of the Tsar. Then he suddenly burst out: "Do you know how you and I are going to address one another in future? I shall call you the *Admiral of the Pacific* and you must call me the *Admiral of the Atlantic* . . ." In other words: Establish your sway over the Pacific Ocean, whilst I make myself master of the Atlantic. We will help each other greatly in this wonderful task.

the recent effrontery of international propaganda-mongers. Having
to choose its president, it has enthusiastically elected Eugène
Etienne, the brave statesman who has devoted himself so tena-
ciously to the defence of our military institutions. He is the leader
of the colonial party and was once a friend of Gambetta.

In his opening speech, the new president referred in lofty terms
to 'all the services which the powerful and faithful friendship of
Russia has rendered to us during recent years,' and wound up with
a declaration that 'the honour and interests of France require us
to allow nothing to shake our loyalty to our ally.' The Union
Démocratique group closed the sitting with an Order of the Day,
categorically reaffirming that loyalty.

Tuesday, February 23, 1904.

This afternoon I presided at a meeting of the *Commission
Secrète des Instructions de guerre.*[1] In attendance; Captain de
Freycinet, departmental director at the Naval Headquarters Staff;
Major Brissé, Director of Intelligence at the Ministry of War;
Captain Nudant, personal representative of the Chief of Staff, and
my colleague, Piccioni, director of our cypher department.

We continued our previous investigation of the various methods
of securing uninterrupted telegraphic communication between
France and Russia in case of a European war; we got the problem
down to three combinations of routes: (1) by the Scandinavian
countries (2) by Turkey and Persia (3) by China and Siberia. We
wound up by organizing a chain of messengers between Paris and
St. Petersburg via Antwerp, Copenhagen, Stockholm and Finland.

At the conclusion of the meeting, Major Brissé reported what
he had learned from one of his secret agents in Berlin; it shows
that the authorities at the Great General Staff in the Königsplatz
believe that the war in the Far East has some "nasty surprises" in
store for Russia. And to think that it is William II who lured Russia into this adventure!

[1] The function of this committee, created in October, 1901, is to plan the measures
(police, intelligence, espionage, *liaison*) which, in case of war, will have to be taken
in concert by the ministries of Foreign Affairs, War, Marine and the Interior It
meets once a month at the Quai d'Orsay. As a rule, only the representatives of the
ministries of Foreign Affairs, War and Marine attend the sittings. The representatives
of the *Sûreté générale* and the Prefect of Police are summoned only when the
matters under consideration require the co-operation of their departments.

Sunday, February 28, 1904.
Musical evening at the house of the Comtesse de Talleyrand, *née* Bénardaky. Smart cosmopolitan audience.

I had a chat with the Baronne de N——, who sees a lot of foreigners, especially Austrians and Germans. She is of a judicious and practical turn of mind:

"The war in the Far East is just madness for the Russians," she said. "Once again the Tsar has revealed his incompetence. He's let the Emperor William fool him completely—you can take it from me that it's the Emperor William who has lured him into this adventure."

Prince Bariatinsky was hardly more comforting:

"Our *mujiks* can't make head or tail of this war," he said, "and I'll admit I'm in the same boat myself. . . . Isn't the territory of Russia big enough already? Why do we need to add Manchuria and Korea? I can only hope that God will protect us!"

But Miquel, the First Secretary at the German Embassy and a fearsome intriguer whom his colleagues dub 'the Emperor's spy,' talked to me in high-flown language of 'this great and most noble crusade on which the Tsar has so bravely embarked.' Then he assumed a professorial tone and explained the present conflict by reference to 'the historic law, the mysterious instinct which has been urging the Russians to extend their power to the Pacific Ocean ever since the sixteenth century and the reign of Ivan the Terrible.' I was itching to tell him that 'this great and most noble crusade' was neither more nor less than a gigantic filibustering expedition in the interests of 'The Eastern Asiatic Industrial and Commercial Company.' I also refrained from quoting Bismarck's pithy comment: "In the Russian barrel there is always an alarming amount of fermentation which may soon cause an explosion. I'd prefer that explosion to take place on the Asiatic side, not the European, as in that case we wouldn't get the cork in our stomachs so long as we kept away from the vent."

Tuesday, March 1, 1904.
That habitual braggart, the Emperor William, is never tired of repeating that he alone directs the foreign policy of Germany, that he keeps a tight grasp on the whole business of imperial diplomacy and his ambassadors and ministers are only the humble

and docile instruments of his august will. The fiction is nothing
but a gigantic piece of swagger.

The real author and sole directing head of German diplomacy
is no other than one of the high officials of the Wilhelmstrasse,
the 'Councillor of the Political Section of the Imperial Department of Foreign Affairs,' Baron von Holstein.[1] A curious character. . . . He had just entered the Prussian diplomatic service when
the war of 1870 broke out. Bismarck, who had already marked him
down as hard-working and quick-witted, took him with him into
the offices of General Headquarters where he came to value him
more and more and soon employed him on the most delicate missions. After peace was restored, young Holstein was appointed
secretary at the imperial embassy in Paris. It was there that he began
to show his true worth by appointing himself, in the Chancellor's
interests, to spy on his chief, Count von Arnim; he displayed positively machiavellian subtlety in accumulating damning evidence
against him.[2]

A little later he resumed these detective operations against his
new chief, Prince von Hohenlohe.

Then Bismarck decided that he must have so valuable an instru-
ment constantly at his side and installed him in one of the highest
posts at the Wilhelmstrasse.

Thenceforth, Holstein was omnipotent because he was known
to be the secret collaborator, confidante, tool and *Eminence Grise*[3]
of the Chancellor.

Over the Secretary of State's head he carries on a private correspondence, distinct from the official correspondence, with all
the ambassadors; he sends them instructions and orders; he lectures
them, snubs them, bullies and terrorizes them. Sometimes, when he
has made up his mind to finish them, he even goes so far as to point
them out to the newspapers as fit subjects for attacks, epigrams and

---

[1] The general policy of the German Empire was the province of the Chancellor,
Count von Bülow. He thus controlled the Department of Foreign Affairs, which
was directed by the Secretary of State, Baron von Richthofen, and the Under-
Secretary of State, Herr von Mühlberg. Immediately after them came the Councillor
of the Political Section, Baron von Holstein.

[2] Prince von Bismarck's jealous and vindictive persecution of Count von Arnim,
whom he suspected of designing to supplant him, is well known. The ex-ambassador
was brought before several courts of justice, charged with 'acts prejudicial to public
order,' and on October 5th, 1876, sentenced to five years' imprisonment. But he
succeeded in escaping to Swiss territory. He died at Nice in 1881.

[3] A term first applied to Richelieu's private adviser, Father Joseph du Tremblay.

abuse—an easy task, as press matters and secret service funds are his exclusive province.

Thus he has gradually made his position so strong that so far nothing has been able to shake it—neither Bismarck's sensational dismissal in 1890 nor the covert opposition of his three successors (General von Caprivi, Prince von Hohenlohe and Count von Bülow) nor the fierce hostility of various persons in high places such as Count von Hatzfeldt, Prince von Münster and Prince Eulenburg.

Admittedly, this privileged position would be incomprehensible if Holstein had not managed to keep himself constantly covered with the mantle of imperial favour. Unstable and capricious as William II may be, he has always kept the *Eminence grise* in office. The explanation of this permanent approval is that the 'Councillor of the Political Section' has never tried to climb any higher; he has never accepted the post of Secretary of State, for instance; he is never seen in society; he refuses all private attachments; no one is known to be his friend or confidante; he never tells anyone what he really thinks; he limits the necessity for human contacts to the indispensable minimum, and in this atmosphere of impenetrable isolation he works with the zeal of a fanatic, putting in sixteen hours a day over his fearsome labours. The theatrical megalomania of William II need fear no rivalry from this obscure official . . .

One foggy day in January, 1899, I was in Berlin and walking in the Wilhelmstrasse with our ambassador, the Marquis de Noailles.

The ambassador suddenly pinched my arm:

"You see that man coming towards us. Have a good look at him—when he's passed us I'll tell you who he is."

Tall, but stooping, the man was walking with quick, firm steps. He was anything but smart in appearance: his old hat was shabby, his coat threadbare, his white hair too long and his beard ill-kempt.

He suddenly recognized M. de Noailles; he bowed to him with studied politeness but simultaneously increased his pace and moved to one side as if to avoid being engaged in conversation.

But I had had time to have a good look at him. He has a high forehead, bony features, an aquiline nose, tight lips, deep-set eyes, and his face wears an expression, compounded of cunning, energy, suspicion and tenacity, which is quite fascinating.

The ambassador then remarked:

"You've just seen our most formidable enemy—Holstein!"
I have also just realized the mysterious power of the *Eminence grise.*

Tuesday, March 8, 1904.
Whilst the flames of a great war are mounting in the Far East and the rulers of all countries are anxiously wondering whether some spark from that quarter may not spread the conflagration to other parts of the earth, our Premier, Emile Combes, can think of nothing but closing religious houses and schools, preventing the recruiting of novices, obliterating the last traces of denominational teaching, removing crucifixes from the law courts—in a word, unleashing the passions of anti-clericalism and destroying the unity of the national faith!

Thursday, March 10, 1904.
Delcassé has been busy with the President of the Republic, arranging the details of their approaching visit to Rome. They anticipate that King Victor Emmanuel and Giolitti will invite them to a frank discussion of our secret agreements of 1900, 1901 and 1902. He has therefore instructed me to prepare a memorandum on the explanations and information we want to obtain from the Italian Government.[1]

I asked the Minister if the President were at last reconciled to the idea of this visit. Until recently he would not hear of it as he has no doubt that it will result in diplomatic relations between France and the Holy See being broken off.

"Yes," he replied, "M. Loubet at last agrees with me that merely to gratify the antiquated claims of the Vatican we have no right to throw away the chance of an alliance with Italy, nor must we

[1] By the first of these agreements (December 16th, 1900) France and Italy granted each other full liberty of action in Tripoli and Morocco respectively. By the two other agreements (June 25th, 1901 and November 1st, 1902) France and Italy mutually pledged themselves to maintain strict neutrality in the eventuality of the provocative attitude of a third power (Germany or Austria) bringing about a European war.

When the fact that France and Italy were becoming increasingly friendly had more or less been revealed, the Chancellor, Bülow, was moved to deal with it in a speech in the Reichstag on January 8th, 1902. He replied: "I do not share the view of those newspapers which appear to be rather uneasy about the Franco-Italian arrangements. . . . In a united household the husband does not lose his head because, for once in a way, his wife dances a harmless waltz with another man. The vital thing is that she should not leave him. And she will not leave him if she is happier in his house than anywhere else."

repeat the mistake of Napoleon III in 1870. But he persists in believing that his presence at the Quirinal will draw down upon him the maledictions of the Church, that our radicals will welcome the opportunity of embittering the dispute and before long we shall have a war of religion in France . . . I don't share his opinion in the least. The Vatican will protest on principle and to save its face—but for no other reason. At bottom, I'm certain that we shall reach an understanding in one of those equivocal transactions in which pontifical diplomacy excels."

Then he suddenly drew himself up and snapped out:

"Anyhow, what we decide in Rome may well prove the salvation of France some day. . . . So the Pope may go to blazes!" [1]

[1] It was not without long and serious consideration that M. Delcassé came to this conclusion. He did not finally commit himself to the view that 'an alliance with Italy is worth the risk of a breach with the Holy See' until July, 1903, when he was influenced by the momentous talks he had just had with Edward VII in London.

On March 21st, 1903, I recorded in my diary:

Saturday, March 21st, 1903.

Barrère, who has just come from Rome, lunched alone with me today. We discussed the great scheme on which he is working with all his usual enthusiasm and pertinacity—the visit of King Victor Emmanuel to Paris.

"Well," he said, the moment he appeared, "what sort of mood are they in here?"

"Beastly. . . . Neither Loubet nor Delcassé will hear of this visit which the President of the Republic would necessarily have to pay the King of Italy—and which in all probability would lead to a breach with the Holy See . . . Only last Thursday, Loubet solemnly told Delcassé: '*Barrère can just shut up! My decision is irrevocable: I don't want Victor Emmanuel to come to Paris as I don't want to return his visit in Rome. I loathe M. Combes' anticlerical policy. I should never forgive myself for lending him a hand by putting the Holy See under a moral obligation to break with France. . . . So don't let me hear any more about this visit!*'"

"What about Delcassé?"

"He doesn't seem as adamant as the President of the Republic, but your ideas don't appeal to him in the least. . . . When he told me of his last talk with Loubet, he said: '*I'm as anxious as he not to give our anticlericals a pretext for a quarrel, if not an open breach, with the Holy See. Anyhow, Italy's still much too tied up with the germanic empires to deserve such a striking mark of distinction from us. . . . Barrère's in too much of a hurry . . .*'"

At five o'clock Barrère, who had just left the Elysée, came to see me in my room. He looked very woebegone and put out:

"You were right," he said in an angry voice . . . "You were perfectly right: the President of the Republic won't receive the King of Italy, because, if he did, he'd be obliged to return his visit in Rome. . . . Well, let's drop the subject. . . . But Loubet will find himself responsible to our country for a stupendous mistake!"

"Yes," I said, "the same mistake Napoleon III committed in 1870 by persisting in making himself champion of Pius IX and the temporal power against the national aspirations of Italy."

Wednesday, March 16, 1904.

Contrary to what might have been expected, the war in the Far East seems to be rousing the Russian people to the highest pitch of patriotic fervour and a superb concentration of all the moral forces of the nation. Our military attaché, Colonel Moulin, who knows Russia so well, has given us a very lucid explanation:

"If events had taken the normal course, and several exchanges of diplomatic notes had preceded the rupture and the ensuing formal declaration of war, the public here, speaking generally, would have remained quite indifferent to what was happening in the Far East. The nation would have confined itself to criticizing the disastrous consequences of a policy of expansion, the object of which is not appreciated by the masses, and the war would have assumed the character of a colonial expedition.

"The sudden attack on Port Arthur has turned it into a national war. All the Russians, apart from a handful of fanatics, are prepared to make any sacrifice to bring it to a victorious conclusion and avenge the insult to the Russian flag. We are witnessing a great outburst of national vigour and the grim determination which animates even the lowest classes—particularly the lowest classes—is most impressive.

"The enthusiasm in the Army is tremendous. All the officers are clamouring to be sent to the front and almost fighting for the available posts. Many of those on the retired list are returning to the service.

"The good humour of the men, and their patience in facing the trials and discomforts of a long journey, are altogether admirable. Every man is calm and collected. There is no shouting or bawling of popular songs and no drunkards are seen.

"The leave-takings at the Moscow station are most imposing. Enormous crowds collect but they are quiet and well behaved. The officers might be off for a holiday. The only people who weep are a few women. Just as the train starts, all the spectators burst into a rousing cheer, which is followed by dead silence as the crowd slowly scatters.

"Donations for the sick and wounded, and particularly for the rebuilding of the fleet, are on the most lavish scale. A great *boyard*, Count Orlov-Davidov, gave a million roubles straight off, but that is nothing compared to the generosity of a certain merchant, a *raskolnik* (an 'Old Believer') who recently called at the Admiralty and enquired how much it cost to build a cruiser. When he learned the figure, he deposited securities to the amount of nine million roubles in order to have the pleasure of calling a cruiser his very own."

As Madame Laetitia, the august 'Madame Mère,' remarked when someone was boasting to her of the glories and splendours of Napoleon's reign: 'If only it will last! . . .'

Nor can I help recalling a disconcerting observation made to Casimir-Périer by our Chief of Staff, General de Boisdeffre, in the far-away days when the final form of the Franco-Russian alliance was being completed: 'We must get an undertaking from our ally that she will go all out from the very start of hostilities. History shows that Russia is at her strongest only at the outset of a war. The vices of her administration and the instability of public opinion confuse and discourage her very quickly.' [1]

At the diplomatic audience this afternoon, the German Ambassador questioned the Minister very politely about the important negotiations which are in progress between Paris and London.

"May I ask you an indiscreet question?" he began. "Is it true that an agreement on general policy has been signed, or is about to be signed, between France and England?"

"Nothing has been signed," replied Delcassé. "But for several months past I have been discussing with the British Government a friendly solution of the problems affecting our two countries. The possibility of an *entente* has been realized; I think we are near to signing."

"I have been told that the agreement covers Morocco."

"Yes, we have dealt with Morocco. Of course you know my point of view on the Moroccan question; I took the opportunity of acquainting you with it when I put the position before the Chambers. We want to maintain the political and territorial status of the Sharifian Empire. But if that empire is to last, it must obviously be supported and reformed. The incessant attacks on the borders of Orania last year gave us the most legitimate of reasons for intervention with our armed forces. I refused to yield to the pressure

[1] It was in December, 1893 that General de Boisdeffre made this apt observation. Casimir-Périer was then Président du Conseil and Minister for Foreign Affairs. I was his *chef de Cabinet*.

of our administrative authorities in Algeria who were anxious to enter Morocco itself with a view to securing a guarantee that our frontier should be respected in future. We must help the Sultan to govern his warlike subjects; but our assistance will be given in such a way as to benefit everybody as we shall scrupulously abide by the principle of commercial equality."

"What about Spain?"

"Spain? . . . She knows that we are her friend, so that she must expect nothing but friendly conduct from us. I'm the last man to ignore her real interests and legitimate aspirations."

After reporting this conversation, Delcassé added:

"Prince Radolin called my statements *perfectly reasonable* and thanked me very warmly."

Thursday, March 24, 1904.

Cogordan's funeral at the church of Sainte-Clotilde. In a snow-storm. The whole *corps diplomatique* was there. Delcassé insisted on delivering the funeral oration himself.

On his return to the Quai d'Orsay the Minister took me into his room; he told me in confidence that he had settled on George Louis to take over the department of *Affaires politiques*.

Then he remarked in a casual tone—which no longer deceives me:

"What has become of Herr von Gröben? . . . Haven't you seen him since last month?"

"No, Monsieur le Ministre."

"It's a nuisance that you haven't been able to continue your conversation with him, as I'd very much like to know whether William is still as anxious to meet the President of the Republic in Italian waters. . . . The more I think of it, the sillier the idea seems. . . . What good could come of a meeting at which the two parties could only look into each other's eyes and say: *We are separated by an unbridgeable gulf!*"

Saturday, March 26, 1904.

Yesterday, Delcassé introduced in the Chamber a bill for pro-viding an extraordinary credit of 450,000 francs for the expenses of the President of the Republic's visit to Rome. "This visit," he said, "is in confirmation of a policy which, irrevocably based on the solid foundation of our alliance with Russia, aims at closer relations with the other powers who are our friends."

The debate immediately opened with a fiery speech by Boni de Castellane. "What!" he exclaimed. "Is not the President of the Republic going to pay a visit to the Pope! Is he really going to reserve his courtesies for the representative of *the dynasty which has robbed the Papacy.*"

Angry protests from the seats occupied by the Left. "Order! Order!"

Old President Brisson, sovereign pontiff of the freemasons, shot up from his chair, his eyes wide with horror as if he had just witnessed an act of sacrilege: "Sir! The entire French nation will protest against your words, words which once again reveal the internal and external dangers against which the Republican Party in all its might is arming."

Cheers from the left; interruptions on the right. In the middle of the hubbub Castellane made some indistinct remark.

But the sovereign pontiff rose again in holy horror: "Under cover of the din, M. de Castellane has just said: *So much the worse for the French nation!* . . . Ordinary disciplinary measures are inadequate for such a remark. In times gone by, it would have been received with silence and contempt. Calm down, please, Messieurs!"

Boni de Castellane, however, continued his speech: "By visiting a King who owes his throne to the freemasons, you will aggravate our disputes with the Holy See. For Italy's sake you will sacrifice a friendship which is older and far more valuable. Besides, your policy has a secret object which has been dictated by freemasonry, so I will not vote for the credit which the Minister for Foreign Affairs is seeking."

Thereupon Pressensé, the radical-socialist *rapporteur*, wound up: "In advising the Chamber to pass the vote of credit, I did not think that my task would be facilitated by the representative of a faction which has always sacrificed patriotism to the interests of religious partisanship."

Castellane's speech, and especially his outrageous attack on 'the dynasty which has robbed the Papacy,' have had the natural result of making the Chamber practically unanimous on a question which worried Delcassé very much.

The really entertaining feature of Castellane's clumsy intervention was that it was insidiously inspired by no less a person than Delcassé himself!

A few days ago, Boni de Castellane called on the Minister to discuss his proposed speech. Delcassé pretended to be very worried and put out. "Do you really mean to say that you're going to use *that* sort of language in the Chamber," he said to his visitor. "*The dynasty which has robbed the Papacy! . . .* You'll cause a riot! . . . You can well imagine that I don't share your opinion. I positively deplore it. But at the same time I appreciate its force and *you* seem to me the only man with sufficient courage and resolution to defend it. But will your friends let you?"

Castellane returned home and secretly prepared his speech, making it even more aggressive in tone. Yesterday, without a word to anyone, he hurled his bomb.

I had all these details, first from the minister, then from Castellane himself and finally from the good Denys Cochin, whom I met at Madame d'Haussonville's this evening.

"We're thunderstruck," Cochin told me. "My friends and I were proposing a discreet qualification of our approval of the President of the Republic's visit to Rome. Castellane's abuse has reduced us to silence."

Sunday, March 27, 1904.

The Emperor William, who is now cruising in the Mediterranean, has just arrived at Naples.

He invited King Victor Emmanuel to lunch with him on the *Hohenzollern* yesterday. Tittoni, the Foreign Minister, accompanied his sovereign.

At dessert the two monarchs exchanged the classic toasts, with the inevitable reference to the alliance which ostensibly makes Italy a vassal of the Teuton Empires.

To give the reference its full flavour, I am producing from my safe the secret correspondence which passed between Barrère and Prinetti on November 1, 1902; let me quote the following paragraph:

> *If France is the object of aggression, direct or indirect, Italy will preserve strict neutrality. The same shall apply if France, in consequence of direct provocation, finds herself reduced to declaring war on her own initiative for the defence of her honour or her security.*

Tuesday, March 29, 1904.

This evening I discussed with Delcassé some of the matters I have on hand at the present moment. He had what I call his headache face; his skin was sallow, he looked worried and his eyes were swollen. I cut short my story, as he was not listening, but obviously thinking of something else. When I had finished and was on the point of leaving:

"Don't go," he said. "Sit down a minute. I've something to say to you . . . alone. . . . It's this. For some time I've been feeling horribly tired: I can't sleep and I've lost my appetite; something always seems to be hammering in my head; when I'm in the dark I see sparks and lights flicker across my eyes. It's absolutely essential for me to have a rest."

"Yes, there's no doubt whatever that you must knock off for a bit. . . . Why don't you go off to the Riviera for a fortnight's holiday? You've plenty of time before going to Rome with the President of the Republic."

"No; it's not just a holiday I mean. I need rest for an indefinite period . . . quite seriously, I'm thinking of throwing up office."

Leaving me no time to expostulate, he continued:

"I've been at the ministry for six years; for six years I've filled the breach. I think I've done one or two useful bits of work: I settled the Fashoda incident; I've tightened the bonds of our alliance with Russia; I've restored the old friendship between Italy and France; I've just settled the broad basis of a general understanding between France and England: I've a right to let someone else take up the running."

I protested that the Franco-British *rapprochement*, which is his great achievement, is as yet little more than a project; that he alone can make it yield its full benefits; that in any event the public simply would not understand his throwing up office merely because he is suffering from overwork and strain, which a few days' rest would certainly put right.

After a long pause he hesitatingly continued:

"My task has got too much for me . . . it gets more complicated every day . . . *they* will soon make it impossible."

His words gave away his secret:

"It's clear that you're not getting any help from the President of the Council, the War Minister or the Minister of Marine."

Then he let himself go:

"It's not merely that they don't help me in my efforts; they positively work against them, paralyse and frustrate them. All M. Combes thinks about is downing the clerics and fomenting religious strife; General André is preparing the way for a reduction of military service to two years and meanwhile allowing freemasonry to run riot in the army; M. Pelletan is disorganizing our navy and recommending the workmen at our arsenals to strike. All that's the very negation of my policy. . . . I tell you I've had enough! I'm not going to go on covering up their beastly work. They can shoulder the responsibility alone!"

It is the first time he has let himself go before me on so delicate a subject. But I did not know what to reply, for in theory he is perfectly right. A country's foreign policy is simply the external expression of the results of its domestic policy; in the eyes of the foreigner, it so to speak embodies all the moral and material forces of that country; to try to make its diplomacy vigorous and creative is illogical and a paradox when the nation is torn by internal strife, the army, diseased in its very vitals, has lost its *esprit de corps*, and anarchy reigns among the ships' crews and the workers at the arsenals.

But my answer was inspired by other elements in the situation:

"Well, supposing you do let overwork and pessimism get the better of you and throw up your office. What's going to happen? Your resignation will do us an enormous amount of harm in Europe. No one is in the least bit likely to swallow the story about your health; everyone will at once guess that you're feeling your task is beyond you, in the present state of dissension and weakness to which the Radical-Socialists have reduced France. . . . Who's to be your successor and what will he do? What *can* he do, even if we credit him with the best of intentions? Neither at St. Petersburg nor in London, Madrid nor Rome will he find anyone prepared to deal with him. The whole network of friendships and understandings you've built up so patiently would break at once. What foreign government will join up with us after you have personally announced that France is obliged to refrain from any sort of action beyond her frontiers? . . . In present circumstances your resignation would be a diplomatic disaster. You have no right to withdraw. The very fact that you remain a member of the ministry will secure the essential benefits of the good results you have achieved in the last six years. . . . But obviously you'll have to go carefully in future, leave the bigger schemes alone and wait for better times."

He wore a sulky air as he listened to me, as if he had been expecting different advice. He said sharply:

"But I've told you that my task will soon be made impossible. I can't look forward to better times; much worse times are ahead. At the rate we're going, the whole future of France will be at stake before long."

"In that case, there's only one course open to you. Put the whole matter before Parliament. Let it see for itself that it's impossible for you to carry on our foreign policy while your colleagues in the ministry are feverishly engaged in wrecking our national forces. If the Chamber doesn't agree with you, at any rate you'll have salved your conscience. Then you can appeal from the Chamber to the country; your resignation may have a salutary effect on the nation . . ."

Delcassé's reaction was a tense, solid silence—as much as to say that my words had not failed to impress him but he must be on guard against himself. I have often seen him in that frame of mind!

Suddenly his features relaxed. After a few kindly words of thanks he dismissed me.

Thursday, March 31, 1904.

Someone has just quoted a fine and profound remark of Leo XIII.

One day he was granting an audience to Blowitz, the famous Paris correspondent of *The Times*. Their conversation soon turned to the state of public opinion in France and the conversion of the Catholics to republican principles. The journalist was warmly congratulating the Pope on finally releasing himself from the hold which the old monarchist parties claimed to have over him:

"I know France well," he said: "She is democratic out and out. Her former dynasties mean nothing to her now. . . . Please take it from me, Holy Father, that French royalty is not only finished; it's dead."

"That's my opinion too," replied the Pope. "And that's why I advise the French Catholics to support the republican cause, and support it sincerely. In doing so, I am only following in the footsteps of all my predecessors. *All down the centuries there is only*

*one corpse to which the Church has ever attached herself . . :
the corpse on that cross."*

Friday, April 1, 1904.

Continuing his Mediterranean cruise, the Emperor reached
Messina on the *Hohenzollern* yesterday evening.

During the last few days he spent at Messina he showed signs of
extreme excitability on many occasions. We also know that he was
woefully disillusioned by his conversation with King Victor Emmanuel on March 26th, when the Italian monarch wrapped himself
in a mantle of chilly and taciturn reserve. It is reported that he
went so far as to say to several people: "I suspect that Delcassé
is trying to entice Italy away from me . . . I'll never allow it,
never!"

I am not surprised that Victor Emmanuel adopted an attitude
of chilly reserve towards William. One of my Roman friends, a
lady whose husband occupies a high post at Court, remarked to me
recently:

"Our sovereign can't bear the Kaiser. You know the sort of man
he is—simple, open and honest but uncommunicative; he weighs
every word he utters and seldom says anything. The airs William
gives himself, his perpetual emotionalism and bragging, his interminable monologues, his craze for lecturing everyone, his taste for
theatrical outbursts, not to mention his assumption that he can
keep Italy under his heel, as in the good old days of the Hohenstaufens—it all makes him perfectly odious to our King . . ."

I may add something which my friend did not say—that, on the
political side, Victor Emmanuel's views are very liberal and advanced; he is thoroughly imbued with modern ideas, whereas the
haughty William is only at home with the trappings, *bric-à-brac*
and reveries of Teutonic feudalism.

Sunday, April 3, 1904.

The Franco-British agreement, which will be Delcassé's *magnum
opus,* is approaching finality; Lord Lansdowne and Paul Cambon
are engaged in putting the finishing touches to it.

So all the chanceries of Europe are agog to learn the exact extent
of this great and mysterious agreement which has been gestating
for the last nine months.

The *Popolo romano,* always well informed, announces that the coming event is "without precedent or parallel in the annals of diplomacy." It adds prophetically:

The whole course of politics in the twentieth century may be influenced by it, for the arrangements which are on the point of materializing will make common action between France and England a certainty for untold years to come . . ." It concludes with a judicious comment: "The Franco-British *entente* does not seem in any way likely to prejudice the Franco-Russian alliance. . . . Since the Russo-Japanese conflict began, France is, so to speak, the central point of a vast combination, a combination such as Europe has never known."

Monday, April 4, 1904.

Side by side with the Franco-British agreement, Delcassé is engaged in negotiating with the Madrid cabinet an agreement which, while defining the rights and interests of Spain in Morocco, will recognize the claim of France to the privilege of political supremacy in the empire of the Sharifs.

The negotiation is exceedingly tricky, for, ever since the expulsion of the Moors and the reign of Isabella, the Spaniards have always considered Morocco as their special preserve, their promised land. This political utopia they can pursue only upon the terms that their object remains unavowed. Now what we are asking of them is officially to admit that they have failed in their historic mission and must make way for us.

The ambassador, Leon y Castillo, Marquis del Muni, is exhibiting remarkable energy and subtlety in pleading his cause—which has all the realities of the situation against it.

Tuesday, April 5, 1904.

The Baron de Courcel has just been to see me at the ministry to inspect certain secret files which Delcassé instructed me to show him. Delcassé has a very high opinion of the political intuition, sound and discerning judgment and wealth of experience of our former ambassador in Berlin and London.[1]

He was representing us in the latter post in November, 1898 during the Fashoda crisis and admires Delcassé all the more for

[1] He was ex-Director of Political Affairs at the Quai d'Orsay, ex-ambassador in Berlin, then London; senator and member of the Institut. He died on June 13th, 1919.

having so skillfully effected a reconciliation between France and England.

"But even all M. Delcassé's courage and tenacity," he said, "would not have sufficed to make friends of two races who have hated one another for centuries, had not the English begun to fear the rivalry of Germany and, what is more, the *menace* of Germany. The English brain, as you know, does not work very quickly. But ultimately the Emperor William's mischievous intrigues opened their eyes to the ominous greatness and prosperity of the Reich. They immediately remembered Lord Chatham's maxim: 'We have nothing to fear until we see France emulating this country as a commercial, naval and colonial power.' They have now applied this remark to Germany, not France. Fear of the *menace* of Germany was what drew England and France together . . ."

Recalling his memories of Berlin at the final apogee of the glorious Bismarckian era, Courcel went on to say:

"Bismarck would never have allowed us to arrange political agreements with Russia and England. At the first suspicion of an impending alliance, he would have called upon us to break off negotiations. If we had not given in, he would have made war on us. . . . One day, during one of my visits to Friedrichsruhe, he asked me abruptly, *Do you know Moltke is a dreamer?—Field-Marshal Moltke a dreamer! But his is the coldest, the most methodical, balanced, ultra-realist mentality I have ever come across!—Nevertheless, he is a dreamer, a great dreamer. Not that his dreams vary much; his imagination is vivid, but limited, as a soldier's should be. He has but one dream, always the same, which recurs every night with obstinate regularity. First he dreams that he has gone to bed in boots and sword. Suddenly he sees a hirsute Cossack slink stealthily into the room and try to pull off one of his boots. At the same moment, a small, dishevelled French soldier appears and seizes the other boot. Then Moltke leaps out of bed, draws his sword and cuts the two intruders to pieces. . . . Every night it begins all over again; every night the Field-Marshal slashes furiously right and left with his sword. . . . Isn't this an odd dream? . . .* And the Chancellor regarded me steadfastly, with a jeer on his face. I had no desire to pay any attention to the ominous significance of this speech and merely replied, *How terrible for the illustrious Field-Marshal Moltke to end his days with such a frightful night-*

mare.[1] But Bismarck was no doubt determined to frighten me that day for he continued in the same mocking tone, puffing away at his huge pipe:

You Frenchmen don't know your geography.

You're wrong there, you're talking at this very moment to a Frenchman with a very good knowledge of geography. Perhaps even better than your own. Just ask me a few questions.

Well, which is the shorter distance? From Paris to London or Berlin to London?

That's an odd question! You're joking, aren't you?

No, I'm not joking and I want you to answer.

I always carry the map of Europe in my head and I believe I'm correct in saying that it is 350 kilometres from Paris to London, which must be at least a thousand from Berlin.

'At this my grim companion burst out laughing:'

I was quite certain you didn't know any geography. The distance is three times shorter from Berlin to London than from Paris to London. I'll prove it if you like. Let's try an experiment, to give you time to consider the matter: We will leave at the same time, you from Paris, I from Berlin, and I guarantee that I'll be in London before you've even crossed the Channel.

'In this picturesque, ironic fashion, Bismarck was giving me a solemn warning. It was as good as saying, *Don't try to form an alliance with England, because the day I see you are doing so I shall be in London before you with such attractive offers and concessions that the British Government cannot fail to prefer an alliance with us. And you can be quite sure that such an alliance will be at your expense.*'

Then we talked about the 'Eminence Grise,' the omnipotent Holstein; I asked Courcel:

"How do you account for this mysterious person having been so long in complete control of German diplomacy, and the fact that, hated and distrusted as he is, no chancellor has dared to fight him?"

"It's a thing I have often wondered. The only possible explanation was given me by an Englishwoman, a close friend of Queen Victoria, whom I used to see very often in London. Holstein, who has a detective-like mentality, is supposed to have collected a file of

---

[1] Field-Marshal Moltke died in 1891, aged 92. The conversation chronicled above was approximately in 1885.

damning documents on William's abominable behaviour during the last illness of his father, and which he repeated some months later, just before the dismissal of Bismarck. Holstein is supposed to have put those papers in some safe place and there is no doubt that he would publish them if necessary. He has often shown that he's capable of doing anything for revenge."

"What a terrible creature!"

"Yes, but there's something of a caricature, something Satanic about him. I can see him in one of Hoffman's "Tales."

Chapter III

APRIL 8TH—MAY 2ND, 1904

Friday, 8th April, 1904.

TODAY, Paul Cambon, our Ambassador in London, and Lord Lansdowne, Secretary of State for Foreign Affairs, signed the Anglo-French agreement, comprising:

1. *a Declaration with regard to Egypt and Morocco*
2. *a Convention with regard to Newfoundland and Africa*
3. *a Declaration with regard to Siam, Madagascar and the New Hebrides.*

This great diplomatic achievement embraces innumerable problems and solves them in most equitable spirit. Every subject of difference and dispute between the two countries has been dealt with. The most important provision is that covering Egypt and Morocco. We are to give up Egypt to England in return for which she gives up Morocco to us.

The agreement which has just been concluded does not merely liquidate the past; it opens a new era in Anglo-French relations. It is a preliminary to common action in European politics. Is it directed against Germany? In terms, no. But by implication, yes, in that the principle of the balance of power in Europe is set up as a barrier to the ambitious aims of the German *bloc* and the programme of expansion of which it makes no secret.

Wednesday, 13th April, 1904.

At the session of the Reichstag yesterday, the Chancellor, Bülow, was questioned by the National-Liberals about the Anglo-French agreement of 8th April. They alleged that this agreement will put Germany in a difficult and humiliating position, especially in view of the enormous advantages conceded to France in Morocco.

Count Bülow's reply was most sagacious: *We have no reason to assume that this agreement is aimed at any particular power.*

It would seem that it simply represents an attempt to compose

39

*all existing differences between France and England by means of
a friendly arrangement.*

*As far as German interests are concerned, we can have no objec-
tion to this agreement. Indeed we ought not to desire strained
relations between France and England, if only because they would
imperil the peace of Europe, the maintenance of which is our
earnest endeavour.*

*With regard to the primary object of this Morocco Agreement,
our interests in that country are, as in the Mediterranean generally,
and particularly in Morocco, mainly economic. Tranquillity and
order in that country are thus of vital interest to us also. Nor have
we any reason to fear that our economic interests in Morocco will
be disregarded or injured by any power whatever.*

Friday, 15th April, 1904.

The Japanese fleet, under the command of Admiral Togo, is
endeavouring to blockade the Russian Squadron in Port Arthur,
thus repeating the operation executed with such consummate skill
by the Americans against the Spanish at Santiago-de-Cuba in 1898.
The day before yesterday the Russian battleship "Petropavlovsk"
(12,000 tons), flying Admiral Makarov's flag, sank in two minutes.

Tuesday, 19th April, 1904.

In spite of Bülow's sensible speech in the Reichstag a few days
ago, public opinion in Germany does not agree with him about the
Anglo-French compact, which it still regards as an intolerable
slight to Germany: "We cannot let France and England settle
such serious matters without reference to us. . . . We cannot let
France have a free hand in Morocco."

Nationalist circles profess to believe that the Chancellor's speech
in the Reichstag in no way squares with the Emperor's ideas, and
are hoping that he will issue a prompt *démenti.*

Wednesday, 20th April, 1904.

I have given the following secret note to the Minister:

*The person who recently supplied the information about the
quarrel between the German Ambassador in Paris and Count
von Gröben, asked Prince von Radolin yesterday how much truth
there is in the rumour that the Emperor William will call on*

*the President of the Republic during his stay in Naples. "I'm
afraid there's something in it," the Prince replied. "If it materializes, you may be quite sure that the Emperor will try and talk
politics with M. Loubet."*

I expected M. Delcassé to greet this note with a furious outburst
against the Kaiser. I was wrong! He was quite unmoved, and his
comments were as judicious as if he had had plenty of time to
weigh his words.

"This idea of a meeting with the President of the Republic vio-
lates common sense. You have often reproached me for always
refusing to entertain the notion of making confidential approaches
to Germany, either the Emperor or Bülow. . . . But let's begin
by seeing things as they are. There's no doubt that France and
Germany have a most serious quarrel, the most serious that has
ever kept two nations apart. It is of thirty-three years' standing
and cannot be cured by time. France will never renounce her claim
to her lost provinces . . . if she did, there would be no more
France. . . . Let me assume, however, that the Emperor William
and President Loubet casually meet at sea, or in some Italian port.
What would they have to say, what *could* they say to each
other? . . . Of two things one. They might be perfectly candid, in
which case the relations between the two countries would immediately become embittered. Alternatively, they might exchange
vague platitudes, in which case their conversation would end in
quibbles which would also result in a fresh outburst of hatred
between the two nations. Surely you can see that I'm right, *cher
ami!* But, to please you, I'll take the matter a step further. Let me
assume that, after thirty-three years of ill-feeling, Germany honestly
wants to effect a reconciliation between our two countries. Isn't it
obvious that such an attempt, the failure of which might have the
most disastrous consequences, should be accompanied by the most
elaborate precautions? If the Emperor William is a real lover of
peace and wants to make overtures to us, why doesn't he make a
start through the ordinary channels? Why doesn't the Berlin
Chancery put up some straightforward proposition if they imagine
close and lasting co-operation between France and Germany is
possible? . . . Not a bit of it! What William is after isn't a gen-
uine, definite reconciliation but a 'sensational' interview, some
coup de théâtre in the Bay of Naples or elsewhere in the Medi-

terranean. . . . It's all nonsense, bunkum! My dear Paléologue, I've told you till I'm tired that *William's just a pompous ass and a charlatan*,[1] and nothing will convince me that I'm wrong!"

Thursday, 21st April, 1904.

Yesterday, the Russian Ambassador, Nelidoff, asked the Minister to take 'immediate' action to deport a refugee, Vladimir Burtzev, whom he describes as a 'revolutionary of the most dangerous, reckless and incorrigible type.' The memorandum submitted by the ambassador in support of his request, ends as follows:

"Burtzev has an amazing gift for rousing the evil instincts of young revolutionaries and rapidly turning them into fanatics capable of frightful crimes."

According to Nelidoff, Burtzev is supposed to be on the most friendly terms with our Socialist leaders, Jaurès included, who are said to have induced Combes, the Minister of the Interior, to make the French police turn a blind eye to the presence of Burtzev in Paris, where he is actively engaged in secret plots against tsarism.

Delcassé at once sent for me to commission me, in Nelidoff's presence, 'to insist in the strongest possible terms on the deportation of Burtzev.'

I accordingly got into touch with Cavard, head of the *Sûreté Générale*, and am seeing him this afternoon.

Rataieff, the foreign representative of the Russian police, handed me a voluminous file this morning in order that I should know all about the Burtzev case. The main facts are these:

"Vladimir Lvovitch Burtzev was born in 1862 at Fort Alexandrovsk. His family were landed gentry. At the age of twenty he

---

[1] We believe that the Chancellor, Bülow, like Delcassé, realized that it was morally impossible to effect a reconciliation between France and Germany so long as the two nations were divided over the question of Alsace-Lorraine. He actually wrote in his book, *German Policy*, published in 1913:

"*In my opinion, the hope of effecting a reconciliation with France is a forlorn and foolish one, so long as we have no intention of restoring Alsace-Lorraine. We have no such intention. . . . We must always try to maintain polite, unruffled and peaceful relations with her. It is useless for us to pursue a will o' the wisp or we shall suffer the fate of La Fontaine's astronomer, who fell down a hole because his eyes were fixed on the stars. The hole in question is 'the Vosges' . . . In any case, if a nation is so deeply hurt by an injury to its pride that revenge becomes its dominating passion, it is proof of a very keen sense of honour.*"

Count Bülow, who was steeped in the Bismarckian tradition, obviously did not share the fantastic, histrionic notions indulged in by the Emperor William of a possible meeting with the President of the Republic.

was imprisoned for revolutionary propaganda. He was released after one month and arrested again in 1885 and sentenced to seven years in Siberia. A year later, he escaped from the penal settlement and fled, first to Geneva and then London. Although the English are traditionally extremely hospitable towards political exiles, he soon got into trouble with the British police for publishing in his review *Narodno Voletz* (*The Will of the People*), a series of articles exhorting the youth of Russia 'to imitate the glorious assassin of Alexander II.' This incitement to regicide earned him eighteen months' *hard labour*. When he had served his sentence, he returned to Switzerland where his first act was to publish an article, 'Down with the Tsar!' which would in itself have justified the English judge's decision. He passed his spare time in editing an extremely interesting review, *Byloie,* (*The Past*) which was devoted to the history of liberalism and seditious movements in Russia.

"But his detestation of tsarism, the lust of battle and his positively romantic taste for conspiracy and violence did not allow him to remain inactive for long. In December, 1901, he co-operated with Guerchuny, Azeff, Khernov, Dora Brylliant and Savinkov to found a *Fighting Organization,* the purport of which was to centralize and direct all the militant activities of the Socialist Party. A plan of campaign was drawn up. Three victims in high places were selected: Pobedonostseff, the Procurator of the Holy Synod, (the rabid theoretician of autocracy), General Prince Obolensky, Governor of Kharkoff, and Sipiaguin, the Minister of the Interior.

"The attempt on Pobedonostseff's life failed owing to treachery. Prince Obolensky was only slightly wounded. But on April 15th, 1902, Sipiaguin was shot through the heart and died instantly. From that moment Terrorist activities increased.

"At the end of 1903, the Russian Government protested to the Swiss Government against the facilities enjoyed by the revolutionaries on Swiss soil for hatching their plots. The facts on which this protest was based were very convincing. Burtzev and his accomplices were thereupon deported and took refuge in Paris. Burtzev took a small house in the Boulevard Avago and affected to lead a very quiet life, devoted entirely to historical research. But he gradually and secretly transferred the whole *Fighting Organization,* with its records, meetings and stock of explosives, under his roof."

The file also included a photograph, to help our police in their enquiries. What I saw was the picture of a man, still young, frail in appearance, pigeon-chested and narrow-shouldered. His face made a great impression on me: it was haggard, sickly and ascetic, though illumined, or rather transfigured, by his eyes—eyes so full of fire and tenderness as to be quite fascinating. I at once understood the man's ascendancy, his genius for suggestion and temptation, the strange magnetism which fires imagination and stirs to action and makes him such a formidable apostle of the revolutionary gospel. On the back of the photograph I read the following dedication:

> *Never forget the great names of Jelaboff, Sophie Perovskaia, Khalturin and Grinevitsky.*[1] *Their names are our banner. They died firmly convinced that we would follow in their glorious steps.*

At five o'clock this afternoon I went to see the Director of the *Sûreté Générale.* Fixing his wicked little eyes upon me, he listened to what I had to say. He made no comment at all but merely remarked:

"I'll ask M. Combes to sign an order for the deportation of Burtzev tonight and the Prefecture of Police will advise him as soon as they're able to get hold of him."

Saturday, 23rd April, 1904.

At 9.50 this morning, the President of the Republic left Paris for Rome, accompanied by M. Delcassé. He will arrive there somewhere about 4 tomorrow afternoon.

We understand that both the Italian Government and the nation have a very warm and impressive welcome in store for him. The prospect does not attract him in the least.

For over a year he has been dreading and opposing this visit to Rome, because he thinks it is bound to result in diplomatic relations between France and the Holy See being broken off. All the same, he has yielded to the entreaties of his Foreign Minister, whose main argument seems to me unanswerable: 'A visit of the President of the Republic to Rome is a *sine qua non* of a Franco-Italian alliance. The state of Europe makes it imperative for us to make sure of that alliance. We must not repeat our mistake of 1870.'

[1] The murderers of Alexander II.

As for the danger of diplomatic relations between France and the Holy See being broken off, Delcassé is still convinced that at the last minute some official euphemism, some polite formula, which will meet all the difficulties, will be found.

Sunday, 24th April, 1904.

The President of the Republic arrived in Rome at 4 o'clock this afternoon in glorious weather.

Victor Emmanuel's welcome at the Termi Station was almost effusive for one usually so phlegmatic, surly and irritable.

All along the route to the Quirinal palace, the procession was greeted with a storm of cheering. A few of the spectators struck a discordant note with cries of *Viva la Republica!* and *Abasso il Papa!* but they found no echo.

At 8 o'clock there was an unofficial dinner at the Quirinal. In the evening a torchlight procession, which was followed by a vast crowd, filed past the palace.

Monday, 25th April, 1904.

In Rome, the President of the Republic is going from function to function and everywhere received with enthusiasm. The Franco-Italian *rapprochement* is, so to speak, acquiring the seal of popular approval, having hitherto been nothing but a cog, or invisible spring, in our diplomatic machinery.

When proposing the official toast at tonight's state banquet, Victor Emmanuel made a happy reference to 'the unforgettable memories' linking the two races, memories which today provide another opportunity of reaffirming their friendship.' No doubt the Franco-Italian alliance is far from being a *fait accompli*, but it is now a possibility—and that is a great step forward. The Anglo-French agreement of 8th April has certainly contributed to this result; Italy knows that in future she has both Paris and London behind her if she wishes to escape from her condition of subjection to the Central Empires.

Delcassé was even wiser than he thought when he pressed the President of the Republic to accompany him to Rome and tried to convince him 'that the state of Europe makes it essential for us to make certain of an alliance with Italy,' sticking obstinately to his point of view. Here is the proof:

Our Chief of Staff, General Pendézec, asked me to call at his

office this afternoon to talk about the Russian alliance, the military
value of which is obviously greatly diminished by the colossal task
facing our ally in the Far East. We have discussed the matter many
times before and always come to the same conclusion; 'While the
Russians are at grips with the Japanese, French diplomacy must
carefully avoid quarrels, *a fortiori* a war with Germany.'

After swearing me to secrecy, Generl Pendézec spread out before
me a large map of Belgium, the Rhine Provinces, northern and
eastern France.

"Listen carefully," he continued. "I'm going to show you the
new plan of concentration which the German General Staff have
just adopted against France."

Greatly amazed, I interrupted him:

"How have you found out?"

"I'll tell you afterwards . . . but I'll guarantee that everything
I say is absolutely true."

The broad outlines of his detailed account are as follows:

"In case of war with France, Germany would reduce her covering troops on the Russian front to six army corps; she would mass
thirty-six on her western front, or, to be more accurate, the
equivalent of thirty-six corps, as there would only be twenty-six in
the front line, the rest consisting of reserve divisions. These twenty-
six corps would be grouped into four armies. Their geographical
distribution would be as follows: One army of nine corps and two
armies of four corps in the Moselle and Saar regions, with the
valley of the Meurthe as their objective; one army of nine corps in
the Aix-la-Chapelle and Malmédy region, with the valley of the
Oise as its objective. The latter would advance through Liège,
Stavelot, Namur, Charleroi, Maubeuge and thence by Guise,
Noyon and Compiègne straight on Paris, while the other three
armies, operating towards the Meurthe, would tie up all our
North-Eastern forces."

The smouldering fires in General Pendézec's eyes contrasted
strongly with the complete absence of emotion in his voice as he
added:

"I need hardly tell you we couldn't resist such an attack? . . .
We should be overrun at once."

He then disclosed the source of his information:

"A short time ago, an officer, who appears to be one of the generals attached to the Great General Staff in Berlin, wrote to us

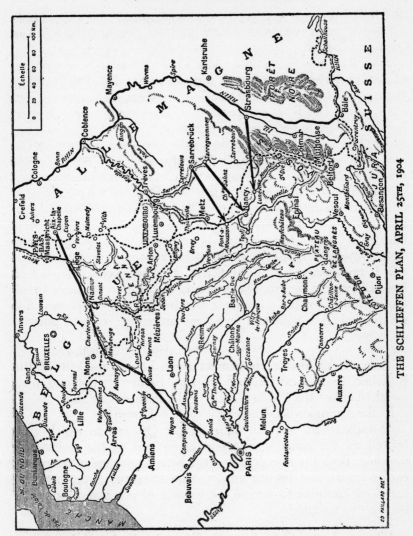

THE SCHLIEFFEN PLAN, APRIL 25TH, 1904

from Liège offering us *some documents of the highest importance.*
Our Intelligence got in touch with him through Captain Lambling,[1]
whom you know. The traitor handed over the entire new plan of
operations devised by the German General Staff, with a detailed
map of what is technically known as the *zones of concentration.*

[1] Captain Lambling, 25th Artillery Regiment, was at that time seconded to
Intelligence. He attained the rank of Colonel and died in 1917.

We have been able to check up on the documents he had got hold of, and his oral comments on them: I am absolutely satisfied of their genuineness.

"We have not the remotest idea who the traitor is; as a matter of fact, we have lost touch with him altogether. He gave Lambling three rendezvous, each by letter addressed from Liège; the first was Paris, the second Brussels, the third Nice, and each time at a smart hotel. But Lambling never saw him except with his head swathed in bandages, as if he had just had an operation; a grey moustache and piercing eyes were the only features visible. At their first interview, he made Lambling swear to respect his incognito and not to have him followed by our police. He said: *I have arranged to leave the hotel in an hour's time. If I find that you're having me followed, you'll never see me again and never know all the rest I have to tell you.* He several times remarked to Lambling: *I fully realize my infamy, but I've been treated even more infamously and this is my revenge. . . .* The three letters we received from him from Liège were signed: *The Avenger.* Yet he didn't hesitate to ask 60,000 francs for his documents and his travelling expenses. But we didn't haggle with him as his revelations are beyond price." [1]

Tuesday, April 26th, 1904.

Today King Victor Emmanuel treated the President of the Republic to a great military review. Eighteen thousand men marched across the Piazza d'Armi in the Prati di Castello.

In the afternoon M. Loubet visited the Forum.

At night there was a banquet at the Quirinal to which were invited all the generals who had taken part in the review this morning. Both the President and the King made cordial references to the Italian and French armies, 'expressing the hope that they may long continue to remain a guarantee of peace and prosperity for the two nations.'

After a short call at Bari, the Imperial Yacht *Hohenzollern* reached Venice yesterday evening. The Kaiser expects to stay there two days; he has to be at Karlsruhe on 28th April for an official function.

[1] For the authenticity of these revelations, see *Un Prélude à l'Invasion de la Belgique; le plan Schlieffen,* page 27 *et seq,* Paris 1932, published by Plon.

This morning, the Prefecture of Police notified the Russian terrorist, Vladimir Burtzev, of the cabinet order for his deportation. He has been given three days in which to leave the country.

Wednesday, April 27th, 1904.

During the three days which the President of the Republic has spent as a guest at the Quirinal Palace in Rome, the Vatican has done nothing to indicate its displeasure at this 'unholy visit.' Its only step has been to forbid the Catholics of Rome to take any part in the welcome to M. Loubet.

We nevertheless know that the Holy See adheres rigidly to its standpoint: "for the head of a Catholic nation, such as the President of the French Republic, to pay an official visit to the despoiler of the Papacy, and stay at the palace which was once the residence of the sovereign pontiffs, is a very grave insult to the head of the church and a criminal infringement of his right both now and always to complete political independence, in the interests of all Catholic nations and as befits the dignity of the Roman Church . . ." For the time being, Pius X is therefore affecting to ignore the presence of M. Loubet in Rome.

The Holy Father must none the less have seen him from his window during a long drive which Victor Emmanuel took with his guest the day before yesterday, when, apparently by chance, they passed the Vatican basilica.

This drive was the result of a sudden inspiration on the part of the King. The day was glorious, but very hot; the President had spent four whole hours at a series of tiresome and tiring receptions at the Farnese Palace; he was only too glad of a breath of fresh air. The pair were in a phæton, driven by the King in person. There was no escort. They went by the Via Nazionale, the Corso Vittorio Emmanuele, the Campo de Fiori, the Ponte Garibaldi, the Transtevere, the Janiculum hills, the Piazza S. Pietro, the Ponte Cavour, the Piazza del Popolo, the Castello S. Angelo embankment and the Borghese gardens, ending up at the Porta Pia, through which the victorious Italian troops entered Rome on September 20th, 1870.

In selecting this route, the King showed himself to be the perfect cicerone, but I doubt whether the Vatican will think much of his taste in passing St. Peter and stopping at the Porta Pia.

Yesterday, our ambassador in Berlin tried to broach the Moroccan question with Baron von Richthofen, the Imperial Secretary of State; he had been instructed to repeat the statements made by Delcassé to Prince von Radolin on March 23rd. But our ambassador, Bihourd, is the victim of a painful and progressive nervous malady, and once again he lacked the necessary self-confidence and resolution:

'From the first moment,' he wired us, 'I knew from Baron von Richthofen's icy manner that I should have to do all the talking. I therefore confined myself to the remark that I personally was very grateful for the Chancellor's speech in the Reichstag in which he admitted that the Anglo-French agreement was not aimed at any other power and in no way endangered German commercial interests.'

It would therefore appear that the Berlin Cabinet also intends to make us pay for our free hand in Morocco; but I imagine that in settling the account we shall have less trouble agreeing on the *price* than the *form*.

Thursday, April 28th, 1904.

At nine o'clock this morning, Victor Emmanuel and M. Loubet left Rome for Naples where the Presidential visit will end tomorrow with a naval review. They arrived at 2.30 this afternoon.

Streets gay with bunting, triumphal arches, the wildest enthusiasm—all in accordance with the classic traditions of Neapolitan demonstrations. Gala performance tonight at San Carlo Theatre.

Friday, April 29th, 1904.

This morning, King Victor Emmanuel and the President of the Republic reviewed the Italian and French squadrons in Naples harbour, after which came the farewells.

At 11 o'clock the President of the Republic embarked on the cruiser *La Marseillaise* and the French squadron put out to sea, making for Marseilles where it is due at 4 p.m. tomorrow.

Yesterday evening, i.e. twelve hours after the President of the Republic had left Rome, the Cardinal Secretary of State, Merry del Val, handed a formal protest to our ambassador, Nisard. It ends as follows:

It is hardly necessary to remind you that it is the duty of the heads of Catholic States, bound as they are by special ties to the Supreme Pastor of the Church, to pay greater regard to his dignity, independence and inalienable rights than the rulers of non-catholic countries. This duty, hitherto admitted and observed by all, is in a special degree incumbent on the first magistrate of the French Republic, the head of a nation which by tradition is very closely associated with the Roman Pontificate. . . .

It is a grave offence to the Sovereign Pontiff for any head of a Catholic country to do homage in Rome (the pontifical seat itself)—and in the apostolic palace itself—to one who, in violation of the law, denies him his temporal powers; but in M. Loubet's case the offence is doubly grave. The undersigned Cardinal Secretary of State, in the name of his Holiness, makes the most solemn protest against such a lamentable occurrence.

The Director of Political Affairs has been discussing this serious document with me; we have both come to the same conclusion: 'A rupture between France and the Holy See is now inevitable; for, on the one side, the Vatican has burnt its boats and, in the other, our Radicals will be only too glad to seize on such a favourable pretext to repudiate the concordat.'

Turning to the personal feelings of Pius X towards France, I mentioned two significant incidents to Georges Louis. Denys Cochin, the Conservative deputy, recently went to Rome in the forlorn hope of arranging a meeting between Delcassé and Cardinal Merry del Val. He came back 'very disappointed' with his visit to the Secretary of State. 'I found,' he told me, 'that the Vatican no longer likes us, nor even acknowledges our existence.' Another deputy of the Right, Count Caraman, also went to Rome a few weeks ago and returned 'highly incensed' at his visit to the Secretary of State. He confided his sorrows to Nisard: 'I did not go to the Vatican to be blackmailed with eulogies of Germany and the Emperor William.'

I wound up by telling Georges Louis of the outburst of a young writer who was so carried away by his catholic and monarchist sympathies that he could think of nothing strong enough to express his horror at President Loubet's visit to Rome. 'Do you mean to tell me that fine fellow Caserio has left no descendants!' [1]

[1] The Italian Anarchist Caserio, who assassinated President Carnot at Lyons on June 24th, 1894.

Saturday, April 30th, 1904.

The cruiser *La Marseillaise*, with the President of the Republic and the Foreign Minister on board, arrived at Marseilles at 4 o'clock this afternoon.

Loubet and Delcassé at once left by train for Paris where they are due tomorrow at 8 a.m.

The day before yesterday, April 28th, the Emperor William, addressing the Burgomaster at Carlsruhe, made a bellicose speech, —one of his 'brass band' efforts:

> *The affectionate welcome which the people have given me here is a worthy successor to the many enthusiastic receptions which were my lot in Italy. I visited the lovely coast where the Hohenstaufens once lived, and where their memory is still kept green. The numerous speeches and addresses, the many artistic monuments, seemed to bring back the great days of Frederick II. You were right, Herr Burgomaster, in saying that the task before the German people is a heavy one. Let us recall the great epoch when the unity of our nation was restored. Yes, let us recall the battles of Woerth, Wissemburg and Sedan. And let us recall the cries of joy with which the Duke of Baden greeted the first Emperor of Germany.*
>
> *I should like to hope that peace will not be troubled. But I also hope that present events will put Germany on her guard and steel her courage.*
>
> *My last hope is that we shall find ourselves of one mind if we are obliged to intervene in world politics.*

This speech, the outburst of a mountebank and bully, is the effect of all the snubs which the Kaiser has met with of late.

At first, he accepted Prince von Radolin's assurances and hoped that the President of the Republic would consent to meet him during his visit to Italy. From a deciphered telegram, we know that shortly before April 15th, the Chancellor, Bülow, made three alternative suggestions to the ambassador: (1). a meeting between the Emperor and M. Loubet off the coast of Italy: (2). a meeting in Italy: (3). a meeting off Algiers, where the Imperial yacht was to call, but 'without anchoring.' The ambassador, caught in the trap of his own lies and toadyism, replied that, on reflection, he could not accept any of the three. But the Kaiser stuck to his guns.

He hung about Italy throughout the President's visit, not daring openly to admit his desire to meet M. Loubet, but looking to his ally, Victor Emmanuel, to find some subterfuge to bring about this meeting. Victor Emmanuel, however, does not like crooked methods and said nothing. William then suddenly changed his itinerary. The *Hohenzollern* should have steamed from Bari to Corfu, returned to Naples and then up the coast to Genoa. She went straight to Venice.

At Venice, further trouble. The *Hohenzollern* cast anchor at 9 p.m. on April 25th, in Malamocco channel. The next day the Emperor paid an unaccompanied call on a very distinguished and beautiful lady, Countess Morosini, with whom he has been on terms of platonic friendship for a very long time. After lunch he remained with her for the rest of the afternoon; in the evening she dined with him on his yacht. The next day, the 27th, he lunched again at the Morosini palace and from there went to the station to catch his train to Carlsruhe.

The Venetians have been greatly shocked by this sentimental episode which is reminiscent of the 'courts of love,' celebrated in the epics of Petrarch, Guido Cavalcanti and the troubadours. They considered it very bad taste on the Emperor of Germany's part to spend the whole of his time on his short visit alone with Countess Morosini, without sparing a moment to see the repairs to the Campanile on the Piazza San Marco, where all the civil dignitaries were waiting for him.[1]

The Venetians are fiery-tempered. The Socialist newspapers ignited the train.

As early as April 26th, the *Secolo nuovo* announced:

"The moment the *Hohenzollern* cast anchor off Malamocco last night—a dark night—a mysterious gondola was seen hailing the Imperial yacht and a veiled woman went on board."

The next day, the 27th, the scandal was out. The moment the Kaiser had left Venice, a rumour spread like wildfire through the whole city: 'The Emperor was seen sneaking out of Morosini palace this morning.' In the streets in the vicinity of the palace, some bold hand had scrawled obscene remarks.

Simultaneously, the principal socialist paper, *Secolo nuovo*, threw mud at another and equally blameless lady, Countess Branolin da Balmarino. She had made a third at the Morosini palace

[1] The Campanile of St. Mark suddenly collapsed on July 14th, 1902.

luncheon. This lady's two sons lay in wait for Marangoni, the editor of the *Secolo nuovo,* in the Piazza San Luca, and beat the life out of him. In the evening there was a fearful *fracas* in the Piazza San Marco between the lower orders and the smart set.

The next day, the demonstrations became more violent than ever.

Before long, even the police and the garrison found themselves incapable of restoring order and had to be reinforced by regiments hastily called in from Verona and Padua.

It was with this news still buzzing in his ears that the Emperor William made his fiery speech at Carlsruhe.

Sunday, May 1st, 1904.

The President of the Republic and Delcassé reached Paris at eight o'clock this morning.

Among the high officials who met them at the Gare du Lyon was Georges Louis, the Director of Political Affairs. He was invited by the Minister to return to the Quai d'Orsay in his carriage, and lost no time in telling Delcassé of the formal protest presented by the Holy See to our ambassador, Nisard, on April 28th.

Delcassé received the blow quite unmoved: "How stupid of them to protest! There'll be no difficulty about the reply. . . . Does the Holy See think it's going to dictate our relations with Italy? Its grievances against the House of Savoy are no concern of ours. If it wants to break off diplomatic relations with France, it can go ahead! . . . You know very well that I don't want a rupture and have done all I can to avoid it. But before making it inevitable, the Pope would be well advised to consider what it may cost him. For us it will have at least one compensation, the possibility of a Franco-Italian alliance. I feel in my bones that I can even now call that possibility a certainty."

At 7 o'clock Delcassé sent for me to tell him about the *Avenger's* disclosures which Georges Louis had just mentioned to him.

The Minister, pursing his lips and keeping his eyes fixed on me, heard me out. When I had finished, he said:

"It's all very serious! But doesn't it show that my policy is absolutely right! Compare the *Avenger's* revelations with the Carlsruhe speech. You find the same idea, the same objective: war on France, provocation to France, the annihilation of France. Our need of

fresh allies is greater than ever, because it'll be a long time before
Russia recovers her freedom of action in Europe."

Monday, 2nd May, 1904.

I dined very quietly *chez* the Comtesse Jean de Castellane with
Prince and Princess von Donnersmark.[1]

The Prince, a man of splendid presence, carries his seventy-four
years remarkably well. He has a fine head and his eyes are full of
intelligence, mockery, courage and fire. His wife is thirty-nine, tall
and slender with graceful, rhythmical movements. She sings when
she speaks and has delicate features, shadowed, shrivelled eyelids
and very long lashes. Her tawny eyes have such a magnetic quality
that each glance seems like a gentle touch or a caress. At the time
of her first marriage in St. Petersburg, she was so feline, bewitching
and irresistible that her admirers nicknamed her 'Cleopatra' or
'Circe.' . . .

Above our heads at table was the portrait of another Circe, the
Duchesse de Dino, Talleyrand's Egeria. As we left the dining-room,
we fell to talking of Thiers of whom Donnersmark saw a lot in
1871, during the tiresome negotiations at Versailles and Frankfurt:

"The correspondence between Thiers and Manteuffel is a document of great importance—a perfect model of political literature.
The more I know, the more I admire Thiers' patriotism, his personal prestige and the amazing resource of his mind. . . . I have
a very high opinion of his chief colleague, Saint-Vallier, too. . . .
They were the real architects of the peace."

"What about Pouyer-Quertier, the Finance Minister," I asked
the Prince: "I understood that he managed to win Bismarck's
confidence, and even his friendship, before those unhappy negotiations were over."

"Yes, Bismarck quite liked him, but only because he didn't
whine, and put a good face on his painful job. But there was something else. Like Bismarck, Pouyer-Quertier had a colossal appetite.

[1] In 1901 Count Henckel, the descendant of an old Silesian family, was granted
the Prussian title of "Prince von Donnersmark," with the right to be addressed as
"Serene Highness."

During the Second Empire he cut a great figure in Paris. In 1871, he married the
notorious Madame de Paiva, *née* Lachmann, who died in 1884. He was very
friendly with Bismarck and played an important part—as go-between doing all the
dirty work—in the negotiations which culminated in the Treaty of Frankfurt. In
1887 he married a Russian, Catherine Slepzoff, the divorced wife of Count Muravieff.
The mines he owned in Silesia brought him in an enormous income.

They had lots of wonderful duels with fork and beer mug. Their friendship stopped there. . . . At bottom, only Thiers and Saint-Vallier counted in Bismarck's eyes."

I then asked Donnersmark about the Arnim case.

"Why did Bismarck choose a moment when he was absolutely omnipotent and just at the height of his power to start such a scandalous case for such futile reasons?"

"Because Bismarck was a tremendous egoist, a monstrous egoist; if he hadn't been, he would never have carried through the colossal task of creating German unity. . . . Conscious as he was of his own superiority and intoxicated with pride, he could not tolerate an equal, much less a rival. It occurred to him one day that Arnim might become a possible rival, so he trod on him as if he'd been a worm. . . . If you're trying to understand Otto von Bismarck, don't forget that he was primarily a *savage*. That was the secret of his strength. He elevated the two outstanding characteristics of the *savage*—violence and cunning—to the level of genius."

Donnersmark is full of stories of that great epoch which settled Germany's future for many years to come. He ended with an amusing anecdote.

"After we returned to Berlin in the spring of 1871, the Chancellor, Marshal von Moltke, Marshal von Roon and I met in Bismarck's drawing-room, a little room in which we had not foregathered since that critical week in July 1870. After dinner, Bismarck said: *We've done great things; the results have surpassed all our calculations, all our anticipations, all our hopes. Now let's talk about ourselves. Let's think: what else can we want?* I modestly said nothing. The two marshals gravely cogitated. Then the Chancellor broke the silence with the remark: *There's only one thing more I want—that the heir of our revered Emperor will not undo my work—And I,* said Moltke, *want our army always to be the first in the world.* Roon was still lost in thought. We pressed him to speak out. At length he said: *After all I've seen happen, I have nothing further to wish. I can't imagine any other interest in life beyond sitting by a tree and watching it grow.*"

"Fundamentally," I said to Bismarck, "that's the same view, the same philosophy, as Napoleon's when, having achieved all his ambitions and attained all the heights of glory, he planted an oak at Longwood."

Then we fell to discussing the difficult problems of the hour. Jean de Castellane bluntly asked:

"Why was the Emperor William such a firebrand in his speech at Carlsruhe? Why the trumpet blast? Why the cruel allusions to our defeats in 1870?"

"The Emperor is very angry with France. He has seen the failure of all his efforts to bring about a reconciliation and work with her. All his advances, however friendly and tactful, have come up against the systematic opposition of your statesmen. Every time he has offered you the hand of friendship you have contemptuously thrust it aside. Your press does nothing but make fun of him. And now his patience has given out; his nerves are on edge. M. Delcassé would be well advised to be careful!"

"The Emperor William's ambition to bring France and Germany together is doubtless a very noble ideal," I replied. "But it's an insoluble problem while Alsace-Lorraine remains a gulf separating the two countries."

Donnersmark reflected for a few moments and then said: "All the same, it may well be that this reconciliation, which you think impossible, will materialize before long—and on a *terrain* very different from Alsace-Lorraine—the *terrain* of the *Yellow Peril.*"

Here, Princess Catherine, who, lost in thought and seeing Heaven knows what visions in her cigarette-smoke, had not said a word during this conversation, interrupted in her singing voice:

"Questions of race and territory are of no importance to us westerners—none at all—What should bring us together is the Cross . . . the Cross of the Redeemer . . ."

Chapter IV

Tuesday, 3rd May, 1904.

THE war in the Far East has begun badly for the Russians.

Yesterday, May 1st, the Japanese Army, commanded by General Kuroki, crossed the Yalu which is the frontier between Korea and Manchuria.

The Russians, commanded by General Zassulitch, are retiring on Feng-hwang-cheng.

Wednesday, 4th May, 1904.

I have lately been reading a book, published recently, by the great Polish historian, Waliszewski. It is one of his fine series on the *Origins of Modern Russia* and deals with *Ivan the Terrible*.

Speaking of the terrible anarchy into which the Empire of the Muscovite tsars sank in the time of Boris Godunoff, towards the close of the sixteenth century, the historian writes:

> *The internal and external development of the great empire of the North seems to have much in common with the behavior of an avalanche. At prolonged intervals the centre of gravity suddenly shifts, producing a swift advance which is then followed by a more or less lengthy period of inactivity. This phenomenon has already recurred several times and appearances point to another repetition. . . . At the present moment (1904), and for the last twenty years, the progress of the Russian nation along the lines previously indicated seems to have been suspended at home and arrested abroad. The explanation is that their energies have been absorbed and deflected by the conquest of a new realm—a realm which is likely to extend their field for evolution to the China seas and the Persian Gulf. But the problems they have temporarily laid aside are none the less slowly but surely coming to a head and, when they do, beware of the avalanche!*

It may be true that, in the domain of politics, history never repeats itself exactly, but I firmly believe in historical determinism, the internal working of the great fundamental and permanent forces which govern the evolution of a nation.

When the war in Manchuria is considered from that point of view, it is impossible not to have misgivings about the future of Tsarism.

I discussed the matter with Delcassé and showed him this passage from Waliszewski. He read it through, shrugged his shoulders and snapped out at me:

"Why do you make me read such stuff? . . . You know I don't consider history of any practical use. . . . All historians are false guides because they are out of touch with reality, or rather, because they see it *a posteriori,* in retrospect, after events have happened and it is no longer possible to change their course. . . . It is just the opposite for the statesman: he sees events *on their way,* with all the risks, openings, possibilities and opportunities for skilful handling which they offer. . . . Can you see me consulting a history book in a crisis? Not I! At such moments what counts most is flair, a cool head, courage, resolution and nimble wits. . . . Beware of history, my dear Paléologue!"

All the same, Waliszewski's ominous prediction seemed to have got home; twice did he mutter in gloomy tones: *Beware of the avalanche!* . . . . *Beware of the avalanche!* Then, with an irritable frown, he turned to the business of the day.

Friday, May 6th, 1904.

When Delcassé, on his return from Rome, heard of the protest of the Holy See against the President of the Republic's visit to the King of Italy, he scornfully remarked to Georges Louis: "Their protest is absurd; . . . I shall find it quite easy to reply. . . ."

The actual reply is as follows:

As the French Minister of Foreign Affairs was careful to explain to Parliament the exact nature and object of the visit of the President of the French Republic to Italy, he can only protest in the name of his Government against the arguments put forward in the note from the Cardinal Secretary of State, and the form in which they are presented.

This reply is caustic, brief and uncompromising and, in view of the fact that it amounts to a blunt "rejection" of the pontifical note, I can see no hope of conciliation.

Saturday, May 7th, 1904.

Pius X, reminding the Catholic world of the inalienable rights of the Papacy to the Eternal City, has made an emphatic protest to the great powers against the President of the Republic's visit to the King of Italy.

I am not at all surprised at his desire to reaffirm those fundamental rights, and protest once again against the "sacrilegious spoliation of 1870." But he might have adopted some other method and refrained from attacking France; after all, she is in no way concerned in the quarrel between the Italian nation and the Apostolic See. It is quite certain that a diplomatic and far-sighted Pope like Leo XIII would have gone to work differently; he would probably have waited for the next consistory or encyclical and then solemnly affirmed *in abstracto* the immutable doctrine of the Roman pontificate.[1]

However that may be, a breach with the Vatican cannot be delayed much longer.

Monday, May 9th, 1904.

The Holy See and the Government of the Republic are no longer on speaking terms, literally at any rate, for communication is now confined to the exchange of formal documents, as if a legal action were in progress. The Nuncio, Monsignor Lorenzelli, handed us the following note today:

> *In the name of his Eminence the Cardinal Secretary of State to his Holiness, the Apostolic Nuncio begs to inform his Excellency the Minister of Foreign Affairs that the meaning and implications of the note delivered by the Ambassador of the French Republic are not understood, since there is no reply to the arguments set forth in the note from his Eminence the Cardinal Secretary of State, under date of April 28th 1904.*

On receiving this document, the Minister shrugged his shoulders: "They can't have understood the note of May 6th . . . I'm not surprised. They don't understand because they don't want to understand. All right! They can shoulder the responsibility to history! . . . The Holy See thinks it can intimidate me by making me break with it. All right! We'll break! But I refuse to sacrifice

---

[1] Everyone knows that, in 1920, the Vatican abandoned its doctrinal intransigeance and has since been completely reconciled with the Savoy monarchy.

the fundamental interests of France to the obsolete utopia of Temporal Power!"

As he uttered this high-sounding phrase, I had a feeling he was rehearsing for a speech in Parliament.

After a moment's reflection, he said to Georges Louis in haughty tones:

"The pontifical note will remain unanswered."

Tuesday, May 10th, 1904.

General Moulin,[1] our Military Attaché in Russia, just back from St. Petersburg, has been to see me at the Quai d'Orsay. He confirmed his official dispatches and embellished them with some very gloomy forecasts:

"You ask me whether the Russians won't win in the end? . . . I'm not at all certain. Even if they do, they'll have paid such a price that it will hardly be worth while. They've lost Korea for ever, and all they can do is to get China to delegate them some sort of suzerainty in Manchuria. That's the most they can hope for now . . . and you'll see the reaction within the Empire and the revival of revolutionary fever . . ."

As he was concluding this effort in prophecy, Delcassé sent for me to talk about Germany, the Emperor William and the degree of importance we should attach to his firebrand speech at Carlsruhe. He asked me to get Intelligence to check up on some secret information he has received direct from Berlin.

The conversation then turned to the Japanese offensive in Manchuria and I told him of the talk I had just had with General Moulin. He listened grimly and without comment, then burst out:

"Now I understand William's insolence."

Wednesday, 11th May, 1904.

I met Lardy, the Swiss Minister, on the Quai d'Orsay and we walked a little way together.

I regard him as the most level-headed, intelligent and far-sighted of all the diplomats now resident in Paris. It is said that he does not like France; I know nothing about that: but if so, I should be very surprised if he showed it, because he never allows his sympathies or antipathies to affect his unemotional opinions.

[1] Colonel Moulin had been promoted to the rank of Brigadier-General on March 30th, 1904.

We chatted as we went along. He confided to me how 'very uneasy' he was about the Emperor William's mischievous activities.

"I represent a country," he said, "which has only one guarantee for its independence, its future and even its existence—its neutrality. So you can imagine how the prospect of a great European war keeps me awake at night. . . . Everything I have observed for some time makes me feel very pessimistic; the Emperor William is getting more and more nervy and irritable. Your agreement with England and the President of the Republic's visit to Rome have made him see red. Hence the outburst in his speech at Carlsruhe. . . . What does M. Delcassé think of it?"

"M. Delcassé thinks that the Carlsruhe speech is probably nothing but a pin-prick of no significance. But he doesn't dismiss from his mind the possibility that it may mark the first move in a quarrel. If he's right, we can only cooperate with our friends and allies in standing our ground and, if necessary, submitting the dispute to the judgment of Europe . . ."

Friday, May 13th, 1904.

A few days ago, the Japanese landed in force at Pi-tse-vo, on the peninsula of Liao-tung.

Port Arthur is now invested by land and cut off from communication with Russia. The garrison of the fortress, which is under the command of General Stoessel, comprises about 50,000 men.

Saturday, May 14th, 1904.

I dined with the Grand Duke Paul.

The little coterie which meets in the Avenue d'Iéna has extended considerably in the last few months.

During the evening, the Grand Duke anxiously pressed me for news of the Manchurian campaign.

"Hostilities have hardly begun," I replied. "Kuropatkin has said himself that they will probably be of very long duration . . . perhaps eighteen months. It would therefore be prematiure to make any prophecy. But, if I can accept the opinion of our leading soldiers, Russia's main concern at the moment is to recover control of the sea; one of them told me yesterday that ultimate victory would definitely go to the belligerent which could manage to retain naval supremacy."

At this the Grand Duke closed his eyes and remained lost in thought for a moment: then he crossed himself.

Sunday, May 15th, 1904.

Public opinion in Germany is losing both its nerve and its temper and Bülow is being attacked for the short-sighted clumsiness of his policy—nor is it afraid of including the Kaiser in its criticism.

One important press organ, the *Parliamentary Correspondence*, which more or less represents National Liberal opinion, wrote quite recently:

"The astounding transformation which has just taken place in France's relations with England and Italy inspired the Emperor's speeches at Carlsruhe and Mainz. It would therefore appear that a change is impending in the governing principles of German policy. We certainly could not go on making ourselves the laughing stock of Europe and it is time we stopped running after every power in turn, asking them for favours. Such abject humility is now inconsistent with the sensational speeches in which the Emperor recently reminded us of our victories at Wissemburg, Woerth and Sedan. But it is permissible to enquire whether it was wise, from the diplomatic point of view, to talk in that strain."

Tuesday, May 17th, 1904.

Delcassé is angrier than I ever remember having seen him, even in the worst days of the Dreyfus case.

This morning, *L'Humanité*, the organ of Jaurès, published the protest of the Holy See against the President of the Republic's visit to Rome; I need hardly say that it regards that protest as an intolerable insult, demanding an immediate reply, the recall of our Ambassador, the abrogation of the Concordat and the complete severance of all the ties uniting Church and State in France.

The fact is that Delcassé, cherishing a vague hope of arranging matters privately with the Vatican, had not shown the pontifical note of April 28th to anyone; he had simply 'told' his ministerial colleagues about it and 'read' them only the text of his scornful reply. This morning's journalistic diatribe means the opening of hostilities.

He sent for Georges Louis and myself and gave us instructions for a thorough investigation as to how the note came into the possession of Jaurès:

"Whoever is responsible for this leakage," he said, quivering with rage, "I don't care who it is, even if it's my best friend, I'll smash him!"

Georges Louis was soon able to show him that none of the ministry officials was responsible:

"The note only left my drawer to be put away in M. Paléologue's safe."

"Good . . . then what's the explanation?"

In the Chamber this afternoon Delcassé was told by Jaurès himself that the note had been communicated to him by the Vatican! The Holy See must *want* the rupture.

Thursday, May 19th, 1904.

The Pontifical note is not meeting with approval from any section of public opinion. Even in reactionary circles it is considered inopportune and lacking in moderation and even courtesy. In Leo XIII's time, the draftsmen of the Vatican chancery wrote in a very different style.

The Socialists and Radicals are, of course, exultant:

"They've thrown down the gauntlet. We'll pick it up . . ."

The *Temps*, taking its cure from the Quai d'Orsay, writes as follows: M. Jaurès tells us: *Since the Pope sent his note, the rupture of diplomatic relations between France and the Holy See is virtually a fact.* We do not accept this extreme statement. Because the Vatican has made one mistake, are we bound to make another? Must an ill-timed demonstration of ultramontanism necessarily involve the separation of Church and State? We do not think so. After all, this matter concerns no one but ourselves. It is not from a relic of tenderness towards the temporal sovereignty of the Pope, nor even as an act of homage to his spiritual sovereignty, that we defend the French embassy to the Holy See, the Concordat and the Public Worship estimates. It is because estimates, embassy and Concordat are, and in our opinion will remain, the best guarantee of religious peace in France. It is therefore on our own account, and not on that of the Holy See, that we adhere to this contractual arrangement. Is the fact that the Holy See seems less attached to it at the moment a reason for abandoning it ourselves? Shall we meet it half-way? Shall it be left to the Vatican to decide whether we are to be forced into reprisals which our interests do not require? And do we want to appear to be at its mercy by meekly following in the path it has chosen?

Friday, May 20th, 1904.

The Government has decided to recall our ambassador to the Holy See at once. Diplomatic relations, however, have not yet been broken off. One of the secretaries has temporarily been left in charge of the embassy in Palazzo Santa-Croce.

Saturday, May 21st, 1904.

Nisard left Rome this evening.

I called on Madame d'Haussonville at two o'clock and met a Right Wing deputy, Denys Cochin. Their feeling was that the Holy See has made a tremendous and irreparable mistake in re-opening the question of temporal power:

"The matter was settled thirty-four years ago," said Cochin. "For thirty-four years all the ultra-catholic powers, Spain and Austria, for instance, have simultaneously had ambassadors both at the Quirinal and the Vatican. So why this protest about M. Loubet? . . . After all, haven't we frequently seen the sovereign pontiff receiving the German Emperor and the King of England with every mark of honour and esteem just after they had been officially welcomed by the King of Italy? Why shouldn't the President of the French Republic be treated on the same footing? . . . I believe I'm a good Catholic. Even so, I admit that I'm not in the least interested in the papal rights to the patrimony of St. Peter . . . any more than its rights to Avignon and the Comtat Venaissin . . ."

Monday, 23rd May, 1904.

I have no doubt that the agreement of April 8th contains within itself the germs of an Anglo-French alliance. But I am afraid that Delcassé's lively imagination is running away with him.

Let me record a little incident which shows that even now Fashoda is not quite forgotten at the *War Office*, though it may be at the *Foreign Office*. Our counter-espionage agents have just caught a retired artillery colonel named Gordon in the act of making plans of the fortifications of Belle-Isle.

Thursday, May 26th, 1904.

Delcassé, in talkative mood, has been prophesying the future of Europe. His predictions may be summarized thus:

"Henceforth, nothing will keep German megalomania in check and it will inevitably lead to a general war which will be a matter of life or death to France." As usual, his conclusion was that it is necessary to organize a vast coalition which could stand up to Germany if the necessity arose. He wound up with the following remark:

"What proves that my deductions are perfectly logical is the fact that King Edward said the same thing during our talks at Buckingham Palace last summer.[1] You know how sensible, practical and thoughtful Edward VII is . . . I couldn't ask for anyone better to back my opinion."

Then he told me of some remarks which King Edward volunteered: "Russia is indispensable if Germany is to be kept in awe of us. I can only beg you, Monsieur le Ministre, to make your allies in St. Petersburg realize that from now onwards France, England and Russia must go hand in hand. If you do that, you will have done great work for the world's freedom."

By way of epigraph to this conversation, I should like to add Vauvenargues' fine thought: *War is less onerous than servitude.*

Friday, May 27th, 1904.

The Chamber discussed today the interpellation to the Government with regard to the pontifical note of April 28th. I was present.

After a violent attack by the Radicals and Socialists, Delcassé, a model of self-possession, coolly replied:

"The President of the Republic's visit to Rome was a demonstration by the Government that French policy is wholly independent; it has further showed that that policy is dictated solely by the interests of France. In recalling our ambassador, the Government has done all that our honour required."

Combes mounted the Tribune to close the debate: 'The recall of our Ambassador shows that we were not prepared to allow the Papacy to interfere in our international relations and that *we wished to have done with the obsolete fiction of temporal power which crumbled thirty-four years ago.'*

Although the language was rather blunt, this speech is really most opportune. The President of the Council has not denounced the Concordat; he has promised to look into the serious problem of separation, but not at present; he has realized the necessity of

[1] July 7th and 8th, 1903.

continuing diplomatic relations with the Vatican; he has not even undertaken not to send back the Ambassador. He has therefore conceded practically nothing to the demands of the Radical and Socialist group. When he denounced the 'obsolete fiction of temporal power which crumbled thirty-four years ago,' not a single Right Wing deputy protested.

Saturday, May 28th, 1904.

By dint of superhuman heroism, the Japanese have carried the formidable Kin-chau positions, which bar the approaches to the Liao-tung. The whole Kwang-tung peninsula is now cut off from the continent of Asia.

Melchior de Vogüé, Othenin d'Haussonville and Nisard lunched with me. The conversation was very animated and we found ourselves constantly returning to the subject of the war in the Far East. D'Haussonville asked me to what I attributed the succession of Russian reverses:

"There must be some major reason for this long and melancholy series of defeats!"

"I do believe there's a fundamental explanation. I don't think it lies in the defects of the Russian Army; it lies in the unanticipated vigour, skill and superiority of its adversary. There's no doubt now that as regards courage, daring, armament and training, tactics and strategy, the Japanese army has an unsuspected advantage. The Russians are today paying a heavy price for their jokes and jeers about *the nasty little Nippon monkeys*. . . . Yet, even in St. Petersburg, there was one high officer, the War Minister, General Kuropatkin, who held a different opinion of the Japanese army. During the weeks preceding the outbreak of hostilities, he often said to our military attaché, General Moulin: '*God save us from war; it would be very long and perilous, and there would be no glory in it!*' . . . More recently he said: '*I don't suppose the war can end before eighteen months and I calculate we shall have to employ three hundred thousand men.*'"

Nisard voiced his conclusion:

"It means that in a military sense the Franco-Russian alliance is paralysed for eighteen months! . . . Germany will have an easy job!"

Vogüé looked very grave and said nothing for a moment. Then his cavernous voice was heard prophesying a great European tragedy in the very near future. I comforted my guests by telling them that Delcassé, on the contrary, thinks that what he calls "a supple combination of the Franco-Russian system with the Anglo-French system" will provide a means of preserving the peace of Europe "for and against everyone."

"Well, if he manages that," cried Nisard warmly, "he'll have earned a high place in the history of French diplomacy."

We then broached the subject of yesterday's debate in the Chamber.

D'Haussonville claims that the separation of church and state is now inevitable, although 'our masters at the moment' do not want it.

"I admit I want it myself. The Catholics are only a minority in France. I don't deny it; but this minority counts for a lot and it is courageous and united; it can play a great part, politically and socially. We shall be much stronger when we are as free as the American Catholics. . . . Of course the change will involve a lot of hardship and sacrifice. But anything's better than the present system. We've had enough of obeying bishops whom we don't like."

Nisard and Vogüé, on the other hand, thought that the abrogation of the Concordat would mean the collapse of Christianity in France, because, from the religious point of view, the French are still steeped in the Constantine tradition.

D'Haussonville and Vogüé pressed Nisard to tell them about M. Loubet's visit to Rome and the negotiations with Merry del Val which have resulted in the present breach.

I have recorded Nisard's statements under their appropriate dates. He added these two interesting sketches:

Merry del Val: thirty-eight; Spanish father, English mother; from the former he gets the uncompromising arrogance, from the latter the Puritan bigotry, from which we are suffering now; *Pius X*: would make an excellent bishop, pious and *borné*. Puts all his trust in God and spiritual forces, and totally blind to political considerations and human calculations . . .

Wednesday, June 1st, 1904.

On April 26th the Prefecture of Police notified Burtzev, the Terrorist, of the order for his deportation. But he is still in Paris, thanks to the all-powerful protection of Jaurès.

The Russian Ambassador is so furious with Delcassé about it that the latter took the matter up with the Cabinet. After a heated dispute, the Cabinet ordered Burtzev's immediate expulsion.

Thursday, June 2nd, 1904.

For some time, I have been observing with some surprise the growth of a new mentality in Germany, a sort of national mysticism, crediting the German race with a special and divine mission to take over the future government of humanity, and having the following practical effect; the rulers of Germany must develop to the full those powers of expansion inherent in Germanism and not be afraid of voicing its just claim to world hegemony—*Weltkaisertum.*

It is sheer megalomania; that most dangerous of mental afflictions, 'egocentric psychosis,' 'obsessional paranoia.'

The first symptom which I observed was in 1900, at the time of Marshal von Waldersee's much-advertised expedition to China.[1] Since then, the disease has made continuous progress and taken firm hold on German mentality. Quite recently, its ravages have been manifested once more at Stettin and Lübeck in the arrogant resolutions passed by the Colonial Union and the Pan-German League. After a long discussion about Morocco, these two great associations carried the following motions: 'That Germany feels herself humiliated at not having been consulted during the negotiation of the Anglo-French agreement. She considers she has quite as much right as France to develop her commercial interests and political rights in the Empire of the Maghreb; she therefore demands equal treatment in every respect; she further claims for the Imperial navy the concession of a Moroccan port on the Atlantic coast.

I pointed out to Delcassé the significance of these resolutions as symptoms. He shrugged his shoulders:

"It's ridiculous! Just megalomania! . . . What does Germany

---

[1] In the Spring of 1900 an anti-foreign revolution, the "Boxer" rising, broke out in the whole of northern China. The foreign legations in Peking had to stand a very long siege. An expeditionary force, comprising French, Russian, English, German and Japanese troops, had to be sent to Pechili. The Emperor William had cunningly induced his simple-minded cousin, the Tsar Nicholas, to agree that Field-Marshal von Waldersee should be put in command of this force. The Marshal's departure for China had provided William II with an opportunity for one of his pompous and theatrical outbursts.

really want? Her interests in Morocco are purely commercial. Doesn't the Anglo-French agreement safeguard them? I personally gave Prince Radolin explicit assurances that it did and, a few days later, the Chancellor, Bülow, told the Reichstag that he was perfectly satisfied with my statements. I'm quite all right with Berlin. If Germany is now saying that she has *political* rights in Morocco and claiming an equal position with ourselves, it can only mean that she's after something much bigger than Morocco. . . . It isn't very difficult to guess: it will lead Germany straight into war."

As I seemed somewhat taken aback at such an emphatic conclusion, he repeated:

"Don't forget what I say: William's vainglorious policy can only result in war."

Friday, June 3rd, 1904.

On the 30th of last month the Emperor William, after reviewing the Potsdam garrison, invited all the foreign military attachés to luncheon.

On rising from the table, he had a long talk with our military attaché, Major de Laguiche, who is in high favour at the court of Berlin, owing to his marriage to the daughter of Prince Augustus von Arenberg. The Emperor abruptly switched off to the topic of the causes of the Russo-Japanese war:

"In 1895 the Tsar foresaw the extremes to which a policy of ambition would carry Japan. But, having clearly seen *the yellow peril*, my dear cousin then went to sleep, lulled into the most incredible sense of security—Time and again I have tried to open his eyes to the determined preparations being made by the Japanese army. But each time Nicholas II, annoyed at my persistence, merely told me he already knew all about it . . ."

As regards the operations in progress in Manchuria, the Kaiser thinks they bode ill for the Russians; it is doubtful whether they will win at all and, in any case, they will have to make a tremendous effort to do so.

Again reverting to his 'craze,' *the Yellow Peril*, the Emperor said he was sorry we had not sent our squadrons to the assistance of Port Arthur and Vladivostok, if only to protect our possessions in Indo-China. Here it occurred to him that French intervention in the Russo-Japanese War would necessarily bring England into the fray on the other side, so he went on to remark with a leer:

"You needn't have worried about your friends coming in. I know the state they're in. They haven't yet recovered from the nasty knocks they got in the Transvaal; they're tradesmen, *business men,* first and foremost; they'd have left you to do what you liked."

Friday, June 10th, 1904.

The prolonged investment of Port Arthur and the idea of this great stronghold, 'the golden mountain on which the cross of the Saviour gleams,' falling into the enemy's hands have made the entire Russian nation angry and apprehensive; no one understands why the armies in Manchuria have not long ago driven the Japanese out of the Liao-tung Peninsula.

So the Tsar has just wired to General Kuropatkin: *I hold you personally responsible for the fate of Port Arthur.*

The Generalissimo has therefore given General Stackelberg's army instructions to take the offensive in the direction of the Liao-tung.

"This offensive seems to me extremely risky," said General Pendézec to me. "You know what usually happens when the civil authorities interfere with the conduct of military operations. Let me remind you of the march on Sedan in 1870!"

Wednesday, June 15th, 1904.

From time immemorial, but particularly during the last few months, the Moroccan Empire has been in financial difficulties. It could not find anyone to borrow from; it has exhausted every expedient, including fraud, confiscation and spurious notes. It has been a case of chronic insolvency.

For a long time, too, our minister at Tangier, Saint-René Taillandier, has been sagely insisting that the whole future of our policy in Morocco would depend on what we could do to relieve the poverty of the Maghzen.

We thus had an opportunity of making ourselves useful to the Sultan, Mulai Abd-el-Aziz, and thereby acquiring the official right to intervene in the administration of his states.

Under pressure from Delcassé, a group of French banks has just signed a contract at Fez, placing 62,500,000 francs at the disposal of the Sharifian Treasury. It will bear interest at five per cent and be redeemable in thirty-six years. It is pledged on the entire customs revenue of the empire. To make this guarantee effective, the

banks will have a representative of the bond-holders in every port
to collect the receipts and see to the strict application of the tariffs.
What is more, the banking group is to have the first call of any
further loans.

From now onwards, Morocco is financially under our thumb.

Thursday, June 16th, 1904.
This morning, General Bobrikov, Governor-General of Finland,
was shot twice through the chest in a Helsingfors square and died
almost immediately. The assassin, a Finnish aristocrat, committed
suicide; a few days earlier, he had said openly that Russian tyranny
had become intolerable to the Finns and he would soon avenge
his down-trodden compatriots.

Friday, June 17th, 1904.
General Stackelberg's army, which had been sent from Man-
churia to the relief of Port Arthur, was defeated at Vafang-u by
General Oku's army. I am now certain that the investment of Port
Arthur cannot be prevented.

Monday, June 20th, 1904.
The quarrel between the Holy See and France is entering on a
new phase. No doubt it will be the last, as the stage of open breach
has almost been reached already.

Today the President of the Council, who is also Minister of
the Interior and Minister of Public Worship, has made a protest
against 'a very serious breach of etiquette' which the Papal Nuncio
has just committed in personally remonstrating with two French
bishops, the bishops of Laval and Dijon, and also issuing orders
to them direct. He considers these actions an obvious violation of
the Concordat. 'At all times and under all *régimes*, the Nuncio's
sole function vis-à-vis the French Government has been that of an
ambassador. At all times and under all *régimes*, the French Government has refused to recognize any claim by the Nuncio to correspond direct with the bishops. . . . I think it opportune to remind the Holy See of these principles.'

So the polemics between France and the Holy See have begun
again.

Friday, June 24th, 1904.

Garden-party at the Austro-Hungarian Embassy. Francis Joseph's new ambassador, Count Rudolf von Khevenhüller, who has been in residence in Paris for six months, has just had the magnificent Galliéra house (in the rue de Varenne) sumptuously restored.

Glorious weather, with a soft blue sky. The reception was in the grand manner and perfect in taste. It seemed as if all the pretty women in Paris must have arranged to meet there, for the lawns of the enormous garden were gay with charming frocks which, from a distance, could hardly be distinguished from the flowers in the beds. As a matter of fact, a very large number of good-looking women turned up; they were attracted by von Khevenhüller's reputation as a lady's man whose successes in gallantry have often been the subject of gossip in cosmopolitan high society.

He is sixty, but has kept amazingly young, with his slim figure and upright carriage, his bright eyes, quick wits and a voice which is warm and vibrating. This cadet of a great German house knows how to ally the most exquisite manners with the most audacious conduct. With his combination of honour and swagger, boldness and fatuity, he always seems to me to belong to the world of Versailles and the Trianon in the days of Marie-Antoinette. I can see him taking his place and playing his part beside Lauzun, Coigny, Besenval, Vaudreuil and Fersen. . . .[1]

The Ambassador was too absorbed in his social duties, and too busy acknowledging the charming smiles he received, for me to bother him.

As it happens, I have often met him at dinner at Madame de Fitz-James', and sometimes on occasions when she had deliberately invited no other guest so that we could talk freely. These *tête-à-tête* have enabled me to verify and supplement most of the reports we have received from the Marquis de Reverseaux, our judicious ambassador in Vienna.

Let me record what I believe to be the aims and tendencies of Austro-Hungarian policy in Europe at the present time.

(1) Francois Joseph is scrupulously loyal to the *Dreibund* pact, engineered by Bismarck twenty-five years ago. But the old confi-

---

[1] The Princes von Khevenhüller-Metsch are descended from a landgrave of Franconia, Richard von Khevenhüller, who lived in the eleventh century. The family subsequently acquired lands in Carinthia, Bohemia and Austria.

dence and intimacy between the courts of Vienna, Berlin and Rome have ceased to exist. The 'ménage à trois' is patently changing and breaking up. For one thing, Italy is daily becoming more aggressive in her claims to Trieste and the Trentino. Germany, on the other hand, is flirting outrageously with Russia in order to keep France in check; the 'underground wire,' which the astute Bismarck established between Berlin and St. Petersburg, has never been kept so busy before. The result is that Austria-Hungary no longer considers the Triple Alliance an adequate security.

(2) Franco-German rivalry does not unduly worry the statesmen at the Ballplatz; as a matter of fact, they exploit it to make Berlin realize the value of their backing.

(3) Since Russia has been at war with Japan, the Austro-Hungarian press of all shades of opinion has brought up the Macedonian question again and is dangling the prospect of Balkan hegemony before the eyes of the public. The General Staffs, and those circles in which the Archdukes Francis-Ferdinand, Otto and Frederick and Count Khuen-Hedervary, etc., move, are again canvassing their great ambition of a march on Usküb. There is open talk of giving the odious Italy such a caning as she is not likely to forget for a long time to come.

(4) But, to my way of thinking, the crux of the foreign policy of the Dual Monarchy is the complexity and bitterness of its internal feuds. The fierce campaign against the prerogative of the Crown, in which the Party of Magyar Independence has been engaged for months, seems to me completely to paralyse Austria-Hungary's activities in the foreign field.

(5) Lastly—and even more influential and important—both the German minority which rules Austria and the Magyar minority which rules Hungary are absolutely compelled to look to Berlin for support—it is a *sine qua non* to them. The result is that the Hapsburg Monarchy has never been so completely under the thumb of the Hohenzollern Empire.

Chapter V

JUNE 25TH—AUGUST 5TH, 1904

Saturday, June 25th, 1904.

KIEL REGATTA has provided the Emperor William with an excuse to invite 'Uncle Edward' to a 'friendly' meeting—a meeting for which, however, the King had felt no desire whatever.

The interview took place today, on board the *Hohenzollern,* in Kiel roads. The wording of their respective toasts corresponded to the difference in their characters. The Kaiser said:

'The German Fleet is delighted to welcome its honorary Admiral. This fleet, one of the youngest in the world, exists to protect German commerce and defend German territory just as the *German Army, for more than thirty years, has preserved the peace of Europe. . . .'*

The King replied as follows: 'May our flags float side by side, as they do today, for the welfare of both our countries and that of *all the other nations!*——'

Monday, June 27th, 1904.

Si-el-Menebbi, ex-Minister of War in Morocco, arrived in France from Mecca a few days ago. A luncheon was given in his honour at the Quai d'Orsay this morning and I was among the guests.

Menebbi, thirty-five, tall and slim, was elegantly swathed in his white burnous and had a gold dagger in his belt. He is not of pure Arab stock, but obviously has a little black blood in him —so, for that matter, have all the personnel of the Sharifian Court, who hail from the Tafilet.

Delcassé had invited some thirty guests, including General André, Minister of War, Gaston Doumergue, Minister of the Colonies, General Pendézec, the Chief of Staff, General Brugère, our future Generalissimo, Jonnart, Governor-General of Algeria, and, last but not least, all the hot-heads of the Colonial Party, such as Etienne, Paul Bourde, Chailley-Bert, etc.

After lunch I had a chat with Etienne and General Pendézec:

75

"This luncheon," I told them, "will perhaps mark a great day in the history of our Moroccan policy."

"Don't say *perhaps*; say certainly . . ." replied the excited Etienne; "I'm going to christen this luncheon *the Morocco luncheon* straight off!"

"In that case I'd better get on with my preparations," said the sage Pendézec.

"I take it that you mean something more than preparations in the Sahara and round Tlemcen?" I said.

"Oh, yes!" He roared with laughter. "I'm thinking of preparations far more important!"

We went on to discuss the rapidity with which this great problem of Morocco has developed; it has only become practical politics—or at any rate amenable to primary treatment—since December 16th, 1900, the day on which Delcassé roped it into the Franco-Italian agreement covering Tripoli.

Wednesday, June 29th, 1904.

The Russians have suffered a serious reverse at Mo-tien-ling, on the road between the Yalu and Liao-yang.

Thursday, June 30th, 1904.

I met Francis Charmes.[1] We talked about Morocco. He is always very doubtful and pessimistic about what he scornfully terms 'the Morocco adventure . . . the Morocco folly.'

I replied:

"Of course it'll take a long time to establish French supremacy in Morocco and all kinds of obstacles will have to be surmounted. But if we hadn't taken the job on, you may be quite sure that others would. Do you like the idea of England or Italy settling down on Algeria's doorstep? . . ."

Friday, July 1st, 1904.

I often hear the comment: 'The Russian reserves don't matter much. The Japanese won't have the money to carry on after October or November. . . .' It's all wrong. Machiavelli, that great master of political science and fencing, wrote one of his shrewdest

---

[1] Editor of the political chronicle in the *Revue des Deux Mondes*. His work on it has earned him a world-wide reputation. He represented the department of Cantal from 1881, first as deputy and then as senator. He was elected a member of the *Académie Française* in 1908 and died on January 4th, 1916.

aphorisms on the subject: *Money is not the sinews of war, but good soldiers. Money does not procure good troops, but good troops always procure money.*

Thursday, July 7th, 1904.

My relations with the agents of the *Okhrana* have given me an insight into the new Russian penal code which was ratified by Nicholas II on March 22nd, April 4th, 1903. Up to last year, the scale of criminal penalties was that prescribed in the *Ulojenie*[1] of 1845, which was still inspired by that old Muscovite spirit of severity, fanaticism and cruelty which justified the description, 'pitiless as the wrath of the Tsar,' applied to the *Sudebnik*[2] in Ivan the Terrible's day. The new code, on the other hand, asserts a claim to have brought the criminal law into harmony with modern principles of state and society. But I also find two species of clauses which assert the doctrine of autocratic absolutism in all its pristine purity and force. They lay down the penalties for the crimes of sacrilege and high treason.

As regards the crime of sacrilege, Article 73, covering the subject, reads as follows: *Anyone found guilty of sacrilege towards God as represented by the consubstantial Trinity, Our Most Holy Sovereign, Our Lady and Eternal Virgin Mary, the Immaterial Celestial Powers or the Saints—profanation or blasphemy in relation to the Holy Sacraments, the Holy Cross, the Holy Relics, the Holy Ikons—attacks upon the Holy Writings, the Orthodox Church or religion in general, will be sentenced to penal servitude. . . .*

As regards the crime of high-treason, Article 99 reads as follows: *Anyone who makes an attempt on the life of the sacred person of the Tsar, the Tsaritsa or the Tsarevich, or who does anything with the object of deposing the Tsar, or restricting his supreme authority, will be punished with death. . . .* Article 100 adds: *Anyone who attempts to change the form of government will be punished with death. . . .* Lastly, Article 103 reads as follows: *Anyone found guilty of outrages against the Tsar, Tsaritsa, or Tsarevich, whether by threats to their persons or insults to their portraits, will be punished with penal servitude. . . .*

These clauses of the penal code seem to me to summarize the two fundamental principles of the Russian state, principles so

[1] Decree (Tr.).
[2] Judge (Tr.).

closely interwoven that each involves the other and cannot be imagined apart—I mean orthodoxy and autocracy.

There is no doubt that such a conception emanates from Byzantium and through Byzantium from the Asiatic monarchies. But to what extent is it still the expression of Russian mentality? How much of it does the Russian nation still accept? We were discussing the point quite recently at Eugène-Melchior de Vogüé's with one of his Russian friends, a liberal, broad-minded old *tchinovnik*:[1]

"I have spent almost the whole of my active life in the provinces," he told us; "I didn't know the splendours of Petersburg and Moscow until the end of my career. So I've always been in direct touch with the Russian masses. I can only tell you that to a man they all believe in the divine origin of the imperial dignity . . . I'll go further. To our simple-minded peasants, the Tsar comes immediately after the Holy Trinity; it is God himself who has given him his power and commands them to obey him. To the pious minds of these humble folk, such radiance thus emanates from his sacred person that he appears to be the image of Christ on earth. . . ."

"Then how is it that, among a people so steeped in this theocratic conception of supreme power, revolutionary factions find so much sympathy, connivance and complicity in all quarters? . . ."

Turgenieff once said: "The Russian soul is a dark forest. To the Latin mind it is incomprehensible, with its tangle of contrasts and paradoxes, mysteries and complexities."

Saturday, July 9th, 1904.

I dined with Baroness de Courcel at the Château d'Athis, near Juvisy. Comte and Comtesse Jean de Castellane, Georges Pallain, Governor of the Bank of France, and his wife, Henri Germain, President of the Crédit Lyonnais, and his wife, were also among the guests.

Before we went in to dinner, I strolled on the terrace with its trim hedges, the view from which embraces the confluence of the Seine and the Orge. The day was dying in an ætherial dusk, a magic blend of crimson and gold. We might have been a thousand leagues from Paris, looking at a landscape by Claude Lorrain or Turner. . . .

[1] Official (Tr.).

All during the dinner we talked about nothing but France's quarrel with the Holy See. It gets more acrimonious every day and now can only end in a sensational divorce. The general opinion is that it was very stupid of the Papacy to provide our anti-clericals with such an excellent excuse for denouncing the Concordat. It is also argued that the elimination of the Public Worship estimates will make support of the churches and recruitment of clergy impossible—the result of which will be the speedy, wholesale and final decay of religious sentiment among the masses in France.

Courcel, ever accurate and far-sighted, emphasized the exaggerated pessimism of these predictions. Yielding to his natural tendency to look at political and social problems from the historical angle, he continued:

"As far as I am able to see into the future, I'm convinced that Christianity will remain the only element capable of preserving and inspiring great human societies. It will develop and adapt itself to new circumstances; but it will endure."

Towards the end of the evening, the ambassador took me aside to question me about King Edward's meeting with the Emperor William at Kiel. I told him that Edward VII, with the greatest possible tact, had most skilfully evaded all the more or less delicate matters into which his imperial host had tried to draw him.

"My idle hours at Athis," said Courcel, "have given me plenty of time to ponder over the political situation in Europe and the possible eventualities involved. . . . I've come to a conclusion: You will remember that I've always regarded Anglo-German rivalry as the greatest menace to the peace of Europe—yes, indeed, even greater than Franco-German enmity. To my way of thinking, the antagonism between Germany and England has entered upon a new phase since our agreement of April 8th. It had previously been vague, latent, spasmodic; it is now crystallized, concrete. What is more, Anglo-German rivalry and Franco-German enmity are now linked up; each intensifies and embitters the other. Their convergence must logically end in war."

Monday, July 11th, 1904.

Paul Cambon has just had an audience with Edward VII, who wanted to tell him about his recent visit to Kiel.

"I had a long talk with the Emperor William and Count von Bülow," the King said; "I found them both very worried by our friendly relations with you; they have even put an unfavourable construction on our agreement of April 8th. I reassured them by reminding them that England and France had many interests in common and some that conflicted; they had settled all outstanding questions in a spirit of equity; their good understanding was one more guarantee of peace in Europe. . . ."

Paul Cambon congratulated the King on a choice of words so well calculated to allay William II's suspicions and soothe his nerves; our ambassador continued:

"The real cause of the nervous irritability from which the Emperor William seems to have been suffering for the last few months is that he has always been reluctant to admit that an Anglo-French understanding was a possibility; he has always banked on the feud between our two countries, as indeed on every apple of discord between any of the powers; he has been trying to compel recognition as the supreme arbitrator of Europe, the sword and shield of European peace; in a word, he claimed the right to play the lead everywhere. Now, to his chagrin, he sees that Your Majesty is stealing his thunder. . . ."

"Yes," answered Edward VII, laughing, "he likes getting himself talked about. He has been completely dumbfounded by the arrangements we have made without him, and without asking his aid and permission. It has left him with an unfamiliar sense of isolation. That's why he's so fretful and angry, and why I thought it would be a good thing to see him."

"Such is the interpretation which the Government and public opinion in France have placed upon Your Majesty's visit. The Emperor William required a sedative; you've given it to him. . . . We also noted the skill with which your toast was phrased and the tactful way in which you intimated that your visit did not in any way impair the binding force of our agreements. . . ."

"It was a ticklish business," the King replied. "I was skating on very thin ice. I got out of my difficulty by emphasizing the family and sporting side of my visit. The Emperor seemed satisfied. . . . Between ourselves, I became aware that the Emperor is still haunted by his desire to visit Paris. Herr von Bülow even asked me if I thought the idea feasible. I replied that it might become so some day, but that day had not yet arrived. What do you feel about it?"

"My own opinion is that William II's visit to Paris would be

premature, to say the least; it would only revive our national
resentment . . . and thus defeat the Emperor's very object. . . .
I doubt whether the proposal is feasible for a very long time to
come."

"I quite agree with you," concluded the King, "but we mustn't
discourage hopes of a reconciliation."

After reading me a record of this conversation, Delcassé remarked:

"The Emperor William is at his old game. . . . You can see
what a coxcomb he is at heart. His great ambition is to pay an
official visit to Paris and see himself the centre of a cheering crowd
of Parisians. It's a silly, childish notion! Even assuming that he
really came to France to celebrate the political reconciliation of
the two nations, tom-toms and a brass-band reception are hardly
a suitable preamble. . . . If the Emperor William really wants to
bring France and Germany together, let him start by refraining
from further insults; let him stop rubbing in our 1870 disasters, as
he did recently at Carlsruhe, and cease his bluster for a few months.
He should get his Chancellor to put clear-cut, concrete propositions
before us; I would consider them with a perfectly open mind. . . .
Of course there could be no question of anything but a special
agreement covering points which had been clearly defined. I don't
see any other possibility of a *rapprochement* between France and
Germany for a long time to come."

Monday, July 18th, 1904.

Relations between France and the Vatican are reaching the
breaking point.

Ignoring our protests, the Holy See has just summoned the
Bishops of Laval and Dijon to appear forthwith before the "Sacred
Tribunal of the Holy Office" to answer the complaints which the
Sovereign Pontiff has laid against them. If they fail in immediate
obedience to the summons, 'there will be no need to acquaint the
said bishops of their suspension *latæ sententiæ ab exercitio ordinis
et jurisdictionis.*'

Combes has immediately retorted with a furious note which we
are sending to the Holy See: "By summoning direct to Rome two
bishops who come under the jurisdiction of the Minister of
Public Worship, the Holy See is disregarding the rights which it

recognized when it signed the Concordat. . . . By threatening to suspend the two bishops *ipso facto* if they do not appear at Rome, the Holy See is disregarding those clauses of the Concordat in which it is laid down that a bishop can only be suspended if both the authorities who concurred in his appointment are in agreement. . . . For this reason, the undersigned, Chargé d'Affaires of the French Republic, is instructed to inform his Eminence the Cardinal Secretary of State that, if the injunctions addressed to the said bishops are not withdrawn, the Government of the Republic will hold the Holy See responsible for the decisions to which it will have been driven."

Thursday, July 28th, 1904.

Plehve, the Minister of the Interior, was assassinated in one of the most crowded streets in St. Petersburg shortly before ten o'clock this morning. He was blown to pieces by a bomb thrown at his carriage. The assassin was arrested on the spot.

There is no doubt that the 'crimson stream' is flowing on. This is at least the sixth political crime of violence in the last twelve months. Rataieff, the head of the Russian *Okhrana* abroad, said to me the other day:

"My life is one long worry. Under the direction of Burtzev, the *Fighting Organization* has become very formidable. The man's audacity is astounding. I can assure you he's made good use of his time in Paris. . . ."

Today I repeated to Delcassé what Rataieff had said. I advised him to bring pressure on his colleague, the Minister of the Interior, to stir up the heads of the *Sûreté Générale* to show rather more diligence in keeping observation on the Russian refugees.

"I'll bring the matter up at the Cabinet meeting tomorrow," he answered.

For his personal edification I showed him a document I had taken from my safe, a document proving that the Russian Government has always attached great importance to the co-operation of our police in its war against the revolutionary parties. It is a letter dated May 29th, 1890, and therefore several months before the first hint of the Franco-Russian alliance. At the request of Ribot, Minister of Foreign Affairs, his colleague, Constans, the Minister of the Interior, had just carried out a great round-up of all the Russian anarchists in Paris; the Government had thus acquired knowledge of every detail of the party organization and had transmitted it to the imperial police. Our Prefect of Police, Lozé, had displayed no less skill than energy in this affair.

The Russian Ambassador, Baron Mohrenheim, had sent him a lyrical letter of thanks:

Paris, May 29th, 1890.

Monsieur le Préfet, and, may I add, my dear, sincere and worthy friend!

I thank you with all my heart. The signal services you have rendered my country can never be adequately appreciated, and never forgotten. Thanks to the incomparable energy and extreme skill of your dispositions, frightful calamities have been averted. I shudder to think of the catastrophies from which the Emperor and the entire country have been saved, thanks to the friendly intervention of the French Government. Neither will ever forget it. My own personal feelings count for little on such an occasion; but permit me to tell you what happiness it gives me to thank you with all my heart. I am looking forward to having the opportunity of greeting you and remain, with the greatest affection, undying friendship and deepest devotion

MOHRENHEIM.

Friday, July 29th, 1904.

As was to be expected, the Holy See maintains in the most uncompromising language the right of the Sovereign Pontiff to summon French Bishops direct before the "Sacred Tribunal of the Holy Office" and to declare them "suspended *ipso facto*" if they do not obey.

At a meeting of the Council at the Élysée this morning, it was decided "to break off official relations which, by the choice of the Holy See, now serve no useful purpose. . . ."

Saturday, July 30th, 1904.

The terrorist Burtzev is still in Paris, quietly directing the operations of the *Fighting Organization* and the sanguinary exploits of his comrades in Russia.

Jaurès, who is protecting him, has persuaded Combes not to carry out the deportation order which was signed on April 26th.

On Delcassé's instructions, I made a further protest to the Director of the *Sûreté Générale* who simply threw up his hands:

"M. Jaurès is the man to apply to!" [1]

Monday, August 1st, 1904.

A fresh development has occurred to strengthen our influence in Morocco. In future, the police and garrison of Tangier will be under the command of a French officer.

Saint-René Taillandier, to whom we owe this excellent achievement, is right in thinking that it shows that the Sultan and his viziers now accept as inevitable the predominating position in the Maghreb which was granted us by the Franco-British Agreement of April 8th.

Friday, August 5th, 1904.

Consummatum est! . . . Diplomatic relations between France and the Holy See have now been broken off—a climax which cannot fail to involve the separation of Church and State in France. I think the judgment of history will be that the French Radicals and the Roman Die-Hards must be held equally responsible for the event we have just witnessed.

Pius X and his counsellors—if indeed he has any—continue to repeat that the Church has triumphed in many worse trials; that, anyhow, France today counts for little in the Catholic world and that the tribulations in store for the faithful and the clergy in France will at least have the advantage of showing mankind the diabolical wickedness of atheist governments.

Our ministers, for their part, are saying that they are more determined than ever "to go ahead with the task of ensuring the predominance of lay and civil society over an autocratic and clerical society."

[1] In February, 1915, my duties as ambassador at Petrograd involved my concerning myself with Burtzev once more.

At the outbreak of war, this terrible foe to tsarism, who was then in exile in Paris, boldly proclaimed that all Russians should unite against Germany; he believed that the sentiment of working-class solidarity would be strengthened in battle and that the internal freedom of his country would be the result of victory.

He immediately started for Russia to preach his new ideas in working-class circles. He had no sooner crossed the frontier than he was arrested and sent to Turukansk on the Ienissei, on the confines of the Polar region. When the news of this stupid deportation reached France, our Socialist party was naturally indignant and began to declaim against the Russian alliance. The Minister of Justice, Viviani, asked me to use all my influence with the Tsar to obtain Burtzev's pardon. I therefore appealed to Nicholas's feelings and he immediately ordered Burtzev's liberation.

In October, 1917, Burtzev was imprisoned by the Bolshevists, whom he loathed. In 1918 he took refuge once more in Paris.

(V. *La Russie des Tsars*, Vol. 1, p. 292.)

The masonic lodges are going still further and demand the complete elimination of the Public Worship Estimates. "The Republic should cease to defray the cost of the scandalous exploitation of human credulity and degrading fanaticism. It must refuse to pay stipends to thieves in cassocks any longer. . . ." Homais[1] himself could not have put it better!

The crisis of this last few days has overwhelmed President Loubet. He had sworn: (1) That he would not receive King Victor Emmanuel if he visited Paris; (2) That he would not return such a visit in Rome unless he was assured beforehand that he would be able to pay his respects to the Pope immediately afterwards; (3) That he would not have the Concordat denounced on any ground whatever. He had many a time made this perfectly clear to our ambassador, Nisard; on one occasion he added: "Make a point of telling the Holy Father that I am a Catholic. . . . The Free-Masons accuse me of clericalism because I occasionally go to Mass. The clericals accuse me of atheism because I don't go regularly. The truth is that I am a believer—a lukewarm one, but still a believer. . . . Don't forget to let the Holy Father know; tell him all about my religious views. . . ." Nisard, ever tactful, replied: "I won't fail to do so, Monsieur le Président; I'll remind the Pope that Louis Philippe's ambassador to Gregory XVII couldn't have said as much."

Notwithstanding all these assertions, Loubet did not say a word when the Council of Ministers finally decided that relations with the Holy See should be severed. He has since given a confidential account of the sitting to one of his friends:

"I was expecting to oppose it, availing myself of the strong protest Delcassé had promised to make on behalf of the national interests of which he is the guardian. So I let the discussion go on, waiting for the moment to intervene. . . . I looked hard at Delcassé three times. He didn't say a word. . . . The vote was taken. He didn't raise the slightest objection and voted straight off with the rest. . . . I could only hold my peace."[2]

[1] Homais. A character in Flaubert's novel, *Madame Bovary*. Type of smug bourgeois with a veneer of education.

[2] Sixteen years later, in 1920, Alexandre Millerand, who was then President of the Council and Minister of Foreign Affairs, courageously took the initiative in restoring diplomatic relations between France and the Holy See. In my capacity as Secretary General at the Quai d'Orsay, I was privileged to take an active part in the negotiations.

Chapter VI

AUGUST 6TH—OCTOBER 14TH, 1904

Saturday, August 6th, 1904.
THE German General Staff is spending a lot of time in *Kriegs-spiel*, the 'war game' of operations and manœuvres in miniature on the map. The greatest problems of strategy are handled and adapted, as far as possible, to the most likely contingencies of the next war. The future army commanders are thus being prepared for their prospective functions and duties. As a rule, General von Schlieffen is in charge of the *Kriegs-spiel*, and it is his great brain and strong will which dominate the proceedings.

Our Secret Service has recently obtained some interesting "notes" on these theoretical exercises. They show that in the event of a war with France the *Oberste Heeresleitung*, the supreme directors of military operations, would act on the following principles:

'(1) The priority of his offensive gives the attacker an appreciable advantage: it is therefore a matter of launching one's offensive at the earliest possible moment in overwhelming force and with enormous numbers; (2) the essential aim of the attacker must be to destroy the enemy; (3) this destruction can only be brought about by means of enveloping movements on the largest possible arc, and with such strong wings that no obstacle can withstand them; (4) an enemy is not conquered so long as he is still in a position to select his line of retreat.'

General Pendézec, who showed me these notes, looks on them as a further reason for accepting the authenticity of the *Avenger's* disclosures.

Monday, August 8th, 1904.
Spain, ever drawn by the mirage of her historic ambitions, cannot bring herself to recognize our priority, both as to influence and action, in the Sharifian Empire. After a long and stormy meeting, the Council of Ministers has just decided 'that the Moroccan question shall be the object of special investigation.'

86

We are, however, vigorously pursuing our task on the spot: French customs officials are getting to work in the ports and we are organizing the police at Tangier.

Queen Maria-Christina's private secretary has been deploring the illusions with which the Royal Government is toying: he said to Paul Cambon:

"Our inability to make up our minds lost us Fez two years ago; if we're not careful, it will cost us Tangier before long."

Friday, August 12th, 1904.

After ten years of marriage, the Empress Alexandra-Feodorovna, who already has four girls, has just given birth to a Tsarevich, or, to use the word in fashion at the court of Byzantium, a Porphyrogenetos.[1]

The Emperor is overjoyed. But will this event be enough to rehabilitate Tsarism and the Romanoffs? . . .

To obtain this much-desired son, they resorted not only to the usual resources of human weakness—prayers, vows, adorations, penances and pilgrimages—but even to the most extravagant practices of occultism and thaumaturgy.

Eighteen months ago, I was confidentially told the most astounding stories about these mysterious happenings by the police officer, Ratchkovsky. A nondescript individual, a butcher-boy from Lyons, "Philippe the Magician," has played an unprecedented part in the private lives of the sovereigns during the last few years. Sorcery and incantations have figured in the proceedings. Even in the darkest days of the Middle Ages in Russia, the barbaric times of Simeon the Proud and Vassili-Dimitrievitch, I doubt whether magical rites had a greater hold on popular imagination. I do not suppose that the sinister women's apartments at the Kremlin in Moscow[2] have ever witnessed weirder scenes or more fantastic liturgies.

At the present time, Philippe the Magician, persecuted by what he calls 'the wicked jealousies of the Court and the Holy Synod,' is insane (melancholia) and has had to bid farewell to imperial splendours. He is living in retirement at l'Arbresle, near Lyons; the post often brings him letters from St. Petersburg.[3]

---

[1] The Greek word means: 'born in the purple.'
[2] Cf. *La Russie des Tsars*, Vol. I, p. 215.
[3] He died at Arbresle on August 2nd, 1905.

Saturday, August 13th, 1904.

Yesterday, while the bells in all the churches of Russia were ringing and *Te Deums* being sung for the birth of the Tsarevich Alexis, public rejoicings were suddenly interrupted by a very depressing piece of news.

On August 10th, the Port Arthur squadron, comprising eighteen ships, put out to sea with the intention of reaching Vladivostok. It was immediately attacked by Admiral Togo's Fleet.

After considerable fluctuations, the Russians lost the battle. It was more than a defeat; it was a disaster. The Commander-in-Chief, Admiral Witgheft, was killed; the cruiser division fled helter-skelter to Chinese ports, where the vessels were disarmed.

The Japanese will now be able to concentrate all their ships against the Vladivostok Squadron.

Tuesday, August 16th, 1904.

The day before yesterday, the Vladivostok Squadron, in an attempt to reach Port Arthur, was completely defeated in the Straits of Korea by Admiral Kamimura's cruisers. The crew of one of the battleships, the *Rurik* (11,200 tons), scuttled their ship rather than surrender.

The Japanese now have complete command of the sea from the Gulf of Pechili to the Kamskatka. I could not help recalling General Pendézec's words to me a few months ago: "In the war in the Far East there is no doubt that ultimate victory will fall to the belligerent which has gained and maintained naval supremacy."

Saturday, August 20th, 1904.

I have had a talk with Paul Cambon about the Moroccan question. He asked me if Delcassé was genuinely anxious to come to terms with Spain.

"Certainly: he wants to arrive at an agreement with Spain which will be the natural complement to the Franco-Italian and Anglo-French Agreements; he has often said to me: *The friendship of Spain, the support of Spain and the collaboration of Spain are indispensable for the development of our Mediterranean policy.* That has been his standpoint throughout. But, though he sincerely desires an agreement, I must admit he's taking his time about it. While the Spanish ministers are haggling over diplomatic formulæ, we are getting a firm hold in Morocco; every day we are asserting the priority of our rights and interests. So I think that Delcassé must mean the negotiations to drag on until the autumn at least . . . Spain should turn up Machiavelli's chapter: *Weak states are always irresolute and delay in coming to decisions is always harmful.*[1]

"Delcassé is decidedly more astute than I thought, *cher ami.*"

Monday, September 5th, 1904.

Since August 25th, the Japanese armies, now united under the command of Field-Marshal Oyama, have been employed in a vast offensive against the massed Russian armies under General Kuropatkin, which are entrenched south of Liao-yang. More than 400,000 men have been engaged.

After a stubborn resistance and enormous losses, the Russians have had to retreat and take refuge behind the Sha-ho lines, about twenty kilometres from Mukden.

Saturday, September 24th, 1904.

I have had to curtail my cure at Vichy to devote myself to an urgent, secret job which Delcassé has asked me to take in hand personally.

Ever since the Japanese obtained the command of the sea by their victory of August 10th, every mouthpiece of public opinion in Russia has been pestering the Imperial Admiralty to make a supreme effort to regain naval supremacy at any cost: the result of the war depends on it. And as the Port Arthur Squadron is at the bottom of the sea and the Vladivostok Division now reduced to a handful of cruisers, it is absolutely essential to send out a new fleet.

The public has given the idea an enthusiastic welcome; it is all the more attracted by it because it evokes all those grandiose, hazy, distant visions so dear to the Russian imagination. The technical departments at the Admiralty, which have to take a severely practical view, obstinately declined to consider the scheme, fortifying their decision with various circumlocutions and allusions which defied comprehension. But at last, the Imperial Admiralty, yielding to public pressure, has had to decide to send to the Far East a large naval force which is to be known as the "Second Squadron of the Pacific Ocean."

The arsenals at Kronstadt, Reval and Libau have been hard at

[1] Essay on Titus-Livius, II, 15.

work and, sooner than anyone expected, have managed to mobilize twenty ships—seven battleships, six cruisers and seven destroyers. In mere numbers, this fleet, though it has not yet reached full strength, is undoubtedly imposing. . . . But what is it worth as a fighting force?

According to our naval attaché at St. Petersburg, the naval and military value of the 2nd Squadron is less than mediocre. It is not a homogeneous, cohesive organism but a motley collection, a hodge-podge of ships of all ages and types. Two of the battleships are nothing but respectable veterans, almost in the 'crock' class; most of the cruisers are either slow or their armament is out of date; the tonnage of the destroyers is not big enough for such a long voyage, nor are their engines good enough. What is more, the heterogeneous character of this naval troupe will be accentuated by all the cargo boats, colliers, hospital-ships, repair-ships, etc., which it will have to take with it.

The efficiency of the crews is no higher than that of the fleet. There are few experienced officers; the engineering staff is of poor quality; there are no petty officers and most of the sailors have had no military training nor ever been to sea. So the fortnight's manœuvres and gunnery-practice which the squadron has had in the Gulf of Finland have revealed lamentable inefficiency.

But all these defects, grave though they are, may in time be remedied, or, at any rate corrected to some extent, by the prestige and personal qualities of the Commander-in-Chief, Admiral Zinovei-Petrovich Rojdestvensky—a first-class man.

He is fifty-six. He distinguished himself by his heroism in the Russo-Turkish War and has since held a succession of difficult posts and responsible employments. He is a sailor to his finger-tips, with all the virtues of honour and loyalty, courage and boldness, endurance and self-sacrifice, which are the pride of the naval profession. He therefore seems eminently fitted for the formidable task which the Tsar has set him.

On a voyage of 34,000 kilometres he will have to solve the navigational problems of all the oceans and all climates, without finding a single port flying his country's flag, or anywhere he can put in for shelter or repairs. He will always be sailing under observation, and in danger, from a bold, cunning and resourceful enemy who is past master at *ruses de guerre*. He will perpetually have to reckon with the ill-will of England, nominally neutral but secretly hostile, and in any event the official ally of Japan. He can therefore only shelter in uncharted waters and off uninhabited coasts. He will often have to meet his cargo-boats in mid-ocean to take in fresh supplies and coal. It would seem that the burden laid on his shoulders is superhuman.

We know all about his programme from a conversation the Russian Ambassador had with Delcassé a month ago.

Nelidoff explained in the greatest detail that, without the clandestine assistance of the French authorities, the 2nd Squadron of the Pacific Ocean could never reach its destination. Throughout the voyage, it will have to apply to our consular or colonial agents for help with regard to ports of call, anchorages, supplies, repairs, the transmission of telegrams to and from St. Petersburg, not to mention certain police matters. Delcassé pointed out to the ambassador that this secret aid—a very tricky business which must be kept up for months—seemed to him *a priori* incompatible with the duties of a neutral; but he promised to look into the matter. Then Nelidoff added in grave and almost pleading tones:

"The veiled cooperation of the French Government is a *sine qua non* in this great adventure, which is our last chance of salvation. The Emperor has instructed me to tell you that, from the bottom of his heart, he appeals to your friendship."

To show his goodwill, the Minister immediately sent for me to give him my opinion in the ambassador's presence. I told them that, in the interests of our own fleet, we had ourselves already given much thought to the problems with which the Russian squadron would be faced and which would crop up again at every stage of its long voyage. The Ministry of Marine and the Ministry of Foreign Affairs had therefore secretly devised a complete plan for facilitating the operations of our naval forces in distant waters. This plan could be adapted to meet the needs of the Russian squadron: but it would be necessary to take the most stringent precautions to prevent Japan from discovering our connivance.

Delcassé approved at once and Nelidoff was overjoyed.

As the sequel to this conversation, I was instructed to take the matter in hand in co-operation with a naval officer, Captain de Saulces de Freycinet, Director of the First Section of the Naval General Staff, and my colleague on the War Preparations Committee.

Our first task was to decide upon the route to be taken by the

Russian squadron from the Baltic to the Yellow Sea. Captain Yepantchin, naval attaché at the Russian Embassy, our *liaison* officer with the Admiralty at St. Petersburg, told us that the itinerary of the 2nd Squadron had not yet been fixed. As a matter of fact, Admiral Rojdestvensky would be glad if we would put forward our suggestions!

Captain de Freycinet, to whom I naturally left this part of our work, studied three routes; the first *via* the Suez Canal, the second round the Cape of Good Hope and the third round Cape Horn; from the geographical point of view, these were in fact the only alternatives.[1]

What were their respective advantages and disadvantages from the tactical point of view? Looked at from that angle, there was one paramount consideration. Admiral Rojdestvensky's main object must be to evade the enemy's traps, conceal from him his plans and the date and place of his arrival at the theatre of war and keep him in ignorance, or better still mislead him until the very last moment, as to the exact spot where the final shock would take place.

Seen in that light, the Suez Canal route was obviously the worst; it is more or less lined with signalling stations, and all the ports of call, Gibraltar, Malta, Port Said, Perim, Aden, Ceylon, Nikobar and Singapore, are in British hands; what is worse, the traffic is so heavy that every movement of the Russian *Armada* would be observed every day.

The Cape of Good Hope route, though longer, seemed to have more in its favour. From Ushant to the approaches to Madagascar, the Russian ships should have no difficulty in evading Japanese observation. No doubt their tracks would be picked up there, but they could then scatter to cross the Indian Ocean and reunite only at the moment of entering the China Sea by one of the many Insulinde straits, the Straits of Torres, Timor, Lumbok, the Sound, etc. There is equally little doubt that thereafter their line of approach will soon be discovered by the enemy, who will shape his course accordingly.

There only remained the Cape Horn route, which was far the longest but quite the most favourable, having regard to the special circumstances of the expedition.

After leaving European waters, the Russian squadron would

[1] See Map 3, p. 93.

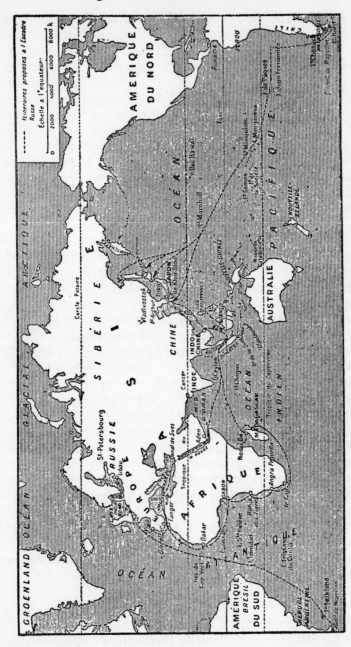

ALTERNATIVE ROUTES SUGGESTED TO THE RUSSIAN PACIFIC SQUADRON, SEPT. 24, 1904

make for the Cape Verde Islands where it would find some deserted harbour 'for coaling and rest.' It would then proceed to the little Island of Trinidad, which is tucked away four hundred leagues from Brazil, or, further south, to the Island of Tristan d'Acunha, a thousand leagues from any land . . . *ultima Thule.* Further on, east of Tierra del Fuego, the Falkland archipelago would offer an excellent anchorage for repairs and taking in supplies. Thence, rounding Cape Horn and ascending the desolate coast of Western Patagonia, it would strike north-west, through waters first explored by Magellan's caravels, and then coal at Easter Island. Five or six days later, it would find a quiet bay at Mangareva, where its presence would be noticed by no one except a few pearl-fishers. It would have to make further calls at the Marquesas and the Marshall archipelago. There its voyage, merely as a voyage, would end. It would be entering upon the zone of military operations, a vast area offering unlimited scope for stategy. With 2,000 kilometres of ocean between the Islands of Kiu-siu and Kamskatka, it would have the choice of alternative approaches to Vladivostok—the Straits of Korea, the Straits of Tsugar, the Straits of Perusia or the Straits of Tartary. Thus the Japanese would not know until the very last moment from which direction the attack was coming.

I did not conceal from Captain de Freycinet that I was wholly in favour of this vast odyssey, because it would reduce to the very minimum the hospitality we should have to offer the Russian squadron in French waters—one stop at the Marquesas archipelgo.

The stages of the Cape of Good Hope route, on the other hand, would be marked by our colonies, Senegal, Gaboon, Madagascar and Indo-China. Would Japan tolerate so many flagrant breaches of our neutrality?

This was Delcassé's opinion also.

We therefore pressed the Imperial Admiralty to adopt the Cape Horn route.

In anticipation of its decision, which cannot be delayed much longer, Freycinet and I have been working out all the details of the arrangements we should have to make if any of these itineraries were selected.

Monday, September 26th, 1904.

Yesterday, 500 reservists mutinied at Kharkov, 'as a protest against the accursed war.' To make them return to their obedience, the employment of Cossacks and brute force was found necessary. The same trouble—with the same result—at Ekaterinoslav.

Monday, October 3rd, 1904.

After negotiating for five months, France and Spain have arrived at agreement over Morocco.

The memorandum which Delcassé and Leon y Castillo have just signed records the Spanish Government's formal acceptance of the 'Anglo-French Agreement of April 8th last, Article 2 of which reads:

> *Article 2. The government of his Britannic Majesty recognizes that it is for France, particularly as she is the neighbour of Morocco, with a very long common frontier, to maintain peace and order in that country and give it all the assistance it may require in the matter of administrative, economical, financial and military reforms.*

In adopting this clause, Spain, like England, recognizes our paramount position in Morocco. Like England, she agrees that we shall give the Sharifian Empire—the whole of the Sharifian Empire—the assistance it requires for its internal reforms.

Unfortunately, this memorandum, though it proclaims the unity of the Sharifian Empire under the Sultan, has a secret supplement, or rather counterpart.

To bring Spain round to his way of thinking, Delcassé has been obliged to leave her a large sphere of influence in Northern Morocco. The boundaries of this zone extend from the Mulina in a westerly direction to the Atlantic Ocean south of Larache; the town of Tangier and the region of Cap Spartel are not included.

Could we have refused to acknowledge rights which Spain has enjoyed for centuries in the north of the Maghreb? Obviously not. Partition into spheres of influence was thus the only way out. I honestly think that we have not paid too high a price for the enormous advantage of being able to intensify our Moroccan policy without always and everywhere coming up against Spanish opposition. Delcassé has frequently said to me during the last few days:

"I shall no doubt be accused of undue deference to the Spanish claims. All I can tell you is that I was contemplating much greater sacrifices to prevent Spain from becoming the tool and champion of Germany in Morocco."

Thursday, October 6th, 1904.

My old friend, Georges-Saint-René Taillandier, our minister in Morocco, has been spending a few days in Paris, preparing for the delicate task immediately ahead of him at the Court of Fez. Sultan Moulai Abd-el-Aziz has expressed a desire to confer with him on the reforms which we think the restoration of order in the Sharifian Empire requires.

Only this morning did he learn from Delcassé of the Franco-Spanish Agreement of October 3rd and its secret counterpart. He is very worried about it.

"Sooner or later," he told me, "the Sultan is sure to hear about this secret counterpart; he'll guess it, anyhow. For that matter, the very wording of the official note, which will be published to-morrow, impliedly admits that France and Spain have reached an agreement with respect to the delimitation of their interests in the Sharifian Empire. Moulai Abd-el-Aziz will certainly think this is the beginning of the partition of Morocco. He will be very wild about it. It will destroy all his confidence in me—it's taken me three years' hard work to gain it. What will become of our sound policy of friendly persuasion, progressive influence and tutelage? . . . Shall not we soon find ourselves obliged to resort to force?"

I replied that, in practice, it was impossible for Delcassé to continue his work in Morocco without compromising with Spanish claims. Could he have compromised on better terms? I do not think so. In any event, he was obsessed by the fear of seeing Spain become the servant and mercenary of Germany in Morocco. Once again he has instinctively followed Cardinal de Retz's excellent advice: 'The whole duty of the statesman is to choose the lesser evil.'

Friday, October 14th, 1904.

When I took my papers to Delcassé for signature, I found him poring over a map of Belgium and Luxemburg; his expression was wrapt, his eyes sparkled, and he held a pair of compasses in his hand. Without giving me so much as a glance, he remained absorbed in his geographical studies, the object of which was not difficult to guess. Quite suddenly he said:

"Do you realize that the reign of Louis XV only just missed

being one of the greatest in the history of the French monarchy? Of course I'm very sorry about the Treaty of Paris and the loss of Senegal and Canada. But three years later we acquired Lorraine, and Corsica two years after that. Louis XV's irreparable mistake was not the Treaty of Paris, but the Treaty of Aix-la-Chapelle. . . . Do you remember? . . . 1748 . . . Maurice de Saxe's victories at Fontenoy, Raucoux and Lawfeld gave us possession of all the Austrian Netherlands. We occupied Flanders, Hainault, Brabant, and had even reached Limburg, for our flag flew over Mae-stricht. . . . We could and we should have kept the greater part of our conquests. International law, so far as it existed in those days, authorized our doing so. In any case, the House of Austria had no better right, ethical or moral, than the House of France to govern the Walloon peoples. . . ."

Bending over his map again, he continued:

"Look at the marvellous frontier we'd have had: Tournai, Mons, Charleroi, Namur, Dinard and the course of the Lesse. . . . Henceforth, the Oise Valley would have been closed to German invasions. Louis XIV's great territorial work would have been consummated. Louis XV didn't realize it. In my opinion, the date of the Treaty of Aix-la-Chapelle was a sad day in our history."

Chapter VII

OCTOBER 15TH—NOVEMBER 9TH, 1904

Saturday, October 15th, 1904.

THE 2nd Squadron of the Pacific Fleet, comprising thirty-five ships, under the command of Admiral Rojdestvensky, traversed Libau Roads this morning and is now in the open sea.

The order to weigh anchor was given by the Admiral three days ago; it was carried out so inefficiently and led to such confusion that the ships had to return to their moorings.

According to a private report, which unfortunately seems only too true, the officers are in deplorably low spirits; 'We shall never see Russia again. We are doomed to the most frightful and futile sacrifice. We are beaten before we start. . . . If only the Japanese would come and finish us off, and get it over!' Every evening they get drunk on vodka and champagne to drown their sorrows, shake off their depression and forget their gloomy forebodings.

Thursday, October 20th, 1904.

The Russian *Armada* has traversed the Sound and the Kattegat without mishap. About noon they rounded Cape Skagen, the most northerly point of Jutland, where the Skagerrak opens out into the North Sea.

Commandant de Freycinet has just been in to ask me if I have been able to obtain any information as to what route Admiral Rojdestvensky proposes to take after passing the Portuguese coast. Has he chosen the passage round Cape Horn?

"I have no idea," I told him, "nor has Ambassador Nelidoff, whom I asked about it yesterday."

"Nor has Captain Yepantchin, whom I was questioning this morning! . . . So I told him quite bluntly: '*If I am not properly informed of your Admiral's plans within three days at the outside, neither Monsieur Paléologue nor I will do anything further for you. We cannot make the necessary arrangements on the spur of the moment. Your delays may have the most serious effect on the movements of your squadron. We're not going to be held respon-*

98

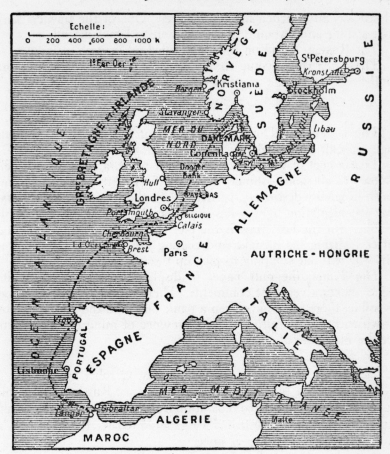

THE DOGGER BANK INCIDENT, OCT. 21ST, 1904

sible. . . .' Yepantchin, very contrite, gave me his usual answer:
'I'll wire St. Petersburg.' "

But we are none the less starting today to make preparations
for the eventuality of the Russian Squadron putting in at Dakar
or Gaboon.

Sunday, October 23rd, 1904.

During the night of October 21st, Admiral Rojdestvensky's
Squadron, while crossing the North Sea, fell in with a fleet of
English trawlers on the Dogger Bank. Misled by certain indica-
tions, they took these harmless vessels for a ruse by Japanese

destroyers and opened fire immediately. One of the trawlers sank like a stone and several others were more or less damaged.

The Russian squadron then continued on its way.

These first very incomplete details have been transmitted by the authorities at Hull, 150 miles west of the Dogger Bank.

Monday, October 24th, 1904.

The lamentable Dogger Bank incident is causing tremendous agitation all over England.

That a fleet of warships, traversing at night, a fishing bank well known to all sailors, should mistake a fleet of trawlers for an ambush of enemy destroyers, particularly as these trawlers were carrying the regulation lights—has positively dumbfounded the British public. But the last straw is the fact that Admiral Rojdestvensky, after realizing his mistake and ceasing fire, calmly continued on his way without stopping to pick up the unfortunate fishermen.

The Times, the only paper to display any moderation in its tone, makes a very just comment: "There is only one explanation possible; there must have been a panic on board the Russian ships —which says little either for the presence of mind of the officers or the discipline of the crews."

Tuesday, October 25th, 1904.

English public opinion is up in arms against Russia. It is unanimous in demanding signal reparation from the Tsarist Government and even that the British Fleet should chase Rojdestvensky's Squadron unless it stops at once.

Yesterday, Count Benckendorff, the Russian Ambassador in London, was greeted with boos and cat-calls at Charing Cross Station when he arrived back from leave in ignorance of what had taken place. The police had considerable difficulty in protecting him.

This evening, Delcassé has been talking to me about 'the grave situation' which the Dogger Bank mishap has produced between England and Russia.

"In the British public's present frame of mind," he said, "it would not surprise me if war broke out at any moment. I've just been speaking very strongly and plainly to Nelidoff: *It is absolutely vital for your government immediately to send the chivalrous and apologetic message which alone can avert a crisis. There isn't a moment to lose. . . . Just think for a minute; tomorrow morning an English Squadron may very well receive instructions to open fire on your ships as they approach Vigo!* . . . Unfortunately, Nelidoff thinks that public opinion in Russia is equally roused, because it regards England as the traditional enemy, an enemy hated far more than the Japanese. He is afraid that national feeling, which already feels so humiliated by the reverses in Manchuria, would rather run the risk of a quarrel with England than make her the *amende honorable.* I could only protest: *But that is all the more reason for your government not losing a moment in saying the word which can still settle the whole trouble.*"

Wednesday, October 26th, 1904.

Paul Cambon has wired that his Russian colleague is appalled by the violence of the current which is sweeping public opinion in England towards war: 'Count Benckendorff therefore wished me to give Your Excellency a confidential message, asking you to press St. Petersburg to send immediate orders to Admiral Rojdestvensky to put in at Vigo. . . . The Tsar's telegram, expressing regret and promising compensation, has not allayed public excitement. There is a general demand for an enquiry, and that the officers responsible shall be punished. The public is in a mood of grim determination which is far more dangerous than the raging of the Press.'

On receiving this telegram, Delcassé sent for me to ask what information I might have on the subject of preparations by the British Admiralty. I was in a position to tell him there and then:

"There is great activity in all the English ports. The *Home Fleet*, which was exercising in the North of Scotland, is being concentrated in the Channel, at Portland, with a squadron of destroyers. The *Mediterranean Fleet*, which was scattered over the Levant, has been recalled to Malta. The *Channel Fleet*, which is assembled at Gibraltar under the command of Admiral Lord Beresford, is clearing for action; it is even said that this fleet has received instructions to blockade the Russian Squadron in Vigo Bay until England has obtained satisfaction from Russia."

When I had finished my recital, Delcassé's eyelids twitched and he half closed his eyes for a few seconds, as if he were trying to look into the future. Then, without a trace of emotion:

"I can see that there's more to fear from the English side than the Russian at the moment."

And he promptly sent for the British Ambassador.

Thursday, October 27th, 1904.

As was to be expected, the cabinet of St. James's has given up trying to keep the national rage within bounds. Its arguments may be summarized thus: 'In opening fire on English vessels, the Russian squadron inflicted an insult on our flag. It is not merely a question of ascertaining whether the attack was intentional or not; if it had been, His Majesty's Government would not have hesitated for a moment as to the course it should take. But, even if we do not question the fact that the Russian squadron only made a mistake, the offence is in itself so grave that we must insist on an explanation, apologies, compensation, a proper allocation of responsibility and the exemplary punishment of the guilty.'

After informing Paul Cambon of the terms of his last communication to the Russian Government, Delcassé added:

"Will not the British Government also realize the danger of precipitate decisions? They will assume a grave burden of responsibility if they say something irrevocable and, a few hours later, a conciliatory reply shows how disastrously hasty they have been! Would anyone in his senses agree that peace between two great empires depends on a matter of hours? . . . You know what happens in Russia; the Emperor is thirty miles from St. Petersburg and his ministers are always reluctant to disturb him, perhaps even to tell him the unvarnished truth and insist on getting the immediate decision which it calls for. . . . I've no doubt that all this is no news to Lord Lansdowne; but you will certainly be able to remind him of it in terms far more candid and forcible than any your Russian colleague could employ."

Admiral Rojdestvensky's squadron has at last been advised to await further instructions at Vigo before proceeding on its voyage.

Friday, October 28th, 1904.

The Emperor Nicholas has wired to the 'Commander in Chief of the 2nd Squadron,' now anchored in Vigo Bay:

All my thoughts are with you and my dear squadron. The difficulty will soon be settled. Russia places all her faith and has implicit confidence in you.

NICHOLAS.

Admiral Rojdestvensky has replied:

The entire squadron bows as one man before the throne of Your Majesty. Whatever the Tsar may command, we will do. Hurrah!
ROJDESTVENSKY.

There has been a pathetic sitting of the Chamber, at which the young Nationalist deputy, Guyot de Villeneuve, produced documents to show that a system of secret denunciation is in operation at the War Ministry—a regular organization, worked in conjunction with the Grand Orient of France, for spying on officers, suspected of being reactionaries or clericals, in their garrisons. Guyot de Villeneuve has paid F. Bidegain, a low hireling of the Grand Orient, 40,000 francs for the most typical samples from the files of this organization, a mass of notes and reports which he exhibited during his speech. Contemptible revelations, full of all the usual masonic-lodge diatribes against hundreds and hundreds of officers: 'Enemy of republican institutions . . . a foe to the principles of democracy . . . does not believe in the innocence of Dreyfus . . . mocks at free-thinkers . . . a frequent visitor at the bishop's palace . . . has the prætorian and sectarian outlook . . . creature of the Roman sect . . . a Jesuit in opinions and language . . . pillar of the Church . . . better fitted to be a monk than a general . . . is having his son educated at a Church school . . . etc . . . etc. . . .' All these accusations, most of them anonymous, based on tittle-tattle or guesswork, are really nothing but *a priori* charges and unwarrantable interference with the private beliefs of the victim. As a matter of fact, since the excitement over the Dreyfus Case died down, the public attitude of our officers has been unexceptional—as even their detractors are bound to admit.

The excitement in the Chamber was therefore very great when Guyot de Villeneuve proved that, as the result of these loathsome intrigues, hundreds of officers have seen promotion barred, or their careers ruined, without a chance of defending themselves. At first, the Extreme Left shouted that the documents were forgeries; but when proof was produced, they listened aghast.

General André collapsed in his seat, stammering vague excuses; Combes, the President of the Council, vainly tried a few red herrings. Guyot de Villeneuve wound up: "Working hand in glove with the Grand Orient, General André and President Combes

have organized a system of espionage and denunciation against
the army; they have sown discord among our officers. In these
circumstances, General André cannot remain a minister any
longer. As the army has ceased to have a head, it appeals from
him to Parliament." He stepped down from the tribune, amidst
cheers from all sides of the Chamber.

Jaurès, however, in tones of thunder, adjured the Republicans
to keep their heads, 'not to play into the hands of the Imperialists,
and to save the Government.'

Such deputies as are masonic dignitaries maintain that the
Supreme Council of the Grand Orient knew nothing of the
documents with which Guyot de Villeneuve fortified his argument.

The Chamber finally passed a resolution (by a majority of four
votes only) 'deploring the facts to which its attention had been
called, but leaving it to the government to take the necessary
action.'

So General André is saved. But his days are none the less
numbered. As he left the Palais-Bourbon, he looked very crest-
fallen.

To my mind, the most lamentable revelation in this ghastly
debate is that our army is once again divided against itself just at
the moment when the clouds are rapidly gathering on the foreign
horizon.

Saturday, October 29th, 1904.

During the last few months, our ambassador in St. Petersburg,
Maurice Bompard, has been drawing our attention to 'the siege
of Russia by Germany,' and the unceasing efforts of the Emperor
William to get the Tsar 'to destroy the Franco-Russian alliance.'
We have recent proof of these insidious activities:

At the Kaiser's suggestion, the two monarchs have agreed to
second the military attachés of their respective embassies for
personal attendance 'in the capacity of aide-de-camp.' This is a
return to an old practice abolished by Alexander III; its only
object is to facilitate direct and secret communication between the
two rulers.

When the German Emperor received Colonel Shebeko in his
new rôle, he said: "Please thank your August Master for attaching
you to my person. And by way of a start, you might remind him

that though the King of England speaks and writes very well, he never tells the truth."

Sunday, October 30th, 1904.

Thanks to his skilful and energetic intervention, Delcassé has settled the Anglo-Russian dispute most successfully. An international commission, composed of admirals, is to investigate the Dogger Bank incident and suggest what should be done as the result of its findings.

To emphasize the contribution of French diplomacy to this happy ending, Delcassé is this evening sending the following telegram to all our embassies and legations:

From the very outset, my conversations with the representatives of both England and Russia gave me the impression that it was the desire of both powers that I should endeavour to effect a reconciliation. My efforts in London and St. Petersburg have facilitated the necessary exchange of views. It seemed to me unthinkable that they would fail to arrive at a friendly solution, provided they were given time to talk things over. I have been happy to co-operate to that end.

The submission to the Hague Tribunal—a tribute to the noble inspiration of the Tsar at the beginning of his reign—of a dispute which threatened to have incalculable consequences marks the close of an incident which has been settled in a manner satisfactory to the dignity of both England and Russia and to the advantage of the whole world.

In Manchuria the Russians have suffered a further defeat and been compelled to abandon the Sha-ho lines and retire to their trenches round Mukden.

At Port Arthur, the intense and methodical bombardment never ceases. The garrison is at the end of its tether.

Monday, October 31st, 1904.

Orders from the Tsar have authorized Admiral Rojdestvensky to proceed. The squadron will sail for Tangier tomorrow morning.

The Russian Admiralty has at last decided to let us know which route the 2nd Squadron is adopting. In spite of pressure from Commandant de Freycinet and myself, Rojdestvensky has not accepted the Cape Horn-Southern Pacific-Polynesian Archipelago route, which had so many advantages for him from the point of view of freedom from observation and his ultimate strategic deployment—not to mention the advantage to France of being able to keep up at least an appearance of neutrality. Rojdestvensky has shied at the marine perils involved in this plan; he says that his men, and particularly his officers, are in no fit state to face the risks of such an adventurous voyage. He has therefore decided to skirt the West Coast of Africa and spend some time at Madagascar, where he will be joined by another of his divisions which will go out by the Suez Canal.

I have been busy with De Freycinet all day: (1) drawing up instructions for our consular or colonial officials in Tangier, Dakar, Libreville, Mossamedes, Angra Pequena, the Cape, Tanararivo, Sainte-Marie de Madagascar, Nossi-Bé, Port Said and Djibouti; (2) working out a code to disguise Russian telegrams; (3) making all the arrangements for coaling, the transmission of news from spies and certain secret missions.

When I took my work to Delcassé, I pointed out to him once more the immense danger of this underhand business to which we are making ourselves a party.

"How can we help ourselves?" he said. . . . "We have only one alternative: either to carry out our promise, or to refuse. . . . If we refuse, think of the capital Germany will make out of it. It would mean the end of the alliance."

I quoted him Cardinal de Retz's wise words:

'The function of the statesman is to choose the lesser evil.'

Tuesday, November 1st, 1904.

General Silvestre, head of the French Mission at General Kuropatkin's headquarters, wrote to us from Lon-shan-tun on October 13th, giving us a very alarming forecast of the result of the winter campaign to the Russian armies.

His emphatic conclusion is that the Japanese are now bound to win and that Russia should make peace at once on any terms she can secure, because the position can only grow worse from day to day.

Delcassé asked me yesterday to let him have a note on 'the personal relations between the Emperor William and the Emperor Nicholas,' so far as we know them or divine them from our secret sources of information.

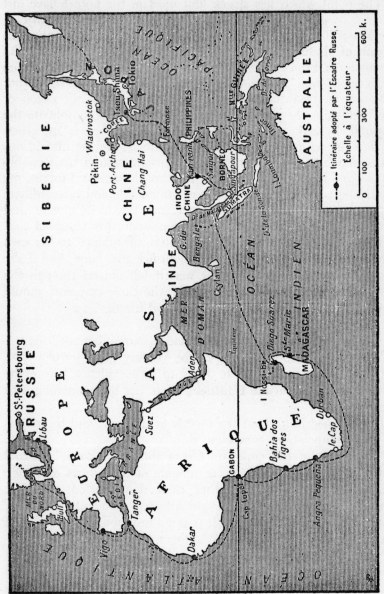

THE RUSSO-JAPANESE WAR. THE ROUTE ADOPTED BY THE RUSSIAN SQUADRON, OCT. 31ST, 1904

The point which has struck him most in the note I have just taken him is that, *ever since Nicholas succeeded to the throne,* the Kaiser has tried to get round him by indulging in a continuous stream of abuse of France. Let me quote, for instance, a remark he made to Prince Lobanoff, Minister of Foreign Affairs, when he received him in audience at Berlin in October, 1905 (our authority is the Prince himself): 'I don't like this succession of royal and princely visits to Paris; their effect is to consolidate the Republic by making it seem just as normal a *régime* as any other, so that the nations forget that monarchies are divine institutions whilst republics are man-made. The consolidation of the Republican *régime* in France is a danger to every throne. And forgive me for telling you that by far the most lamentable and extraordinary feature of the situation is the fact that the most monarchical government in Europe is hobnobbing with this republic! . . . It's all wrong! France should be isolated, abandoned to her own internecine party feuds—*left to stew in her own juice.* And if she showed any inclination to make herself felt abroad through the medium of revolutionary propaganda, the three emperors should at once join forces to crush her once and for all. . . .'

Wednesday, November 2nd, 1904.

My old friend, General de Lacroix, Military Governor of Lyons, who has been summoned to Paris to give evidence before the Consul de Guerre in the Dautriche affair, has been lunching with me.

I questioned him about the morale of the army and the effects of the 'denunciation' campaign.

"The spirit of the rank and file of the *active* army," he told me, "is fairly good. The officers, in spite of this odious campaign against them, are angry rather than downhearted. . . . The reservists, on the other hand, are infected with anti-militarism, internationalism and anarchy. If it came to mobilization, we must anticipate serious mutinies among them. . . ."

We went on to discuss the arrangements which our secret agreement with Italy last year now enables us to make. General de Lacroix told me of the plan which has just been adopted to transfer to the Vosges 40,000 men from the army originally designed to fight the Italians.

The minister sent for me at half-past six this evening. He looked very upset:

"Sit down and take a pen," he said. "I've just had two very serious talks with the German and Spanish Ambassadors; I'll dictate; you can polish it up afterwards."

When I had finished taking down what he said, he added:

"We'll talk about it tomorrow. . . . At the moment, I simply can't. . . . My head is splitting."

I reproduce the two memoranda to which I committed the minister's story.

I

SECRET MEMORANDUM OF M. DELCASSÉ'S CON-VERSATION WITH PRINCE VON RADOLIN, GER-MAN AMBASSADOR.

On November 2nd, 1904, the German Ambassador in Paris, who had recently returned from Berlin,[1] had a diplomatic audience of the minister.

After complimenting M. Delcassé on the part he had played in the amicable settlement of the Dogger Bank incident, Prince von Radolin went on to talk about the Russo-Japanese War:

—"It's no good my trying to conceal my anxieties from you,' he said. "As war has broken out in the Far East. . . . Well! . . . let them get on with it. But we mustn't let the flames spread to Europe. . . . The Japanese are becoming more and more overbearing; they are behaving high-handedly towards neutral powers and always criticizing the way in which they carry out their duties as such. . . . As they are winning, no doubt they are fully conscious of the strength which is bringing them victory. But I hardly think they would assume such a tone if someone was not backing them. England is certainly behind them. . . . And that's what worries me, for England and Germany are not on good terms. The English are jealous of our modest commercial prosperity. Who knows where all these provocations will land us? I don't like it at all. . . . If your impressions differ from mine, I shall be only too thankful. I only ask to be proved wrong."

Reverting to the Dogger Bank incident, Prince von Radolin continued:

[1] Prince von Radolin resumed his work at the Embassy on October 27th, 1904

"It was a very dangerous incident. If it hadn't been for you, England and Russia would have come to blows and the casus fœderis would have arisen. I have been told that Japanese officers, including the naval attaché at Berlin, had laid a trap to catch the Russian Squadron as it was leaving the Baltic: electric torpedoes were to be fired at Rojdestvensky's battleships. So there was reason for the admiral to be on his guard. . . . No doubt vodka also played a part in the business. . . . Just like the Grand Dukes! It horrifies me to see them hanging round restaurants while 40,000 Russians are being killed in battle. If they can't fight, why do they go about in uniform? Why all the braid and decorations? Why all this clanking of swords? I call their behaviour disgusting. . . . It's not exactly calculated to enhance the prestige of the Monarchy! . . . I particularly hate to see it because of our friendly feelings for Russia. Our relations with her are excellent. The two Emperors are on very intimate terms. The Tsar knows he can safely take away all his troops from the western frontier of the Empire."

M. Delcassé simply replied:

"I can't imagine why England should be trying to pick a quarrel. She has only just emerged from a war which has been a great strain on her commerce, and still more her finances.

"She has not—as far as I know—begun to reorganize her army. Anyhow, only yesterday, I had proof of the real attitude of the British Government. So far from wishing to exploit the Dogger Bank incident, it has openly countenanced my efforts to facilitate discussion between the cabinets of Petersburg and London."

II

SECRET MEMORANDUM OF A CONVERSATION BETWEEN M. DELCASSÉ AND THE MARQUIS DEL MUNI, SPANISH AMBASSADOR.

On November 2nd, 1904, half an hour after the German Ambassador left M. Delcassé's room, the Spanish Ambassador entered:
"You've just been seeing Radolin, haven't you?" asked the Marquis del Muni. "I don't know what he said to you. But I must tell you the extraordinary things he has been saying to me."

The Marquis del Muni then repeated the substance of what M. Delcassé had just heard from the lips of Prince von Radolin (except the allusion to the behaviour of the Russian grand-dukes).

*Then he related the end of his conversation with the German
Ambassador in the following terms:*

Prince von Radolin—*"It is impossible to tolerate Japan's insolence towards neutrals: it's aimed at Germany. Japan would certainly never assume such a tone if she were not being backed and
egged on by England. The situation will soon become unbearable.
Now, if war breaks out between Germany on one side and
England and Japan on the other, there will be a Russo-German
alliance within twenty-four hours. That will mean war in Europe
—a general war."*

The Marquis del Muni—*"What! A European war? Why
couldn't France, for instance, remain neutral?"*

Prince von Radolin—*"Oh, no! Impossible, quite impossible!
France will have to make up her mind one way or the other and
side with Russia and Germany or with England. . . . M. Delcassé,
with his universal prestige, is the only man who can save the cause
of peace. He has great influence in London—almost as great as in
Petersburg. He must advise the English to stop playing with fire."*

The Marquis del Muni—*"Have I your permission to repeat what
you've said to M. Delcassé?"*

Prince von Radolin—*"I can't give you permission, because I'm
not speaking officially. I'm just giving you the personal impressions
I have brought from Berlin—I've just come back."*

*After relating this conversation to M. Delcassé, the Marquis del
Muni said:*

*"I'm convinced that Prince von Radolin's remarks are merely
an echo of what the Emperor has told him. The Emperor is
greatly attached to his ambassador (at any rate, the latter says so)
and always speaks his mind to him."*

N.B.—*From secret information from a reliable source which
has come to the ears of the Foreign Minister, it appears that what
Prince von Radolin said both to M. Delcassé and the Marquis del
Muni was anything but the 'personal impressions' of which he
spoke. He was acting on formal and definite instructions from the
German Chancellor.*

Thursday, November 3rd, 1904.

I had a call this morning from our ambassador to Russia,
Maurice Bompard, who has just arrived from St. Petersburg.

"The war in the Far East," he told me, "is getting more and more unpopular with the masses in Russia; they regard it as an enterprise promoted by private interests, a vast filibustering expedition engineered by the Court and the *tchinovniks*.[1] In many villages the departure of reservists has been accompanied by riots. One of the most common phrases to which public discontent has given currency is: *Our masters have declared an unjust war. Is it surprising that God does not bless our arms?* . . . If the disasters continue, and the armies do not soon win some brilliant victory which will enable Russia to secure an honourable peace, I foresee great troubles, and perhaps even revolution, within her borders."

I asked Maurice Bompard about William II's secret and insidious efforts to entice the Tsar away from France and irritate him against England. He replied:

"I see them, or suspect them the whole time; but I have great difficulty in taking any sort of action because the two sovereigns correspond direct and I have been able to satisfy myself that not even Lamsdorf knows what they are writing." [2]

Friday, November 4th, 1904.

At five o'clock I had tea with the Grand Duke Paul at his flat in the Avenue d'Iéna. He questioned me anxiously about the Dogger Bank incident and its possible consequences:

"If war broke out between Russia and England, what would France do?"

"France would always stand by her ally," I replied; "but our compact applies to an attack on Russia by Germany, not by England."

In mysterious tones, he continued:

[1] Officials (Tr.).

[2] The private correspondence of the two sovereigns has now been published by the Soviet Government and shows that at this stage of the Russo-Japanese War William was openly badgering 'his dear Nicky' to form a triple alliance, consisting of Russia, France and Germany, to oppose the insolent English, Japan's accomplice. He wrote, for example: "If you have not sufficient troops at the moment to attack India, at least you have enough for Persia, which has no army. . . . Fear of seeing you enter India from Turkestan and Afghanistan from Persia will immediately cool the heels of the 'jingoes' in London." France, of course, would obviously sulk about the intrusion of Germany into her alliance with Russia. "But once the agreement between us is signed, she would soon have to come in" . . . —the weak-minded Tsar dare not either complete or break off these secret negotiations in which, *vis-à-vis* France, William made him cut such a contemptible figure.

"I know for certain that if we had to fight England we should be supported by Germany."

"What grounds have you for your certainty?"

"This is for your own private ear. . . . I know from a letter from my brother Sergei that the Emperor William recently wrote to the Emperor Nicholas: *If you have war with England, I will put my fleet at your disposal. And I will force France to come in with us.*"

The Grand Duke Paul is extremely fond of his brother Sergei, who is Governor-General of Moscow. His children by his first wife, Alexandra of Greece, i.e., the Grand Duchess Marie (born in 1890), and the Grand Duke Dimitri (born in 1891), are being brought up in Moscow by the Grand Duchess Elizabeth Feodorovna, sister of the Empress.

I went back to the Quai d'Orsay at seven o'clock and told Georges Louis what the Grand Duke Paul had said to me.

"So the veil's lifted at last!" he cried. "This is the beginning of something really serious. We must consider the position at once."

The ever-cautious Georges Louis then asked me:

"Can you absolutely rely on the Grand Duke Paul?"

"Oh, absolutely; he is perfectly straight, and the soul of honour and chivalry."

"Is his brother, the Grand Duke Sergei, really in a position to know about so secret a document as a letter from the Emperor William to the Emperor Nicholas?"

"Oh, yes. . . . The Grand Duke Sergei is Governor-General of Moscow; he married the sister of the Empress Alexandra Feodorovna; he is also head of the reactionary party in Russia and the uncompromising champion of orthodox autocracy. I know that the Emperor tells him—perhaps no one else—his greatest secrets."

Georges Louis started to go down to the minister's room, but stopped for a second in the doorway and said:

"Can you remind me of what was it we learned last spring about Germany's latest strategic plan?"

I gave him a summary of the *Avenger's* revelations, the march of the German armies on Paris *via* Liége, Namur, Charleroi and Maubeuge.

"That seems forcible corroboration," he said, "of the Emperor William's words to the Emperor Nicholas: *I will force France to come in with us.*"

The denunciation affair in the army came up for discussion in the Chamber again this afternoon.

General André made a pitiful attempt to explain away the vile practices discovered by Guyot de Villeneuve; he wound up: "I have remained at my post to defend the Republic and restore the confidence of the republican officers."

Ribot and Leygues made eloquent speeches to this effect: "You claim to be ridding the army of clerical influences; you are really handing it over to informers!"

Millerand himself, socialist though he is, made a fierce attack on the Minister of War: "You claim to be defending the interests of the republican officers; they have not deserved such an insult. You think you are in that way building up a republican army; all you are doing is to put a premium on hypocrisy. . . ."

The humiliated General André stammered but could find nothing further to say, and his downfall was certain until the Nationalist deputy, Syveton, walked up to him and slapped his face so hard that the old soldier fell backwards.

At this brutal insult, the Chamber executed a *volte face* and passed a vote of confidence.

Saturday, November 5th, 1904.

This morning, Delcassé telephoned for me at half-past eight to go and see him at once.

His face was drawn and there was a fevered look in his eyes.

"M. Georges Louis," he said, "told me yesterday everything about your talk with the Grand Duke Paul. I take it that you can implicitly rely on the Grand Duke's statements?"

"Yes, *Monsieur le Ministre*, I have implicit faith in anything the Grand Duke Paul says. Besides, he has told me several times of the Emperor William's emphatic promise to the Emperor Nicholas: *"If you have war with England I will place my fleet at your disposal. And I will force France to come in with us."*

"You needn't be told that it kept me awake all night and made me feel pretty glum. . . . I mentioned the other day that what intrigued me most about Radolin's action was the question whether it was the result of an agreement between Berlin and Petersburg. I've no doubt about it now! So we may well be in for a European war. Where shall we be if, at the last moment, Russia admits that she has formed an alliance with Germany? . . . Of course it will be open to us to denounce our Russian alliance. But in that case we should find ourselves facing Germany single-handed—with twenty-four army corps to their thirty-eight, i.e., 840,000 men to their 1,400,000. As for our navy, perhaps I'd better say nothing: don't I know that we haven't got one, thanks to M. Camille Pelletan!"

He rose, strode up and down his room, sniffing and breathing heavily—signs of strong emotion with him. Then he stopped right in front of me, arms folded, head thrown back and eyes flashing defiance:

"Can you see *me* agreeing to join in a Russo-German coalition! Can you! The Emperor William claims that he will be able to force us to come in. We haven't come to that yet! Anything rather than be tied to Germany's apron-strings! It's about time the Emperor knew something about us! What a fool! . . . And to think there are idiots and weaklings in France who actually admire him!"

Suddenly he recovered himself, sat down at Vergenne's bureau again and continued in measured tones which made his words all the more moving:

"Until the Treaty of Frankfurt has been revised, friendly collaboration between France and Germany is impossible. To associate ourselves with German policy would be tantamount to recognizing the loss of Alsace-Lorraine for good and all. And if, to our discredit, all our national instincts did not promptly revolt at the idea, it would be the end of France. . . . You'd better go now, my dear Paléologue; I want time to think out some means of defeating the Emperor William's machinations."

As I walked back to my room, I reflected that even in our most private talks Delcassé had never before referred to Alsace-Lorraine. I had long thought and felt that the recovery of our lost provinces was his fondest dream, the mainspring of all his actions, the secret goal of all his efforts; but he had never uttered a single word to justify my conviction.

Georges Louis telephoned me just as I arrived home at half-past seven this evening:

"Get ready to leave for London at once. The train goes at 8.40. One of my secretaries is going to the Gare du Nord to take your ticket. I'll be with you in a quarter of an hour."

I dined hastily, while my valet packed my suit-case.

Georges Louis arrived before I was ready.

"The minister," he said, "wants you, as a personal favour, to go to London tonight. That'll show you how worried he is! He wants you to explain the position to the ambassador and ask his advice. I've brought you the secret memoranda you gave me yesterday so that you may have all the facts at your fingers' ends. The minister says you must be most careful to keep them on you throughout the journey. . . . My carriage is waiting; I'll drive you to the station."

On the way, he added:

"The minister leaves M. Paul Cambon an absolutely free hand in deciding how much to tell Lord Lansdowne, or even the King."

London, Sunday, November 6th, 1904.

I arrived in London about six o'clock this morning and am putting up at the Embassy.

Last night I stayed on deck all the time during the crossing from Calais to Dover. The wind was in the north and pretty keen, and a few clouds scudded across the sky.

Above my head the sky was a pure dark blue. I could not have had a more beautiful or stimulating setting for the task of collecting my thoughts and thinking out the problem which I had to put before Paul Cambon.

I was with the ambassador from ten till twelve.

To explain the position to him, I read him four notes on the following subjects: (1) the conversation between the minister and the German Ambassador of November 2nd last; (2) the conversation between the minister and the Spanish Ambassador on the same date; (3) my conversation with the Grand Duke Paul of the day before yesterday, and (4) the revelations of the *Avenger*, of March-April, 1904.

After carefully scrutinizing these documents, the ambassador said:

"Prince von Radolin's words and the Grand Duke Paul's story confirm my own impressions here since the Dogger Bank incident —that the Emperor William is stirring up Russia against England. So the position seems to me anxious, and I should call it serious if (a question the answer to which I don't know) Prince

von Radolin's action was prearranged between Berlin and Petersburg. . . . What's your view on that point?"

"I have no doubt that Prince von Radolin, despite his oral
disclaimer, was carrying out official instructions and not speaking
on his own responsibility. Our own secret enquiries show that his
statements to the Spanish Ambassador had been approved by the
German Chancellor. . . . I hesitate to believe that the matter
was officially discussed by the two governments through the
ordinary channels. What seems to me more likely is that the
Emperor William, with his usual impetuousness, took a step
which he imagined was bound to be welcome to his imperial
cousin. William II is too well informed about what goes on in
Russia not to know that the Manchurian War is becoming more
unpopular with the Russian nation every day, and that the rum-
bling of revolution can be heard even among the rural population.
He therefore imagined that the Tsarist Government would look
favourably upon the idea of a diversion in Europe. . . . On the
other hand, regarded exclusively from Germany's point of view,
wouldn't a great European quarrel provide a magnificent opportunity for the Germanic Empires to shatter the ingenious
arrangement whereby France is assured of the double advantage
of an alliance with Russia and an *entente* with England?"

"I'm very much afraid you're right! . . . But what does M.
Delcassé think?"

"Yesterday the minister talked to me very frankly and made
no attempt to hide his feelings. He thinks that the Grand Duke
Paul's story is proof that the two emperors are engaged in secret
negotiations, and has no doubt that Prince von Radolin's action is
the first symptom that they have come to terms. So he's afraid
that Germany will soon require us to join a Russo-German
alliance which is openly aimed at England."

Paul Cambon reflected for a few moments and then said:

"Do you know what worries me most about all you have told
me?—the revelations of that enigmatic individual you call *the
Avenger*."

He opened an atlas and asked me to explain on the map the
bold plan of campaign, the object of which is to carry the German
armies up to the sources of the Oise *via* Belgian territory.

After another pause, Paul Cambon continued:

"Yes, it all worries me very much. But I can't believe that the

Emperor William really wants war. He's a *poseur*, a braggart and a mountebank; but he's not a fire-eater, because he doesn't know the first thing about strategy and his generals have frequently reminded him of the fact. If he'd had the slightest taste for soldiering, you may be quite sure he would have declared war on us long ago. . . . Well, well! We cannot be too cautious. First of all we must let the British Government know all about this dangerous intrigue to which the Grand Duke Paul has given you the clue. I'll tell Lord Lansdowne about it tomorrow morning; like all self-respecting Englishmen, he's in the country today; the weekend is a sacred institution."

Lunch at one o'clock. Geoffray, the Counsellor of the Embassy, de Seynes and Fleuriau, the Secretaries, and Colonel d'Amade, the military attaché, were the other guests.

At half-past two, the ambassador took me back into his room. We lit our cigars and once again reviewed all the possibilities we had discussed in the morning. The conclusions to which we came were recapitulated by Paul Cambon as follows:

"Simultaneous action in St. Petersburg and London is our best chance of foiling the Emperor William's machinations. At St. Petersburg we must broach the subject quite candidly with the Tsar and tell him: *You must not think that we would ever join a Russo-German coalition aimed at England; we set great store by the friendship of England and shall remain loyal to it. You know that we have several times taken advantage of it for your benefit—in the Dogger Bank affair, for example. So do not destroy the Franco-Russian alliance with your own hands. Don't let the Emperor William entice you into an adventure the consequences of which would be incalculable.* . . . We must simultaneously say to London: *While remaining Japan's ally, try to be more tactful in your dealings with St. Petersburg. Don't give this idiot William the slightest chance of exploiting Russia's rage and humiliation against you. Help us to keep the peace of Europe.* . . ."

"Do you think the British Cabinet would see things in the same light?" I asked the ambassador.

"Yes; but we shan't have an easy task. Since the Dogger Bank incident, public opinion in England has been roused to the highest pitch against Russia. At the least little thing it would get out of hand. And the government would have to give way."

"Have to!—really?"

"Yes. The Balfour-Lansdowne-Chamberlain Ministry is old, decrepit and worn out; its only strength is the weakness of its opponents. It has lost all its prestige in the country. I haven't the slightest doubt that, if the nation took the bit between its teeth, the cabinet would be obliged to follow it."

At four o'clock I went for a walk under a smoky sky with Colonel d'Amade in Regent's Park. I have known him since the days when I was qualifying for the rank of lieutenant of reserve in the mounted batteries of the 5th Cavalry Division. We discussed the problem I had just been debating with the ambassador.

"I think," said our military attaché, "that Europe is on the brink of very grave developments. . . . William II's fretful humour may mean the outbreak of war at any moment. . . . With the English in such a state of hysterical irritation against the Russians, the slightest incident would be enough to fire the train."

I worked at the Embassy from six to seven. At eight I dined at the St. James Club with d'Amade and Fleuriau.

London, Monday, November 7th, 1904.

The ambassador met the Secretary of State at the *Foreign Office* at 10.30 this morning.

When he returned, at about quarter-past twelve, he told me about his conversation:

"I was perfectly frank with Lord Lansdowne as to the object of your visit to me; I kept nothing back. He replied: *It looks very bad, but I am not surprised. I've had a feeling for a long time that Germany was stirring up the Russians against us. . . . Of course, in sizing up the position, we mustn't forget that the Emperor William is impulsive and a born mischief-maker; he has a restless mind and resembles the operatic tenor who must always be singing some great air. At Sandringham recently, I heard him propose a toast which would set Europe on fire if it got to the ears of the public. The next day he couldn't even remember what he'd said; he had a fresh bee in his bonnet. . . . But for all that, what you've told me does show that there's serious danger ahead. I'm*

*most grateful to you for letting me know at once. We are having
a Cabinet Meeting very shortly; I will tell my colleagues about
our talk and then go and see the King. . . .* As for the best way
of thwarting the German move, Lord Lansdowne entirely agrees
with us. He shares our view that the British Cabinet should carefully avoid anything calculated to offend the national susceptibilities of the Russians. His parting words were: *If we want to save
the cause of peace, each of us must do his part. . . ."*

We then went into the dining-room where lunch was served.

At two o'clock I left for Paris, *via* Dover and Calais.

Tuesday, November 8th, 1904.
I arrived in Paris yesterday evening at 9.40.

I went to see the minister at nine o'clock this morning.

I reported my discussion with Paul Cambon and he entirely
approved.

When I had finished, he read me some rough notes he had
made during my absence; they confirm in every way the conclusions to which I told him we had come.

He remained lost in thought for some time, scowling fiercely,
and then continued:

"I can see what I have to do. . . . But shall I have time to
do it? I'll need at least a fortnight to get busy in London and St.
Petersburg. . . . If the Tsar is weak or silly enough to commit
himself to William in writing, or Prince von Radolin meanwhile
faces us with the alternative of friendship with England or a
Russo-German alliance, war will be inevitable. . . . I'll never tie
myself to Germany's apron-strings, and I'll have the whole of
France behind me."

The clock struck ten. Delcassé suddenly left me to report our
conversation to the President of the Republic before the usual
cabinet meeting at half-past ten. In the doorway he turned and
shot at me in a rasping voice:

"Hasn't General André chosen a good moment to ruin our
army?"

"For Heaven's sake, tell that to the President, *Monsieur le
Ministre!*"

Wednesday, November 9th, 1904.

Delcassé had a call from the Russian Ambassador today and thought it his duty to speak very frankly about my recent mission in London.

"I am aware," he said, in somewhat formal tones, "of the private correspondence which has been passing between your sovereign and William II for several weeks. I know the Kaiser is offering him an alliance against England and that he says he can force us to join in."

Nelidoff almost jumped out of his skin:

"You amaze, me, Minister. I have heard nothing whatever about it. . . . Are you sure your information is correct?"

"If I wasn't sure, do you think I'd even breathe a word of such a thing to you? There is something I think it my duty to tell you, in all friendship. So long as I live, France will never enter a coalition with Germany; if she did, it would be tantamount to ratifying the Treaty of Frankfurt a second time. If Russia ignored this warning and made a private compact with Germany, the Republican Government would look elsewhere. After all I've done for your country, I've a right to tell you exactly what's in my mind."

Nelidoff was deeply moved and stammered:

"No, no, what you've been told can't be true. I can guarantee that His Majesty the Emperor is as devoted as ever to our alliance. . . ."

He almost tottered out of the room.

Chapter VIII

November 10th—December 17th, 1904

Thursday, November 10th, 1904.

At eleven this morning, the Japanese Minister, Motono, called on the Director of Political Affairs to lodge a further complaint about the 'supply facilities afforded Admiral Rojdestvensky's squadron in French waters.' He remarked somewhat caustically:

"We know for certain that this squadron could never reach the China Seas if it were not for your help. If it does, all our military plans will have to be changed. So it is a question of vital importance to us. . . . I hope you understand me—*a question of vital importance.*"

Georges Louis replied in his most naive manner:

"I don't understand at all and I won't ask you how you can be so certain; but I can assure you that we are meticulously observing our duties as a neutral."

Motono left without a word.

I ran into him, just as he was leaving the Director's room. We exchanged a few polite remarks for, in his own stately fashion, he is extremely courteous and always very friendly with me. But I trembled to think of his little ferrety eyes piercing through my bag and seeing what I was carrying—three long telegrams from the Russian Admiralty to Rojdestvensky, which I was just about to send on to him at Dakar.[1]

This afternoon Delcassé made a very fine speech in the Chamber, summarizing the main principles which have inspired his Moroccan policy for the last six years, mainly with regard to England

---

[1] In 1914, when I was ambassador at St. Petersburg, I met Motono again. During the Great War, he proved a perfect ally and we became very friendly. We often talked about the years 1904 and 1905. One day he said to me: "My government knew all about the secret help you were giving the Russian squadron; we even knew that you and Captain de Freycinet concocted all the arrangements, because at St. Petersburg we had an excellent informer who had sources of information in all the Admiralty offices. . . . The reason we did not protest more strongly was because, on the other hand—I must admit to our advantage—England did not observe her neutrality very scrupulously either. . . ." I laughed and replied: "Delcassé always pooh-poohed me when I was worried about your complaints; he used to say: *I'm doing no more for Russia than England is doing for Japan.* . . ."

and Spain. It is a great chapter in our history—one which is by no means closed, but has already resulted in the recognition of our supremacy in Morocco by the Spanish and British Governments.

In London last night, as Balfour was ill, Lord Lansdowne made a speech in his place at the Lord Mayor's Banquet. He performed his task with his usual skill and moderation. He devoted himself primarily to belittling the importance of the occurrence which "has brought the possibilities of a great war before our eyes in the last few days." As an honest man, he laid stress on the significance of the assurances which the Russian Government has given England: 'The International Commission will clear up all the causes and circumstances of the disaster and determine all personal responsibilities. . . .' He concluded by congratulating the government of the French Republic on the part it had played in promoting an amicable settlement of the dispute.

Friday, November 11th, 1904.

General Pendézec has just told me of a number of indications observed by our Secret Service men in the vicinity of Crefeld, Cologne, Aix-la-Chapelle, Malmédy, Hellenthal and Saint-Vit, and which tally exactly with the *Avenger's* curious disclosures.

As regards the stategic development of the operation in the direction of Liége, Namur, Charleroi and Maubeuge, it would doubtless be swift and easy. It must thus be assumed that the German forces would reach our northern frontier a fortnight after leaving the Aix-la-Chapelle zone; the distance is only 180 kilometres and the small Belgian Army, completely taken by surprise, would be powerless to stop them.

I asked the Chief of General Staff if our plan of concentration had been already modified with a view to countering this overwhelming eccentric offensive:

"I'm afraid not!" he replied. "No change whatever has been made in Plan XV of 1903. . . . General Brugère refuses to believe that the Germans would risk such an audacious violation of Belgian neutrality; he admits the possibility of their cutting off a corner *via* Luxemburg, but no more. Our concentration zones remain échelonned from Belfort to Bar-le-Duc, behind Toul and Verdun, with a strong reserve at Rheims. If the Germans advanced through Luxemburg, this reserve would at once be despatched to the Argonne to extend and strengthen our left wing. . . . As a matter of fact, I am proposing to bring up the whole question with the Generalissimo in the near future. No doubt you know that the decision rests with him alone. My functions are confined to the preliminaries and the execution of the orders he issues." [1]

The wry smile which wreathed his lips as he uttered these last words once more revealed the sullen, jealous animosity between the Generalissimo and the Chief of Staff [2] and their fundamental personal antipathy.

Saturday, November 12th, 1904.

The Dogger Bank incident is settled, to all intents and purposes. But there is still an undercurrent of bitter feeling amongst the English and Russians alike. The resentment among our neighbours, however, seems to be subsiding. Their national phlegm, common sense and self-control are reasserting themselves.

It is otherwise in Russia. Hatred of England is a national obsession. The public regrets that the Imperial Government did not take a much stronger line over 'the absurd Dogger Bank affair' and it bears a grudge against France for intervening. Responsible papers actually dare to write: "We are not afraid of a clash with England; we are strong enough to hold our own with her and tame her incorrigible pride for ever. . . ."

But far more serious than this rhodomontade is an article such as the following in the *Soviet*: "As the Dogger Bank incident all but ended in war, we have the right to ask what France would have done if the English Fleet had attacked Admiral Rojdestvensky's squadron. This is a matter of vital importance. Why should we hold our peace? Why should there appear to be a conspiracy of silence. . . . We say that if France had proved herself a loyal ally, England would never have dreamed of blockading our squadron in Vigo. But instead of muzzling the English

[1] The generalissimo has exclusive authority in all matters pertaining to concentration and operations. He can please himself as to how much he cares to tell the Minister of War and the *Conseil Supérieur de la Guerre*.

[2] From the historical point of view, these remarks of General Pendézec require correction. It is unfortunately true that the Generalissimo and the Chief of General Staff did not get on well; private grievances complicated differences of professional opinion. But although General Brugère's 'primary reaction' was to refuse to believe in the possibility of a German attack through Liége and Namur, he soon changed his mind. Up to June, 1906, when he retired, he displayed great ingenuity in devising means to "counter the *coup de surprise*" with which we were threatened.

with a stern reprimand, the French Republic merely offered London honeyed words and friendly advice. In this national crisis, it was not France which saved Russia; we understand that it was Germany."

The *Novoie-Vremia* goes even further: "Can we think of no other alliance save that with France? What about a continental alliance? Can no other nation produce a Napoleon in whose brain the idea is taking shape?"

Sunday, November 13th, 1904.

Admiral Rojdestvensky's squadron arrived at Dakar yesterday and is leaving for Gaboon in three or four days. When discussing this latter call with the Russian Admiralty, we had expressed a desire that the squadron should not put in at Libreville, where the governor resides, but at a deserted part of the coast, the excellent roadstead at Cape Lopez. Rojdestvensky, however, insisted on anchoring at Libreville itself. We had quite a battle over it. When our naval attaché in Russia, Captain de Saint-Pair, was arguing our views before Admiral Virenius, the Chief of the Naval Staff, the latter asked him:

"Where exactly is Cape Lopez?"

"I'll show you," said Saint-Pair, "give me a map."

He was brought a Stieler atlas, showing Cape Lopez jutting out from the West Coast of Africa like a nose in the middle of a face. But Admiral Virenius continued:

"Is there a good anchorage at Cape Lopez?"

"First class. I'll show you it too. Give me a chart."

After twenty minutes' search, an officer came in:

"The Admiralty doesn't possess any charts of the African Coast."

Monday, November 14th, 1904.

Ever since hostilities began in Manchuria nine months ago, the Russians have sustained a long series of reverses, both by land and sea, and every day we get further proof of the naval and military superiority of the Japanese. Public opinion in Russia feels the humiliation very deeply. In all ranks of society, including the rural masses, and in every part of the Empire irritation is becoming more and more pronounced. But during the last weeks, public discontent has not confined itself to criticism of the government authorities or fulminations against the vices of the administration and the inexperience of the generals: it is protesting openly in the form of public demonstrations.

At Moscow, for instance, a thousand reservists, after insulting and beating their officers, refused to leave for Manchuria. Cossacks had to charge before the mutiny was quelled. Result: eight killed and twenty-three wounded. In Lodz, Riazan, Lugansk and Tula, mobs of workmen paraded the streets, shouting: "Down with the war! . . . We want peace, peace!"

In St. Petersburg and Moscow, students are organizing seditious meetings at which the *Marseillaise* is sung.

The garrisons on the Polish Frontier are constantly reporting that bands of soldiers have escaped into Germany or Austria during the night. At the little towns of Ottlotshin and Myslovics, the first Prussian stations on the lines connecting Warsaw with Berlin and Breslau, more than fifteen hundred Russian deserters have been seen passing through.

Our Consul in Kharkoff also writes: 'The war with Japan is getting more and more unpopular with the working-class population in the south of Russia. The attitude of the workmen and *mujiks*[1] is actually becoming so threatening that in some districts the authorities have ordered mobilization. I am very much afraid that the disorders will soon become much worse.'

Tuesday, November 15th, 1904.
France is still highly incensed at the recent disclosures of 'spying' activities among our garrisons. Every day, the opposition newspapers, *Le Figaro*, *l'Echo de Paris*, *le Gaulois*, fill their columns with the 'secret reports' obtained from F. Bidegain (he has produced 25,000) which afford undeniable proof that General André and the officials of the *Grand Orient* Lodge are working in concert to spy into the private lives of our officers.

In those daily revelations, the freemasons, spurred on by Jaurès, affect to see nothing but a dishonest campaign on the part of the monarchist, nationalist and clerical reactionaries; they actually congratulate General André 'on having helped so gallantly in saving the Republic from the machinations of its unsleeping enemies.'

But the bitter and universal attacks on General André, the humiliation of Syveton's blow and his breakdown in health have really made him a continual source of weakness and danger to the

[1] Peasants (Tr.).

Ministry. The President of the Council has therefore decided quietly to throw him overboard, to 'strangle him, Turkish fashion'; the poor old fellow has realized the position at last and tendered his resignation today.

His place has been taken by Maurice Berteaux, deputy for the Seine-et-Oise and Vice-President of the Army Commission. The new minister is an extreme Left Socialist; but his family traditions, education and great wealth (he is one of the richest Paris brokers) make his political opinions much less dangerous. At any rate, he is said to be honest and patriotic. If only he can restore *esprit de corps* among our officers!

Wednesday, November 16th, 1904.

In his speech of November 10th on the Anglo-French Agreement of April 8th, Delcassé ingeniously introduced a very kind word for Russia.

Today I showed him a telegram from Prince von Radolin, just decoded, in which the German Ambassador commented on this demonstration of loyalty to Russia, adding: *That's what I call real statesmanship!*

Delcassé's features lighted up at once; his eyes shot flame; he positively glowed with pride and joy, so radiant was his face. I might have been on Mount Tabor, witnessing the Transfiguration.

Thursday, November 17th, 1904.

Bompard, who is just going back to his post, has repeated a long conversation he has just had with Delcassé.

"I found him very pro-English," he said, "because he's heart-broken at the complacent reception given by Nicholas II to the Emperor William's machiavellian enticements. He remarked several times, in indignant tones: *After all I've done for Russia during the last year! What ingratitude!* . . . . He has instructed me to speak to the Tsar very plainly. . . . I told him he needn't have said that, as I should have done so without any prompting. You can't be too firm with Russians. They're naturally so evasive! . . ."

Friday, November 18th, 1904.

Paul Cambon has just had a long talk with the King of England, after a dinner given by their Majesties in honour of the King and Queen of Portugal at Windsor the day before yesterday.

I quote below the principal passages in our ambassador's dispatch reporting this important conversation:

The King made me sit beside him in a quiet corner. Looking more worried than I have ever seen before, he asked me what I thought of the situation. I repeated what I had told Lord Lansdowne. . . . I added that it would be possible, and in fact easy, to improve Anglo-Russian relations if the press would keep out of it. "Yes," he replied, "but we have no means of influencing the press and public opinion may boil over. Besides, we don't know what's happening in St. Petersburg. There is a war-party there which is longing to pick a quarrel with us, by way of diversion after all the disasters in the Far East. The Grand Duke Alexis hates us; the Grand Duke Alexander is pressing for war. The Emperor is a man of peace, inspired by the best intentions: but he always takes the advice of the last person he's been speaking to. War would be absurd. Its consequences to the whole of Europe would be incalculable and you yourselves would be placed in a very awkward position."

I replied that I quite agreed with him, but he had forgotten one vital factor in the situation—Germany, which was working for war and the only power in a position to benefit from a universal conflagration. "I know all that and know it well," His Majesty replied, "I can't understand my nephew's policy at all. He never says the same thing twice. I know what he's up to at St. Petersburg, but it's the Grand Dukes I'm most afraid of."

He reverted to the disasters which a war between Russia and England would involve: "It would be a cataclysm, cataclysm," he repeated several times. . . . "The Russians would stir up trouble on the Indian Frontier. . . . I'm wondering whether I hadn't better write to the Emperor Nicholas! I'll think it over."

The King wound up by saying: "Please tell Monsieur Loubet how grateful I am to him for the attitude France has taken, and the services she is rendering to the cause of peace. And don't forget to tell Monsieur Delcassé that I have implicit confidence in him and rely on his loyalty and experience to save us from the horrors of a war."

Your Excellency will yourself draw the moral of this royal conversation. I think it reveals very real fear of war, grave anxiety

*for India and a sincere desire to facilitate a settlement of the
current difficulties. Ought King Edward's apprehensions to be
disclosed to St. Petersburg? I think not; they would supply the
war-party with an argument, and I feel sure Your Excellency
will think it inadvisable to fan such dangerous flames.*

Saturday, November 19th, 1904.

The Emperor Nicholas has just returned to St. Petersburg after
a tour of inspection to Poland.

While he was staying at Suvalki, in the province of Vilna, General von der Goltz, who commands the 1st Prussian Army Corps,
came to pay his respects and brought him a personal letter from
the Emperor William.

On his return to the capital, Nicholas II read this letter to his
Minister of War, General Sakharoff, who shortly afterwards communicated its terms to our military attaché, General Moulin. They
are as follows: *I hear that certain countries are inclined to offer
you their services in mediating with Japan. I should not venture
to do the same unless I knew beforehand that you wished it. But
in case of need, do not forget that I am at your service.*

By way of comment on General Sakharoff's disclosure, General
Moulin writes: "I have known General Sakharoff too long and
too well, and I have too much respect for his extraordinary dis-
cretion, not to realize that, if he has taken the risk of communi-
cating his Emperor's secrets, it is because he sees some peril ahead,
some peril to the close and friendly relations between France and
Russia."

I happened to be with the minister just at the moment when
this dispatch was brought in. He took a swift glance at it. Then he
made a wry face and a dull gleam came into his eyes:

"This is serious," he said.

He read out the whole dispatch. Then, as if transfigured by a
sudden inspiration, he rapped out:

"Either the Tsar did not tell General Sakharoff, or General
Sakharoff did not tell General Moulin, all that was in William's
letter. . . . But I can guess the rest of the letter—something no
one dare admit—the prelude to a Russo-German alliance and
the destruction of the Franco-Russian alliance. . . . How can
we even be sure that the two sovereigns haven't already signed

something? I must speak to Nelidoff at once. Telephone and ask him to come and see me this afternoon. . . . I'll shake him up properly!"

After a pause:

"For this interview I want you to get out a note in which, without the slightest allusion to General Sakharoff's disclosure, we will say that we have received from Germany the most precise and reliable information about the negotiations in progress between the two emperors. . . . You must make the note very emphatic. I will read it to Nelidoff and I mean to make him think we have proof positive of everything I suspect." [1]

Sunday, November 20th, 1904.

I lunched today with Boni de Castellane at the Château du Marais, between Arpajon and Dourdan. The air was nippy, the sky translucent and the scents of the forest filled our nostrils.

The château was built by the architect Gabriel and is an example of the Louis XVI style in its most elegant and classical form.

It is the old home of the Noailles and the Molés. Shades of lovely Cornélia de Castellane, who was the mistress, first of Count Molé and then Chateaubriand, during the Restoration.

Castellane has restored this magnificent property, both buildings and gardens, in perfect taste. There is a large staff whose liveries are a dream. As I entered the vestibule, I could not help thinking of Louis XIV's contemporary, who, when invited to a magnificent fête at the Duc d'Antin's, spat in the face of the footmen, because, so he said: "Everything here is so beautiful that I daren't spit anywhere else!"

Princess Alexandre de Tour et Taxis, Princess de Ligne, Albert Vandal of the Académie Française, etc., etc., accompanied me from Paris.

After lunch I went for a walk alone with Princess de Tour et

[1] In this case, M. Delcassé's presentiments were correct but a little premature, as subsequent events proved. The Bolshevik Government has now published the correspondence of the two Emperors. The letter which General von der Goltz was instructed to give the Tsar was dated October 30th, 1904. In it William II formulated a plan of diplomatic action whereby Russia and Germany would 'force' France to join them 'openly' against England: 'This would be very important for us, as we should then have her excellent ports and fine navy at our disposal. . . .' The letter ended with a *Draft Treaty* which was a sort of forerunner to the mysterious pact the two sovereigns were to sign at Bjorko on July 24th, 1905.

Taxis, *née* Princess Marie of Hohenlohe-Schillingfürst.[1] She is approaching fifty, but still lithe, slender and charming. Last year, she published in the *Revue de Paris* a fantastic novel called *Le Satyre.* The scene is laid in the marshy plain of Aquileia, north of Venice, and its imaginative treatment reminded me of Merimée's *Lokis,* or even more *La Vénus d'Ille.* During the summer she lives at the old Castle of Duino on the Adriatic, near Trieste. It has a thirteenth-century dungeon with a vault, the door of which has been walled up since the time of the Hohenstaufens. I asked Princess Marie why she had not had the door of this mysterious vault opened. She replied wittily:

"We might well find nothing there—mysteries never improve by being unveiled."

Then she asked me about the European situation, the evergrowing tension between France and Germany, the progress of the revolutionary ferment in Russia, etc. I asked her in turn about the internal condition of the Austro-Hungarian monarchy:

"The Archduke Rudolf's death was a tragic blow to the Hapsburg dynasty," she said. . . . "When our dear Emperor Francis-Joseph dies, we shall be faced with an appalling crisis. . . . Our last chance of salvation lies in the Hungarians. They alone possess the intelligence, energy and courage to save us from total disintegration. . . . But how humiliating for us Germans to have to submit to the Magyar yoke!"

As if her confidence in me were growing, she gradually began to talk quite frankly about the difficult and delicate problem which the personality of the *Thronfolger,* the Archduke Francis-Ferdinand, presents to Austria. In her vivacious, unrestrained tones, though occasionally skimming lightly over some ticklish point, she confirmed all we already knew about His Imperial and Royal Highness—his narrow outlook; his suspicious, irritable and capricious nature; his overbearing manner; his piety—bigoted, superstitious and obsessed by terror of Hell; his aggressive and fanatical clericalism; his implacable hatred of the Hungarians,

[1] The Tour et Taxis family come of very old stock. They had lands in Lombardy in the twelfth century, in the time of Frederick Barbarossa. They were Knights of the Holy Roman Empire and later raised to the dignity of princes with the rank of Serene Highness, "Hereditary Grand-Masters of the Imperial Posts." Today (1904) their chief estates are in the Tyrol, Hungary, Bohemia and Bavaria. One of Princess Marie's cousins, Prince Godefroy von Hohenlohe-Schillingfürst, is the Emperor Francis Joseph's "Military Plenipotentiary" at the court of the Emperor Nicholas.

Italians and Serbs; his jealous animosity towards Francis-Joseph, 'who is taking much too long to die,' and endless quarrels with the aged monarch; his determination, which he makes little attempt to conceal, to apply to the Holy See some day for a release from the solemn oath which he took when he married Countess Sophie Chotek, that their children should never succeed to the throne.[1]

Princess Marie concluded in these words:

"What is he going to do when he mounts the throne? The prospect is as puzzling as it is alarming. We have reason to believe that he contemplates nothing less than the transformation of the constitution of the monarchy by substituting for Austro-Hungarian dualism a vast federation in which the Czechs, Croats, Slovenes, Poles and Rumanians would all enjoy autonomy. Will he embark upon such a crazy adventure? . . . He does not conceal his desire to take advantage of the Russian disasters in the Far East to establish our hegemony in the Balkans. . . . It all seems to me very fantastic, but equally alarming. . . . Yet the Hapsburg dynasty must not die!"

As we went in, the sun had just sunk out of sight in an amethyst sky. . . . I thought of the sorceress, Cornelia de Castellane, who made Madame de Récamier suffer so much.

Monday, November 21st, 1904.

I dined with the Grand Duke Paul and Countess Olga-Valerianovna von Hohenfelsen, together with Countess Herbertstein, the Austrian military attaché's wife, Count and Countess Fersen, Countess Marie Kleinmichel and Nekludoff, Counsellor of the Russian Embassy in Paris.

During dinner, Madame von Hohenfelsen spoke to me about the insidious intrigues of Miquel, the Secretary of the German Embassy, among the Diplomatic Corps and all the Russians resident in Paris, in favour of a Russo-German alliance. "The

---

[1] On July 1st, 1900, the Archduke Francis-Ferdinand morganatically married Countess Sophie Chotek. Before the Emperor Francis-Joseph would consent, or rather resign himself, to his heir's *mésalliance*, he exacted the humiliation of a solemn oath before the whole Court that any children born of the marriage should not succeed to the Hapsburg throne.

Sophie Chotek, made 'Princess' and subsequently 'Duchess of Hohenberg,' was assassinated with her husband at Serajevo on June 28th, 1914.

Franco-Russian alliance," he is saying, "has lost its *raison d'être*, for the ever-fickle France has sold herself body and soul to England."

After dinner, the war in Manchuria became the subject of general conversation. The Grand Duke, Fersen and Nekludoff assured me that 'Russia must fight on, cost what it may, until dirty little Japan begs for mercy, even if the war lasts two more years.'

But Countess Marie Kleinmichel, who has just come from St. Petersburg and is merely passing through Paris, had a very different opinion:

"You have no idea," she said, speaking with much warmth, "of the intensity of the feeling aroused in Russia during the last few months. Our *mujiks* are now objecting to being killed for what they call *a bit of territory we've never heard of.* . . . Not a week passes without a mutiny in the barracks, or riots along the line when reservists leave for the front. . . . In the universities it's even worse; revolutionary demonstrations, provoked by the slighest incident, are everyday occurrences. You can be sure that the peasants will come on the scene before long. That will mean the end of Tsarism and Russia!"

All the guests were struck dumb with horror at this prophetic outburst. The Grand Duke brought the conversation to a close with an exclamation:

"Pugacheff! . . . Pugacheff. . . . We must never forget Pugacheff." [1]

Fifty-eight years of age and a general's widow, Countess Kleinmichel belongs to the nobility of the Baltic Provinces—that caste, of German origin, from which Tsarism has drawn its most intelligent and devoted servants since the time of Anna-Ivanovna. It is the Baltic aristocracy which is chiefly responsible for the conversion of the Russian State into a great police bureaucracy, inspired by Prussian militarism. General Nicholas Kleinmichel, Countess Marie's husband, was the grandson of that Count Peter Kleinmichel who was the chief tool of the ferocious, diabolical Arakcheieff in the reign of Alexander II.

[1] In 1773 the Cossack Pugacheff incited all the peasants in southern Russia to rise against Catherine II and the domination of the aristocracy. There was a frightful civil war for over a year. Pugacheff almost succeeded in seizing Moscow. His memory has an unholy fascination for the *mujiks*, who regard him as an apostle and a portent.

Wednesday, November 23rd, 1904.

I have been working in close touch with Delcassé for the last
six and a half years. I would like to record my impressions of his
character as it has gradually unfolded to me.

Its dominating feature is strength of will; his is a bold, tenacious,
purposeful and inflexible will.

It is beyond all doubt that he is doing great things. Yet his is
not a great brain: it is clear, nimble and accurate, but it has its
limitations and they are soon perceived.

His one and only occupation is politics. Nothing else exists
for him. In spite of his early education, which was sound and
classical, he never gives a moment's thought to literature, philosophy, science, history or art. He is fundamentally practical, essentially the realist. Philosophical speculation and abstract reasoning
mean absolutely nothing to him. He is the least systematic,
doctrinaire and doctrinal of men. The English expression, 'a
matter of fact man,' describes him to perfection.

He has an extraordinary facility for grasping facts with rapidity
and accuracy; he is both far-seeing and clear-sighted. He has, in
Talleyrand's phrase, 'a mind full of the future.' But the habit of
looking at coming events never leads him into the errors of the
visionary or idealist. The 'European Republic' of Henri IV, the
Abbé de Saint-Pierre's 'perpetual peace,' the evangelical mysticism
of the Holy Alliance, merely make him shrug his shoulders.

His literary style is simple, concise and fluent, though colour-
less, and he cares nothing about phrasing; a good business style,
without a superfluous word.

His eloquence is similar: it is virile, sober, forceful, urgent and
always straight to the point, but it is lacking in brilliance, artistry
and all those unexpected, picturesque or glamorous elements which
linger in the memories of an audience.

His only creed is patriotism; the great vision of his country is
ever before his eyes. At one of the worst moments of the Dreyfus
affair, he once said to me: "Ever since I entered politics, I have
made the recovery of France my life's work. I always swore to
myself that, if I ever attained cabinet rank, I would only accept
such office as would enable me to work directly for the national
defence, national expansion and the security and development of
France's position in the world. You can see that I've kept my

word so far; my first post was Minister for the Colonies and my second Foreign Affairs. In any future cabinet I would accept the War Office or the Navy, but no other. . . ." [1] Quite recently, he enlarged enthusiastically on his veneration for Louis XIV and his cult of Joan of Arc: "They are my national divinities: if it had not been for them, France would have ceased to exist."

In the exercise of his ministerial functions, he strikes me as essentially the great negotiator and tactician. Resourceful, imperturbable, keeping his tongue and his features under complete control, equally quick in his questions and answers—though extremely suspicious and always on his guard—he is past master at the game of diplomacy. He is never caught napping because he is thoroughly *au fait* with every question that arises, or is likely to arise. He works at least fourteen hours a day. In spite of the wealth his marriage has brought him, he leads a very simple, homely life. Apart from official receptions, he never invites anyone to a meal. His only friends are two or three old cronies, people of no importance but absolutely devoted to him. The grim solitude which he cultivates corresponds to one of his most peculiar characteristics—which is the source of much of his strength—love of secrecy. He shuns his fellow-men, to whom he is a closed book. Many a time at Cabinet meetings his colleagues have begged, prayed and positively ordered him to give them information about some particular negotiation in progress—but always without success. Even the President of the Republic has not been able to worm his secrets out of him. The nature of my special duties has compelled him to be more communicative with me; I am none the less extremely proud of the confidence he has always shown in me. The result is that I have often known *what he was thinking.* But can I say I have ever known *his real thoughts?* How many times have I heard an anxious voice behind me as I was leaving his room: "Don't put anything on paper!" or: "Forget everything I've told you!" or "Burn it!"

One more trait in his character. He has implicit faith in his work, because he believes it to be not merely useful, expedient and opportune, but essential, dictated by circumstances, the logical outcome of the march of events. "Even if I die or am

[1] He was, in fact, Minister of Marine in the Cabinets of June 27th, 1911 and January 12th, 1912, and Minister of War in the Cabinet of June 8th, 1913. He returned to the Quai d'Orsay in the Cabinet of August 26th, 1914.

thrown out tomorrow," he said to me a few days ago, "I defy my successor not to continue my policy unless he wants to break his neck, and that within six months." By way of peroration, he reiterated his fundamental conviction, which is neither more nor less than an *idée fixe* with him; "Germany's high-handed policy and William's fire-brand buffoonery must inevitably end in a European war, in which France will have to fight for her very existence."

Friday, November 25th, 1904.

I presided at the meeting of the Secret War Committee this afternoon. Commander Malo-Lefebvre, who has just been appointed Director of the 1st Section of the Naval General Staff, will henceforth take the place of Captain de Freycinet.

After dispatching current business (intelligence in enemy territory, the organization of relays in neutral countries, etc.), we resumed our discussion of the instructions to be issued to our naval commanders for the maintenance of their telegraphic communication in time of war. The arrangements and subterfuges to which I have recently been driven to enable the Russian squadron to keep in touch with the Imperial Admiralty have taught me that our own system will have to be modified in many ways.

At the end of the meeting, Lieutenant-Colonel Holender, Director of the 2nd Bureau of the General Staff, on instructions from General Pendézec, gave me a detailed account of the information collected by our Secret Service with regard to the future concentration of nine German army corps in the northwest of the Rhine Provinces. From various indications it would appear that the 'concentration zone' would extend roughly from Aix-la-Chapelle to Malmédy. The invasion of Belgian territory would commence with two simultaneous attacks designed to force the line of the Meuse above and below Liége. The first column, marching along the frontier of Dutch Limburg, would make for Visé, *via* Aubel, while the second would make *via* Stavelot for Huy, where they would meet to close on Namur.

Saturday, November 26th, 1904.

The Chamber of Deputies is now debating the Foreign Affairs vote.

In the course of the discussion, the Socialists have once more protested against the 'alliance between French democracy and autocratic Tsarism,' and so on.

"The Franco-Russian alliance has never been more necessary," Delcassé at once replied; "we shall never have a better opportunity of showing our loyalty to this alliance, the most potent safeguard of the higher interests of our two countries."

This sentiment was greeted with vociferous applause from the whole Chamber, with the exception of the Socialists.

When I congratulated him on his brave speech this evening, he shot at me, with a mischievous wink:

"Take my word for it, *cher ami*, courage is the cleverest thing in the world."

Monday, November 28th, 1904.

The Russian Foreign Minister, Count Lamsdorf, and the British Ambassador, Sir Charles Hardinge, have just signed the "Declaration," referring the Dogger Bank dispute to an International Court of Enquiry which is to meet in Paris.

This procedure—which is that prescribed by the Hague Convention—could not be bettered, as the only cause of the present dispute is 'a difference of opinion on points of fact.'

Wednesday, November 30th, 1904.

A few days ago, while the Chamber was debating the Anglo-French Agreement of April 8th, Jaurès thought he could fortify his *peace-at-any-price* argument by invoking the authority of that excellent and prophetic patriot, Gambetta. After alluding to the possible return of Alsace-Lorraine to the French commonwealth, he concluded: "My friends and I agree with the illustrious director of the National Defence in thinking that the ravishment of our provinces was a *crime of force,* but the reparation of that crime must not be sought in *the hazards attendant upon force. . . ."*

It is true that in 1876, when addressing the electors of Lille, Gambetta solemnly declared: "The only object I have at heart is to further the recovery of France, to see her great and loved, strong and respected, once more, and I hope that some day, *merely by the ascendancy of Right,* we shall be one again with our lost brothers, for the sake of stability in Europe and the triumph of justice. . . ."

Delcassé, who is still a devoted admirer of Gambetta, made the following comment:

"This argument of Jaurès is an odious paradox. . . . Gambetta couldn't possibly have said anything else in a public speech. But his whole life and work are a protest against the abominable pacifism of our Socialists! Jaurès would never have dared to extol the virtues of the Triple Alliance in front of Gambetta, or tell *him* that *it was necessary in order to counterbalance Franco-Russian chauvinism!* What a devastating retort, what a flood of oaths and curses he would have brought down upon his head! . . . No, *cher ami*, take my word for it, Gambetta was not such a simpleton as to think that our provinces would come back to the fold some fine day merely through the effect of *divine justice.* Even in his most fervid moments, he kept a pretty clear head and lots of common sense—characteristics he inherited from his Genoese ancestry. He knew perfectly well that *divine justice* never materializes in favour of nations which lose heart. . . . No might, no right!"

I commented that his argument had been anticipated by Pascal and quoted him the famous thought: *Justice without strength is powerless: that which is just must therefore be strong.* . . . The depth, boldness and clear-cut beauty of this aphorism filled him with admiration. I continued: "In a word, you don't think we could regain Alsace and Lorraine except by war?"

He frowned and rapped out:

"No, no! . . . That's not my idea at all! I've never said that! . . ."

I bowed, but said nothing. He modified his tone and continued, weighing his words as if he were speaking in the Chamber:

"Let me tell you what I really think. . . . I'm absolutely certain that in the near future William II's arrogance and charlatanism will compel him to risk *the hazards attendant upon force* —in other words, declare war on us! When that day comes, I want us to be capable of defending ourselves. This thought is never out of my mind and it governs my whole policy. . . . But I must allow myself one further prophecy. I believe the death of Francis-Joseph will almost inevitably involve the disruption of the Austro-Hungarian monarchy and a great European crisis, which in turn, and equally inevitably, will result in territorial changes, the rectification of frontiers and the loss and gain of colonies. Surely it isn't unreasonable to suppose that in such circumstances, if Germany wanted our help or our neutrality, she would not consider the revision of the Treaty of Frankfurt too high a price to pay for it? History has seen things less surprising. But if Germany is to resign herself to restoring our lost provinces, she must be made to realize that she is powerless to change anything in Europe without our consent and that of our allies. So I think it quite conceivable that we shall recover Alsace-Lorraine some day, simply by diplomatic means alone and the sheer dynamic force of our alliances."

Thursday, December 1st, 1904.

The Italian Government is going to ask the Chambers for an extraordinary credit of 200,000,000 francs, 'to complete the defences of the frontiers of the Kingdom.' The grant is to be divided between the War Ministry and the Ministry of Marine. The expenditure for which it provides is applicable solely to war with Austria. The main headings are as follows:

For the War Ministry: Remodelling part of the field artillery; doubling the permanent way in Lombardy and Venetia: organizing the system of defences in the Alps in the vicinity of the Trentino and Friuli; the construction of a fortified camp at Verona, etc. . . .

For the Ministry of Marine: establishing a great naval harbour at Ancona; the construction of battleships and cruisers of sufficiently low draught to be able to use the port of Venice, etc. . . .

The Premier, Giolitti, is hoping to get this substantial credit voted in a form which will more or less disguise its true application.

Monday, December 5th, 1904.

Since his return to St. Petersburg, our ambassador, Bompard, has had an audience with the Emperor in the hope of drawing him into giving his views about Franco-Russian relations.

"I am amazed at the campaign in progress here against France," he said, quite bluntly. "It is being said that my government is prepared to betray Russia in favour of England. What is more, we are being described as not merely a disloyal ally but a useless one —with discipline non-existent in our army and chaos rampant in our fleet. . . . We know the source of these calumnies; they come from Berlin. We have definite proof. That Germany should show goodwill towards Russia can only be a matter of satisfaction to us; it is an additional guarantee of peace. Unfortunately, this good-will conceals others designs. The Emperor William has an ulterior motive—we know this for certain too; he hopes to drag Russia into the quarrel which Germany is trying to pick with England, and believes that this would simultaneously destroy the Franco-Russian alliance. We have been able to trace his insidious handiwork in certain articles in our Radical and Socialist Press. But it has no chance of success in France. The Republican Government and the French nation are more loyal than ever to the alliance with Russia. M. Delcassé proclaimed the fact the other day in the Chamber of Deputies and his speech was greeted with enthusiastic applause."

Nicholas II interrupted:

"I have read M. Delcassé's strong and noble words; they give me all the greater pleasure because they express my own feelings. I'm just as determined as yourselves to stick to an alliance, the results of which have only been for good during the last ten years. Besides, I am benefiting by it at the present moment. If it were not for our alliance, I couldn't take my troops away from the Polish frontier and send them to Manchuria, could I?"

"So no change whatever has taken place in Your Majesty's policy?"

"None whatever. . . . Please make that clear to your govern-ment. To me the Franco-Russian alliance remains as close and binding as ever it did. If it appears less striking to the imagination at the moment, it is the fault of circumstances. Personally, I am most anxious that it should soon recover all its old lustre."

Delcassé went into transports of delight as he read me these words of Nicholas II; his eyes flashed. But he quickly resumed his wonted air of concentrated gravity as he read the shrewd observa-tions with which Bompard concluded his report on his audience with the Emperor:

'The Franco-Russian alliance is thus intact, but it is living in a new world. The days are past when it was based on a fear of Germany which was shared by France and Russia alike: Germany's tactfulness during the Russo-Japanese War has finally allayed the suspicions aroused against her in St. Petersburg by her attitude at the Congress of Berlin. Further, Germany is no longer in a position to set Austria-Hungary against Russia and Italy against France. As a result of the Austro-Russian Balkans' compact of 1897 and the Franco-Italian Tunis Agreement of 1896, ancient enmities have been converted into friendly relations. The result of the Russo-Japanese War appears to be that England is to inherit the animosity with which Russia favoured Germany for a quarter of a century in consequence of the Russo-Turkish War. These are new elements in the situation which do not in themselves prejudice the Franco-Russian alliance; but we must bear them in mind when making our plans for the future.'

Tuesday, December 6th, 1904.

There was an interesting debate in the Reichstag yesterday.

Taking advantage of a brush with the Socialists, the Chancellor Bülow dealt ingeniously with the criticisms—which are sometimes too severe—levelled at Germany by the press. "I cannot conceive," he said, "that anyone in either country could seriously contemplate the idea of a war between England and Germany. Every reasonable man, whether English or German, must realize the enormous sacrifices and losses which a war, even the most successful war, means to his country. No, indeed! The game is not worth the candle! . . . You will therefore understand, gentlemen, that I do not take a tragic view of the animosity displayed towards us by a section of the English press. I like to think that the destinies of England and Germany will always be in the hands of level-headed men who will ponder the true interests of these two great nations."

Wednesday, December 7th, 1904.

The Senate has just ratified the Anglo-French Agreement. Delcassé seized the occasion to make an excellent speech, in which he recalled and analysed the results of our diplomatic activities of the last few years. Without any attempt at oratory, he summarized the work accomplished in these terms:

"Look at Indo-China, extended or strengthened by the establishment of French authority in the Mekong Basin. Look at Morocco, unfolding to our revitalizing influence. Look at Spain, France's neighbour in Africa as in Europe, who realizes that she has everything to gain from the success of our African enterprise.

Look at Italy, a quarrel with whom is now unthinkable and who knows that her increased prosperity will nowhere be welcomed more than in France. Look at England, who shares our pleasure at having eliminated so many serious causes of estrangement or conflict and looks upon our country—loyal ally of Russia though she is—as a trusty worker for world peace."

There is something so noble, invigorating and incisive about the way in which he has placed each of our alliances and friendships in the hierarchy of our great national interests that his speech might be a page of history.

Saturday, December 10th, 1904.

It is obvious that Delcassé's great speech to the Senate, with its splendid tableau of our diplomatic achievements, was hardly calculated to meet with a good reception in Germany. Count Bülow, who seemed so amenable and friendly only five days ago, has just been addressing the Reichstag in much more fiery terms. In reply to a question by the Socialist, Vollmar, the Chancellor said:

"Herr von Vollmar tells us that the European situation is so peaceful that there is no need for us to increase our military forces. Of course I do not for one moment doubt the sincerity of the pacific assurances repeatedly given us by the governments of the great powers. But I should be failing in my duty if I shut my eyes to the undercurrents of feeling in various quarters which are sweeping Europe into complications which may lead to war. Gentlemen, if you think of those ideas of revenge to which expression is often given on the other side of the Vosges, you will realize that I cannot hold so optimistic a view of the European situation as Herr von Vollmar apparently does. Just think of the commotion in the English press and you will agree with me that there is a good deal of inflammable material in the world. A strong Germany is the best safeguard of European peace."

Saturday, December 17th, 1904.

The question of Morocco led Delcassé to talk to me about our colonial empire—that wonderful empire which the Republic has built up in twenty-four years, having successively secured the Congo, Tunis, the Sudan, Annam, Tonkin, Laos, Madagascar, the Ivory Coast, Guinea, Dahomey and the Wadai for France.

As I was rhapsodizing on this vast accession of territory, Delcassé interrupted me.

"I'm not so enthusiastic as you. . . . I haven't the slightest interest in a large portion of this immense area and, if I could find a buyer at a profit, I'd gladly sell it. Indo-China and Madagascar are too far away and too far apart. They are too difficult to govern and their defence might embarrass us a lot if there was a war. . . . We are essentially a continental power, so we must concentrate our efforts nearer home. Geography, policy, strategy and our material assets determine the limits of our colonial empire. First I see the Mediterranean seaboard, Tunis, Algeria and Morocco; then the Sahara *hinterland*, Tafilet, Mauritania and Touat; behind them, Senegal, the Sudan, the Niger, Tchad, Guinea, the Ivory Coast and Dahomey; lastly, the Wabangi and the Congo. We have enough there to keep us busy for centuries. . . . But don't forget that, in this colonial empire limited to Africa, I necessarily include Morocco."

Chapter IX

DECEMBER 18TH, 1904—JANUARY 11TH, 1905

Sunday, December 18th, 1904.

OUR minister in Tangier, Saint-René Taillandier, was just preparing to leave for Fez when the Grand Vizier unexpectedly told him that, "in view of the impoverished condition of the Sharifian Treasury and the necessity for retrenchment," the Sultan had decided to dismiss our military mission. Thus, on the eve of the French minister's departure for Fez to cooperate with the Maghzen in working out the scheme of reforms, Mulai Abd-el-Aziz informs us, by a mere stroke of his pen and without the slighest warning, that our officers are to be sent home.

When Delcassé received the news, he leaped to his feet as if he had been struck:

"The dismissal of our military mission is intolerable," he bawled, "and I won't tolerate it. Saint-René Taillandier must go straight to Fez and speak very plainly to the Sultan. . . . Force is the only thing the Mohammedans understand or believe in. If they resist, the way to talk to them is face to face, at the top of your voice and cracking your whip."

He has therefore just wired Saint-René Taillandier: "You must make the Sultan understand that he has given France his word and we are holding him to it; that France has already helped him several times and is prepared to do so again in the common interest of Morocco and Algeria; further, that she is absolutely determined to carry on her work in Morocco, and has the power to do so."

Monday, December 19th, 1904.

After twenty-four hours to think about it, Delcassé takes a calmer view of the incident which has just occurred in Morocco. Saint-René Taillandier's departure for the Sharifian court is therefore to be postponed until our legation sees what can be done by persuasion to obtain permission for our military mission to remain. We can see later whether it will be necessary to resort to force.

144

Has Delcassé changed his mind on his own initiative? I doubt it. I imagine he felt he was obliged to inform his fellow ministers of the situation and found that they were all violently hostile to his original intention. The Chambers have been told too often that we were using no coercion in our work in Morocco and that optimistic formula, *peaceful penetration*, has been worked to death. And now that circumstances call for strong measures, public opinion is quite unprepared for them.

But, looking at the matter purely from the Moroccan angle and considering the mentality of the Sultan and his viziers, Delcassé's first thoughts were best: 'Force is the only thing the Mohammedans understand or believe in; if they resist, the way to talk to them is face to face, at the top of your voice and cracking your whip.'

I dined with the Comtesse de Fitz-James. The Grand Duke Paul, Countess von Hohenfelsen, the Marquis du Lau and Melchïor de Vogüé were also there. We talked mostly about the International Commission which is to meet at the Quai d'Orsay tomorrow to investigate the Dogger Bank incident. The Grand Duke and his wife did not disguise their dismay at 'the idea of the Russian Navy—which is answerable to the Tsar alone—having to appear before a foreign tribunal—a tribunal on which an English Admiral is sitting!'

Tuesday, December 20th, 1904.

The International Commission of Enquiry into the Dogger Bank incident held its first meeting today at the Quai d'Orsay.

France is represented by Vice-Admiral Fournier, a member of the *Conseil Superieur de la Marine*, who would command our navy in time of war; Russia by Vice-Admiral Kaznakov and England by Vice-Admiral Sir Lewis Beaumont.

Vice-Admiral Davis, who is to represent the United States, wired this morning from Dover to say that he is coming through Antwerp and will not arrive in Paris until tomorrow evening. He has asked the others to start without him; not a word of apology or explanation. As he was at Dover yesterday, he could perfectly well have kept his appointment. This Yankee casualness has obliged the other commissioners to confine themselves to unofficial conversations for today.

Fournier, Beaumont and Kaznakov have had a 'backstairs' discussion over the choice of the fifth commissioner, whom the commission is to appoint as soon as the arrival of Admiral Davis enables it to sit officially. Kaznakov, looking very sheepish, murmured something about asking the Emperor of Austria to nominate this fifth commissioner himself. Beaumont and Fournier immediately realized that the courts of St. Petersburg, Vienna and Berlin must have secretly arranged for the Emperor Francis-Joseph to appoint a German admiral. As a matter of fact, we know for certain that the Emperor William is furious that his navy is not represented at this great naval enquiry which is about to open. Beaumont and Fournier both protested that the Commission had no right to surrender one of its most delicate duties; they would only agree to the Emperor Francis-Joseph being asked to allow his navy to participate in the labours of the Commission by appointing the *doyen* of his admirals, Baron von Spaun. Kaznakov agreed.

At half-past twelve, Delcassé gave a luncheon to the members of the Commission and their numerous acolytes. I was among the guests.

Admiral Fournier's quick intellect, personal prestige and splendid naval record are a great credit to us.

Admiral Sir Lewis Beaumont is a distinguished-looking man, courteous if cold in manner, who talks little but to the point. When we conversed, I was reminded of the commodore whose phlegmatic economy of words was so much admired by Taine. One day he forced the enemy ship to surrender after a very stiff fight; the unfortunate captain who had been taken prisoner was greeted with the laconic remark: *Fortune of war.*

Admiral Kaznakov, on the other hand, is an object of amazement to everyone he meets. He is round-shouldered and has dull, lifeless eyes, a hang-dog look, drooping lips and moustache. He cannot string a sentence together and seems to see and understand nothing. And it is to this pitiful human scarecrow that Russia has entrusted her cause before the European areopagus—a cause in which nothing less than the honour of her navy is at stake.

Wednesday, December 21st, 1904.

The most important point for the Russians in the Dogger Bank case is to prove that, when they opened fire on the harmless trawlers, they had real grounds for believing them to be enemy destroyers. No one doubts that they were genuinely mistaken; but they must show that the mistake was not simply the result of impulse, gross negligence and panic.

Admiral Rojdestvensky confines himself to saying that he had secret information to the effect that Japanese destroyers had been seen in the North Sea; that he had therefore reason to fear an attack, especially at night, as he emerged from the Skagerrak. But where did he get his secret information? . . . On this point, not a word of explanation is forthcoming. There is evidently some mystery, which both intrigues and irritates the British Government.

The Russian delegates, regarding us as their best advocates before the International Commission of Enquiry, have given us, in the strictest confidence, the clue to the puzzle.

On the morning of October 20th, while the 2nd Squadron was rounding Cape Skagen, at the entrance to the Kattegat, Admiral Rojdestvensky received a very strange communication from his spies: 'Four Japanese destroyers, which were bought in England in the name of a neutral, have been diverted from their pretended destination and are now lurking in one of the Norwegian fjords, watching for the arrival of the squadron in the North Sea. . . .'

The result was that, as the squadron approached the Dogger Bank the following evening, it redoubled its vigilance, for everyone was haunted and hypnotized by fear of an ambush. Hence the fact that the *Souvoroff* and the *Kamtchatka* did not hesitate to open fire at once when—about 1 a.m. in a thick fog—they suddenly caught a glimpse of a number of ships coming towards them and apparently intent on getting in their way. The whole squadron was immediately smitten with panic and fired off all its guns.

I have been able to find out the source of the secret report about the presence of the four Japanese destroyers in the North Sea; it was a pure invention on the part of a contemptible police official, Michael Harting.

This man, whose real name is Abraham Hekkelmann, originally attached himself to the revolutionary party under the *alias* of Arcade Landesen. When he grew tired of making bombs and weaving plots, he joined the imperial police and soon distinguished himself as an *agent provocateur*. In that capacity he employed his talents in Berlin, Stockholm, Geneva, Zurich and finally Paris. There his fertile imagination, low cunning and genius for intrigue brought him such success that he was attached to the head of the Russian police organization in France—the terrible Ratchkovsky.[1]

Last September, he was put in charge of the espionage services of the 2nd Squadron. In this capacity, he explored, or pretended to explore, the fjords of Bergen and Stavanger, where he found nothing suspicious. To justify his employment—and his bill for expenses—he invented the story of the four Japanese destroyers lurking in the vicinity of the Dogger Bank. And so we have to thank him for the fact that, two months ago, Russia and England were on the brink of war. The knavery of a low-down policeman nearly caused a wholesale conflagration in Europe!

Thursday, December 22nd, 1904.

Admiral Davis having concluded his jaunt and turned up in Paris at last, the International Committee of Enquiry has been able to hold its first official sitting.

As arranged by the three admirals, Fournier, Beaumont and Kaznakov, the Commission has requested the Emperor Francis-Joseph to appoint Baron von Spaun, the *doyen* of the Imperial and Royal Admiralty, as fifth member.

The Russian Ambassador has just confided to Delcassé that he has requested the Emperor to recall Admiral Kaznakov immediately, alleging ill-health as an excuse.

His successor has already been nominated—Admiral Dubassov. Pending his arrival, the International Commission has fixed its next meeting for Monday, January 9th.

Friday, December 23rd, 1904.

Delcassé has just given a further demonstration of his new policy of caution and temporization in handling our Moroccan

[1] I never knew Michael Harting personally but have heard a lot about him from Ratchkovsky, his successor, Tataiev, and more particularly, their assistant, Manuilov. I was to meet Manuilov again in 1916, at Petrograd, where he was *chef du cabinet* of the notorious minister, Stürmer (cf. *La Russie des Tsars*, II, 171).

affairs. He now seems to have eliminated from his programme any idea of coercion in dealing with the Maghzen: "Before we make him feel our power, and even before he fears it, we must exhaust every possibility of compromise. Have we not always held ourselves out as the Sultan's best friends and the best advisers he could have in view of his inexperience and irresolution. We must show him—and Europe too—that we meant what we said. . . ."

There is an explanation of this change of front. Five or six days ago, the Socialists let Delcassé know that they had decided to start 'a violent and immediate campaign' against his Moroccan policy which, in their view, must inevitably lead to a military expedition and, consequently, to a recrudescence of militarism in the French nation. The artful minister, pretending to be overjoyed at this opportunity of telling them 'exactly what was in his mind,' convinced them that he was the only man capable of solving the Moroccan problem *by diplomatic means.* "If I go out of office, if I disappear, it is the Colonial Party—Étienne's crowd —which will run our foreign policy, and you'll certainly see the military conquest of Morocco and the revival of chauvinism in France." . . . As the result of this frank suggestion, Jaurès has been busy in the lobbies of the Chamber telling everyone that Delcassé must be left to settle our Moroccan difficulties.

I am reminded of La Fontaine's fable of *The Wolf turned Shepherd*:

> "Aping the shepherd, he wears a smock,
> A twig serves for crook,
> Nor are the pipes forgotten."

Friday, December 30th, 1904.

After calling at Cape Lopez on November 26th, Bahia-dos-Tigres, on the Angola coast, on December 6th, and Angra-Pequena, on the Namaland coast, on December 11th, the Russian squadron arrived yesterday at Sainte-Marie de Madagascar.

Since he left Vigo, Admiral Rojdestvensky has several times pleaded with us to allow him to put in at the port of Diégo-Suarez. He had not disguised from us that 'he would require to stay there a very long time,' as he was proposing to overhaul all his ships and complete the training of his officers and crews by 'systematic exercises in naval operations.' He emphasized that Madagascar 'would be the last place of call where he can remain undisturbed

before he sets out for the China Seas to face the ordeal which
Providence has in store for him.'

Naturally, we can hardly turn a deaf ear to these naval, military
and ethical considerations. But the question is, have we the right
to make them our own? I explained the situation to Delcassé:

"The port of Diégo-Suarez is our naval base in the Indian Ocean.
It has an arsenal, stores of explosives, workshops, an ammunition
depot, an artillery park, a coal depot, barracks and hospitals; if
we admit a belligerent squadron to this fortress and allow it not
only to rest and take in supplies, but to stay a long time and complete its training in combatant operations, we are really placing
our naval base at its disposal and authorizing it to make such use
of it as we should ourselves if we were at war with Japan. Would
not this flagrant violation of international law expose us to all
sorts of perils? . . . While the Russian Squadron was in the
Atlantic, off the coast of Senegal and Guinea, our more or less
disguised hospitality involved us in the risk of getting an official
protest from the Japanese Government, which might even have
favoured us with a haughty summons to desist. Even so, the matter
would have been handled through the ordinary diplomatic channels. But now that the Russian squadron has reached the Indian
Ocean, can we close our eyes to the unpleasant possibility that
Japanese cruisers may slip through the Maldives and Seychelles
and attack it unawares at Diégo-Suarez, in the same way as they
surprised the Port Arthur squadron at the outset of hostilities? . . .
What an affront it would be to us! . . . And you can't see these
cruisers stopping at shelling our forts, can you?"

Delcassé cut me short:

"Go and see Nelidov at once; tell him that I do not wish Rojdestvensky's Squadron to stay at Diégo-Suarez. . . . Suggest some
other anchorage—any you like!"

"I know of a very good one, Passandaya Bay, on the Mozambique Channel, behind the island of Nossi-Bé! It's a roadstead
which . . ."

"All right! All right! Get off to Nelidov quick."

When I had explained the whole situation to the Russian Ambassador, he said with a tragic sigh:

"I must bow to M. Delcassé's ruling. But his decision will be a
very great blow to His Majesty the Emperor!"

Saturday, December 31st, 1904.

From a private letter, emanating from a great Berlin financier (which has come into our possession *by chance*), we know that Baron von Holstein, the formidable *Eminence Grise* of the Wilhelmstrasse, is going strong with his venomous campaign against France. The immediate object of his bitter and biting dialectics is the Franco-Spanish Agreement of October 3rd. He looks on it as not merely a private arrangement covering Morocco, but as the basis of a general understanding on European questions. For the last thirty years, since the accession of Alphonse XII and, more particularly, his marriage to a Hapsburg, the Germanic empires have been pleased to regard Spain as their natural client and ally. Will she not in future gravitate towards the French orbit? Has she not sold herself to the great coalition which Delcassé is plotting against Germany? . . .

Judging by the letter in question, this argument has convinced Chancellor Bülow that Germany cannot tolerate 'M. Delcassé's impudence' any longer.

Sunday, January 1st, 1905.

Better news from Morocco.

The Sultan Moulai Abd-el-Aziz, alarmed about his recent imimpertinence and irresolute as ever, has consented to keep our military mission. Saint-René Taillandier will thus be able to leave for Fez, where the *ulemas*, the chiefs of the Zaouyas, all the supporters of the *ancien régime* and all the beneficiaries of its abuses are raging against us.

Monday, January 2nd, 1905.

Port Arthur, the Gibraltar of the Far East, the great fortress which, symbolizing Russian domination in the China Seas, crowns the extremity of the Liao-tung Peninsula, surrendered this morning.

The news reached the Quai d'Orsay at five o'clock this evening. "What about Rojdestvensky's squadron? . . ." asked Delcassé, with a look of dismay. "Will it be able to continue its voyage? Wouldn't it be better to turn back and retire to the Baltic again? . . . In any case, we can't let it stay at Madagascar any longer; I can't consent to its doing so; in future we shall be running the risk of an ultimatum from Japan at any moment. And public opinion in France wouldn't support me!"

"It's obvious that the surrender of Port Arthur gives the Japanese unfettered command of the sea. The task of the Russian *Armada* is over, as its object was to relieve Port Arthur. In any event, how could it renew supplies and carry out repairs without a fortified base in the Gulf of Pechili?"

"Then let it return to the Baltic and the sooner the better!"

"It might, of course, try to reach Vladivostok. But that would be sheer suicide; the Japanese would never let it get through the Straits of Korea. . . . At any rate, that's what Captain de Freycinet and Captain Yepantchin told me the other day."

At half-past six I called on the Dowager Baroness de Berckheim, whose husband commanded the Guard Artillery in the Army of the Rhine in 1870:

"If only Bazaine had defended Metz as well as Stoessel has defended Port Arthur!" she said. "An eleven-months' siege! Even finer than Masséna's resistance at Genoa!"

Wednesday, January 4th, 1905.

Delcassé has been talking to me about Thiers and his part in the war of 1870:

"A sorry figure," he said. "It shows that, although he wrote a history of the revolution, he never understood it! . . . He never had the slightest idea of the real interests of the nation. . . . All the historians brag about his diplomatic tour to Florence, Vienna and St. Petersburg. It was all wrong! . . . To behave like a beggar and knock at the doors of all the capitals was not the way to persuade Europe to intervene; his first task was to show that we were determined to fight on to the last breath. . . . No one helps those who throw up the sponge. It's only those who help themselves who get helped. After Sedan, only one course was open to us; to fight on, improvise armies and show the world a second edition of the miracle of 1792. . . . It's a miracle France has performed too often in her history for anyone to doubt her ability to do it again. . . . That's what Gambetta felt so strongly, in spite of our disasters, and that's why I regard him as one of the greatest servants of France!" [1]

---

[1] It is interesting to note that on the evening of the Battle of Sedan the future Marshal von Hindenburg, who was then a lieuenant in the 3rd Regiment of the

Monday, January 9th, 1905.

A Russian destroyer, which succeeded in escaping from Port Arthur in a fog yesterday, has brought to Che-fu the following telegram from General Stoessel to the Emperor Nicholas:

> *The Japanese are in possession of all our lines. We cannot hold out much longer; we shall have to surrender. Great Sovereign, forgive us; we have done everything possible. Be merciful in your judgment upon us. The constant struggle for eleven months has worn down our strength. Three-quarters of the garrison are in the hospitals or the cemeteries. The last quarter is holding no less than 27 versts and cannot take turns even to snatch a short rest. The men are shadows.*
>
> STOESSEL.

On the other hand, General Stoessel has received the following message from Field-Marshal Yamagata:

> *His Majesty the Mikado is graciously pleased to advise me that, in view of your gallant conduct, He desires that you shall be granted military honours. His Majesty has therefore commanded that your officers should retain their swords.*

Tuesday, January 10th, 1905.

Judging by the remarks of the head of the Russian detective police, who arrived from St. Petersburg yesterday evening, the conduct of General Stoessel, Governor of Port Arthur, must have been nothing short of heroic.

During the last few days, all the drawing-rooms in Paris have been echoing with the words: 'Stoessel's defence of Port Arthur is a feat of arms as fine as Masséna's defence of Genoa in 1800, or that of Saragossa by Palafox in 1809 . . .' Society has been

---

Prussian Guards, had come to the same conclusion. The famous Marshal tells us in his *Memoirs* how, on September 1st, 1870, when his comrades heard that the enemy had surrendered, they gleefully shouted: "It's the end of the war! . . ." The young Lieutenant Hindenburg, however, thought that the new masters of France would continue the struggle. And, several weeks later, he expressed his approval of Gambetta's perspicacity: "In my opinion, the fact that the French Republic took up arms at the point where the Empire had been compelled to lay them down was not only a proof of ideal patriotic spirit, but of far-seeing statesmanship as well. I firmly believe, even today, that if France had abandoned her resistance at that moment, she would have surrendered the greatest part of her national heritage and with it her prospects of a brighter future."

jumping to conclusions. As a matter of fact, Stoessel lost heart some time ago; his nerves gave way.

The real defender of Port Arthur, the heart and soul of the beleaguered army, was General Kondratchenko, who was killed a fortnight before the capitulation. A sapper, like General Todleben, the defender of Sebastopol, he had his intrepid and infectious courage and the same serene, tenacious and inflexible will.[1]

Since I am recalling the great sieges of history, when human strength was taxed to the very uttermost, should I not add Numantia, Gergovia and Alesia? . . .

Wednesday, January 11th, 1905.

Our minister at Tangiers, Saint-René Taillandier, embarked today on the cruiser *Du Chayla*, which is to take him to Larache. He expects to arrive at Fez on January 25th.

---

[1] After his return to Russia, General Stoessel was summoned before the Supreme Court Martial at St. Petersburg and charged with having surrendered in humiliating circumstances and before he had exhausted all possibilities of further resistance. He was found guilty and condemned to death on February 20th, 1908. The Emperor, however, granted a reprieve and commuted the death sentence to ten years imprisonment in a fortress. The prisoner was finally pardoned in 1910.

Chapter X

Thursday, January 12th, 1905.

YIELDING to constant pressure from us, Admiral Rojdestvensky has abandoned the idea of mooring at Diego-Suarez and gone to Passandaya Bay.

This bay opens into the Mozambique Channel, opposite the Comoro Islands; it provides excellent shelter, as it is twenty kilometres wide and fifty long and lies behind Nossi-Bé, which protects its approaches.

The Russian Squadron anchored on January 9th, and has been joined by Admiral Fölkersam's Division which went out by the Suez Canal and Djibouti.

The 2nd Squadron of the Pacific Ocean is thus assembled in full strength in Madagascar waters; there are no less than thirty-five warships and fourteen transports—a total of approximately 150,000 tons.

From all we hear, it would appear that Admiral Rojdestvensky intends to set sail again in about ten days' time.

Saturday, January 14th, 1905.

Nicholas II is as determined as ever to continue the war against Japan and has just issued the following Order of the Day to his naval and military forces:

> Port Arthur has fallen into the enemy's hands. The struggle for the defence of this fortress lasted eleven months.
>
> For more than seven months the gallant garrison was cut off from the rest of the world and deprived of all means of succour. It endured physical privations and infinite moral suffering whilst the enemy's successes continued.
>
> A handful of Russians, sacrificing their lives and their blood, have held out against the furious onslaughts of the enemy in the steadfast hope that relief would come.
>
> Russia has watched their heroic deeds with pride and the whole world has paid homage to such bravery.

Let us hold in everlasting remembrance all those glorious Russians who perished in defence of Port Arthur and died for Russia's cause, far from home, their hearts filled with love for their Emperor and their country.

We have a strong and courageous enemy whom it is extremely difficult to fight, 10,000 versts from the sources of our strength; but Russia is powerful, and, during the thousand years of her existence, she has faced still graver trials and dangers and always emerged from the struggle even stronger than before.

Like everyone else in Russia, I am convinced that the hour of triumph is at hand.

I pray to God to watch over me, my troops and my fleet, so that together we may vanquish our enemy and save the honour of Russia.

NICHOLAS.

Monday, January 16th, 1905.

The periplus of the Russian *Armada* is providing German journalists with valuable material for compromising France in the eyes of her ally.

One ultra-conservative organ never misses an opportunity of reiterating that 'the fate of the 2nd Squadron is entirely in the hands of the French Government'; it has decided that 'if the government of the Republic refuses help to this gallant squadron, or haggles about it, the Russian nation and posterity will hold it accountable for the terrible trials which the war in the Far East must then hold in store for the Romanoff Empire.'

It is superfluous to add that all these mischievous articles are immediately reproduced and discussed in the Russian Press.

Tuesday, January 17th, 1905.

I referred yesterday to the insidious efforts of the German newspapers to exploit against France the rage and mortification of the Russian nation.

We have just received some information from London which shows up the machiavellian casuistry of this press campaign. The new British Ambassador in Paris, Sir Francis Bertie, who was formerly Permanent Under-Secretary of State at the Foreign Office, has told Paul Cambon that, during the autumn of 1903, the Emperor William said to the Japanese Minister, Inouye: "You are absolutely right in your dispute with St. Petersburg, so refuse to be intimidated by Russia; go one better and attack her. . . . All the odds are on your side; you have England's help; France won't move; I myself will preserve an attitude of benevolent neutrality in our relations. . . ." The Japanese Government, not knowing what to make of this odd outburst, at once reported it to the British Government in the hope of getting an explanation. Lord Lansdowne replied to Viscount Hayashi: "The Emperor William is a mischief-maker who is simply trying to sow discord. You can't be too suspicious about his encouragement. No one can rely on him."

What Sir Francis Bertie tells us is on all fours with a secret report we received from Berlin at the beginning of November, 1903, when Motono officially asked Delcassé for the mediation of the French Government with a view to an amicable settlement of the Russo-Japanese dispute. Delcassé said to me then: 'What a knave William is! . . . Yesterday he was inciting the Russians against the Japanese; today he's inciting the Japanese against the Russians. . . . He is absolutely set on a war in Manchuria so that he can have a free hand in Europe. So I simply must avert it at any price. . . .'

Wednesday, January 18th, 1905.

The Combes Ministry, which was losing votes every day, has now resigned. Its downfall is due, not to an adverse vote in the Chambers, but to the immense revulsion of feeling in the country produced by its support and defence of the system of denunciation in the army.

I lunched at the house of my friend and colleague, Soulange-Bodin, with Admiral Dubassov, who has taken Admiral Kaznakov's place on the Commission of Enquiry into the Dogger Bank incident.

Feodor-Vassilievitch Dubassov is the General Aide-de-Camp of the Emperor and was formerly naval attaché at Berlin. He has the advantage over his predecessor that he has a fine presence and a very bright, intelligent face.

Throughout lunch the conversation was quite general and social.

In the smoking-room, Soulange-Bodin asked the admiral whether he thought the proceedings before the Commission of Enquiry were likely to last long.

"I haven't the slightest idea," he replied.

"But the matter seems to me settled," I said, "by depositions taken by the British authorities from their witnesses; they've been published in *The Times*. Thus half the Commission's work has been done already."

Dubassov seemed lost in thought; he ultimately admitted that he had not opened a newspaper for a long time.

The Commission of Enquiry is to begin its work tomorrow, and the Russian Admiralty's mouthpiece does not even yet know that the vital documents in the case have been published and discussed by the entire English Press!

We went on to talk about Rojdestvensky and his pathetic *Armada*. Between two puffs at his cigar, the casual Dubassov cried: "Dear old Zinovei-Petrovitch! How is he? . . . Where is his squadron at the moment?"

"I think he's all right. The squadron was recently at Sainte-Marie de Madagascar; it has just gone on to Passandaya Bay, near Nossi-Bé, and will stay there until it sets sail for the China Seas."

The vague, far-away look in the admiral's eyes showed that these geographical names meant nothing to him. So Soulange-Bodin took an atlas and showed him a map of Madagascar. In sheer amazement, we watched him tracing the outlines of the great French island, finding considerable difficulty in spelling out such names as Antananarivo, Tamatave, Diégo-Suarez, Nossi-Bé. . . . He was very astonished at the Comoros. One surprise followed another, for he suddenly cried out:

"Oh! . . . the Mozambique Channel . . . I'd no idea it was there! . . ."

Thursday, January 19th, 1905.

By the Orthodox Church calendar, today is the Feast of Epiphany. Its main rite is the "Blessing of the Waters."

At St. Petersburg, a service marked by superb ritual is always held on the quay opposite the Winter Palace, in the presence of the Emperor and all the imperial family.

This morning, while the Metropolitan, Mgr. Antonius, was about to bless the Neva and artillery salvos were punctuating the hymns, the service was suddenly interrupted by a frightful clatter of broken glass, large fragments of which fell on the crowd almost at the Emperor's feet.

When the excitement had died down, it was seen that the first floor of the palace was riddled with shots. It did not take long to clear up the mystery; investigation showed that one of the batteries, employed in the regulation salutes on the far bank of the Neva, had fired with shrapnel.

There can be no doubt that it was an attempt on the Tsar's life; a plot was the only possible explanation of the fact that the guns were loaded with shrapnel; the possibility of mistake was excluded.[1]

The only casualties reported are a few wounded in the ranks of the Guard.

Friday, January 20th, 1905.

During the last few months, or, strictly speaking, ever since the visit of the President of the Republic and Delcassé to Rome, the Austro-Hungarian General Staff has been intensifying its military preparations on the frontiers of the Tyrol, the Trentino, Carinthia and the Isonzo. The Italian General Staff is very concerned about them and has begun to construct a vast defensive system in the Val Camonica and Friuli.

But, to all outward appearances, diplomatic relations between the two *allied powers* continue to be most friendly. Only quite recently, the German Chancellor, Bülow, was loudly congratulating himself on the fact.

Saturday, January 21st, 1905.

General strike in St. Petersburg. Not less than 140,000 workmen are parading the streets of the capital. In spite of the scale the commotion has assumed, no violence has been reported so far.

But a new and very characteristic feature is the fact that the strikers have adopted as their leader a fiery and poverty-stricken young priest, by name Gapon, who was formerly a prison chaplain. They obey him blindly. He is a disciple of Tolstoi: and is always reminding them that a servant of Christ never meets force with force. His influence with the working class is so great that the

---

[1] The officers commanding the battery in question and sixty of their men were court-martialled. On March 18th the Court Martial promulgated the following sentences: (1) Captains Davidov and Kartzev, eighteen months' imprisonment in a fortress: (2) Lieutenant Roth fifteen months; all three to be cashiered. The gunners who were found guilty were sent to disciplinary camps in Siberia.

police have not yet dared to arrest him, though he has just been excommunicated by the Holy Synod.

For tomorrow, Sunday, Gapon has organized a huge procession to be led by himself, with an advance-guard of crosses and ikons. It is to march unarmed, and in silence, to the Winter Palace and hand a petition from the Russian people to the Emperor. "His Majesty the Tsar," he says, "cannot refuse to receive his children. If police and Cossacks bar our way, we will not retreat. If they drive us back by force, we will not retaliate; we will let ourselves be massacred where we stand. As I shall be at the head, I shall be the first to give my blood."

Sunday, January 22nd, 1905.

A tragic day in St. Petersburg.

Led by the priest Gapon, who was carrying a crucifix, 15,000 workmen marched to the Winter Palace to present their moving appeal to the Tsar: *We come to you, our Sovereign, to ask for justice and protection. . . . We are treated like slaves. . . . We cannot bear our suffering any longer. . . . We have reached the extreme limit of human endurance. . . . Sire, do not refuse us your aid. . . . Break down the barrier which separates you from your people. And your name will be carved forever in our hearts.* They were unarmed and singing hymns.

As the procession emerged from the Nevsky Prospekt into the Palace Square, a police officer ordered it to disperse. The priest Gapon tried to parley. But suddenly there was a burst of rifle fire. The ground was soon covered with several hundred dead and wounded. Gapon fell, his crucifix in his hand; his friends carried him away. The crowd, shrieking with terror, scattered in all directions.

Paris learned the news, just after six o'clock, from the evening papers.

I dined with Comtesse Vera de Talleyrand-Périgord, the widow of Napoleon III's ambassador at St. Petersburg, and met the Duc and Duchesse de Bisaccia, Comtesse Robert de Fitz-James, the Comte and Comtesse d'Haussonville, the Comte and Comtesse Arthur de Vogüé, the Vicomtesse de Gaigneron and Comte Louis de Turenne. The Grand Duke Paul and Countess von Hohenfelsen were expected.

They are always the most punctual of visitors and, as they were late, we rather expected to get a message that they were too distressed to dine out. The company lost no time in attacking the Emperor for not having had the courage and sense to receive the perfectly respectful petition presented by the strikers, and ordering the police to fire on an unarmed crowd. I had a further opportunity of observing how hostile Paris society has become towards the Tsarist *régime*.

Meanwhile, the Grand Duke and his wife arrived. Their forced smiles did not succeed in disguising the horror-stricken look in their faces.

Olga-Valerianovna took me aside and said:

"Don't leave me for long tonight; I'm absolutely in the depths. I'd like to bury my head in a pillow and cry my heart out. . . . What a horrible day! Now we shall have revolution—it's the end! . . . I did so hope there would be no bloodshed! Today's disaster is irreparable! . . ."

After dinner, which was a dismal business, the Grand Duke took me away to a boudoir:

"Well," he exclaimed with a heartrending sigh, "Well! We're lost, aren't we? You can see for yourself: within and without, everything's crumbling!"

He could not continue for tears. When I had consoled him a bit, he went on:

"Why in Heaven didn't the Emperor receive the strikers' deputation? There was nothing seditious about their attitude. Whilst we were waiting for news, I prayed all day that not a drop of blood might be shed. . . . And blood has flowed in streams! What has happened is both unpardonable and irreparable. . . . If the Emperor had only deigned to receive the delegates and said to them: *My children, you have appealed to me. I will listen to you because I am the father of my people. I will personally consider the reforms for which you ask. You may be certain I will do everything possible to help you in your misery. Now return home in peace. Trust in your Tsar.* If only he'd talked to them on those lines, a cry of affection for him would have gone up from one end of Russia to the other. We should have been saved!"

Wednesday, January 25th, 1905.

The new Cabinet has been formed with Rouvier, the Finance Minister, as President of the Council.

Delcassé remains at the Quai d'Orsay. Étienne, Chaumié, Berteaux and Thomson have respectively taken over Home Affairs, Justice, War and the Navy. It certainly is hardly a brilliant combination; but we may hope that we have seen the last of the foul denunciation business in the army.

The Grand Duke Paul, Countess von Hohenfelsen, Comte and Comtesse d'Haussonville, Baron de Courcel, General Pendézec and a few close friends have dined with me.

In the smoking-room, the Grand Duke went into a corner with our Chief of Staff and plied him with anxious questions as to 'what chance of victory the Russian Army still has in the Manchurian plains. . . .' General Pendézec, candid as ever, replied:

"If Admiral Rojdestvensky's Squadron recovers command of the sea, I think the Japanese would soon be reduced to suing for peace. Othewise, I can see only one way of achieving ultimate victory: you must retire three or four hundred kilometres, somewhere between Hirin and Harbin, dig yourselves in on a fortified line and wait there until the arrival of large reinforcements enables you to resume the offensive on the grand scale in the spring of 1906."

"But the internal situation will make it impossible to carry on the war so long!" cried the Grand Duke.

"That's a matter of politics, not strategy, Monseigneur. I know nothing about poltics."

After the Grand Duke Paul and Madame von Hohenfelsen had left us, at about eleven o'clock, my guests talked quite freely about the dangers—now only too obvious—to which Tsarism is exposed. But they were nothing like so heated as they were a few days ago about the brutality of the imperial police; they do not feel so sorry for 'the unfortunate St. Petersburg workmen piously marching behind their ikons.' The outrageous abuse of the radical and socialist press has made many critics ask themselves Barnave's question: 'Was the blood that was shed so pure after all?'

Saturday, January 28th, 1905.

The new cabinet met the Chamber yesterday and had a fairly good reception, except, of course, from the radicals and socialists.

In the *Humanité* this morning, Aristide Briand accuses Rouvier of 'having yielded to the demands of the clericals and reactionaries

by sacrificing a general who is "beloved by the whole republic"—
General André. . . .' Then he turns his attention to Delcassé:
'As a crowning piece of folly, the Cabinet has seen fit to remind
us of the compact between this land of freedom and down-trodden,
groaning Russia. An indignant protest by Allard against such strong
language brought M. Delcassé to his feet. The Minister for Foreign Affairs should not have found it difficult to extricate himself
from the awkward situation into which his lack of foresight had
got him. He need only have said that it was our business to keep
out of the domestic affairs of other countries if we did not want
other countries to start interfering with ours. But M. Delcassé
was over-zealous: to the amazement of the whole Chamber, he
appointed himself *official advocate of the slaughter of a nation,*
to use the fine phrase of Jaurès. He tried to plead extenuating circumstances in favour of those responsible for the massacre. This
was too much of a good thing. From that moment, the new
Cabinet was damned in the eyes of socialists and all sincere demo-
crats. It was impossible for them to have any confidence in it.'

Monday, January 30th, 1905.

The Japanese have just won another battle at San-de-pu, in the
region of Mukden.

The government and people of Russia are now pinning their
last hopes to the *Invincible Armada,* which is still at Madagascar.

Admiral Rojdestvensky considers, quite rightly, that the fall of
Port Arthur and the destruction of the 1st Squadron have added
enormously to the difficulties of his task. In view of the supreme
effort Russia requires of him, he is making superhuman attempts
to complete the naval and military training of his crews. He exercises them every day, either in Passandaya Bay or in the open sea
off Nossi-Bé. But not a day passes without Delcassé asking me:

"Well, have they gone yet?"

At the same time, he will not allow us to order Admiral Rojdestvensky to move on. . . . Personally, I agree with him, because
I no longer doubt that the 2nd Squadron is doomed to destruction
and I should hate to think that we could subsequently be charged
with driving it to its fate.

Wednesday, February 1st, 1905.

Saint-René Taillandier arrived at Fez on January 20th; he disembarked at Larache on January 12th and started for the Sharifian capital next day.

Friday, February 3rd, 1905.

When I am talking to the *Okhrana* police, men like Rataiev, Manuilov, etc., I always have a feeling that, beneath the majestic façade of Tsarism and the brilliance and fascination of its aristocracy, civilization in Russia is several centuries behind that of the Western races. I cannot help recalling the profound remark made by Joseph de Maistre during his mission to St. Petersburg: "It's all wrong to write 1815 here; it should be 1515; we're still in the sixteenth century."

Saturday, February 4th, 1905.

The entire German Press is breathing fire and slaughter against England over a speech recently made by Mr. Arthur Lee, Civil Lord of the Admiralty, to his constituents at Eastleigh.

In the course of explaining the redistribution of the English fleets, Mr. Lee had simply expressed the opinion that 'for some time now the centre of gravity of naval power in Europe has shifted; Great Britain must now do more than keep watch on France and the Mediterranean; she must keep a sharp look-out in the North Sea too?'

In London, this speech passed practically unnoticed; but the German Press affects to regard it as 'a challenge to the German Empire . . . a threat of war in the midst of peace.'

Monday, February 6th, 1905.

On January 29th, Mulai Abd-el-Aziz gave our minister a ceremonial reception and next day received him in private audience.

Saint-René Taillandier's first impression was fairly favourable; but the serious and critical business with the Maghzen will not begin for several days.

Tuesday, February 7th, 1905.

The Russian Squadron has now been a month in Passandaya Bay and the Japanese Government's protests are becoming more and more impatient.

This extension of Rojdestvensky's stay in our waters, which is good for another three weeks at least, is becoming a real danger to us. The Tsar has in fact ordered Admiral Rojdestvensky to wait for a reinforcement division (which is to join him in the China Seas) to leave Libau before he continues his voyage.

This division is to be commanded by Admiral Nebogatoff and comprises two battleships, three coast-defence ships and several auxiliary vessels. It is not expected to be fit to put to sea before the end of the month, so that it cannot reach the vicinity of Singapore much before May 1st.

Captain de Freycinet's opinion is that Nebogatoff's division is of no value whatever from the military point of view.

"These two battleships, the *Utchakoff* and the *Nicolai*," he said, "are just old hulks—scrap value and no more. So far from reinforcing the 2nd Squadron, they'll simply get in its way and paralyse its movements. . . . It's just crazy to send such old barges to fight the Japanese Fleet!"

Wednesday, February 8th, 1905.

The International Commission of Enquiry into the Dogger Bank incident is still busily engaged in its task.

The British Government has called as witnesses several fishermen who were on the scene on the night of October 21st. They have all sworn that all the trawlers were showing their regulation lights and engaged in their ordinary work. No suspicious-looking vessel had slipped in among them.

In reply, the Russian Government wanted to produce several Norwegian fishermen whose evidence would tend to show that there really were Japanese destroyers in the North Sea. At the last moment it changed its mind—it had to! For the Imperial Government now knows all about the activities of the secret agent, Michael Harting, in concocting the story of the Japanese decoy: the director of the Police Department in St. Petersburg, Councillor of State Lopukhin, has at length cleared up the whole mystery. So, in order to avoid an appalling scandal at the enquiry, it was decided that Admiral Dubassov should decline to give any information about the source of the reports which misled Rojdestvensky. But, as the matter was too delicate to be committed to writing, Lopukhin has come to Paris in person with his right-hand man, the notorious Ratchkovsky, on purpose to coach Dubassov.

Unfortunately, there is yet another mystery in the Dogger Bank drama.

It was the captain of the *Kamtchatka*, Stepanoff, who first reported the presence of Japanese destroyers and immediately opened fire on the trawlers. At that moment, owing to engine trouble, the *Kamtchatka* was slightly in rear of the squadron and off her course. His frantic wireless messages and the noise of his guns left no doubt in the minds of the others that the situation was extremely critical. It is now known for certain that on this tragic night Captain Stepanoff and his officers, realizing the grim fate—a horrible and inglorious suicide—in store for them, could think of nothing better than trying to escape from their dismal thoughts by getting hopelessly drunk. . . . Hence the stubborn refusal of the Russian Admiralty to produce to the Commission Admiral Rojdestvensky's logs and telegraphic records!

Thursday, February 9th, 1905.

Delcassé is very worried about the critical situation of the Russian armies in Manchuria and the evil portents from Berlin. For the last two days he has taken refuge in gloomy silence and I can hardly even guess at his thoughts. I have noticed again how, when danger threatens, he assumes the mask of tragedy; a sort of tense, aggressive, sullen, suspicious and ominous look comes into his eyes. The explanation is that he is entirely obsessed by his political task, which he regards as nothing less than the salvation of France. To that task he is devoting all his energies; it is engaging every fibre of his being.

Chapter XI

February 10th—March 16th, 1905

Friday, February 10th, 1905.

THE German Press is continuing its diatribes against the recent speech of Mr. Arthur Lee, Civil Lord of the British Admiralty, although an unofficial note from London has explained away anything which might be considered unfriendly to Germany in that piece of hustings oratory.

In all the imperial and pan-German papers the onslaught takes the same form: 'The unofficial note from London is a lie. In speaking as he did, Mr. Arthur Lee can have had no other power in mind but Germany. In any event, does not the redistribution of the English fleets show that, in increasing the strength of the Home Fleet Squadrons, the British Admiralty is now determined to thwart the legitimate development of the German Navy. . . . Anyhow, Germany has had her warning; she knows she must have a navy capable of defending itself against the surprise attacks rashly referred to by the Civil Lord of the British Admiralty. The Reichstag will no longer dare to haggle over the grants for the necessary expansion of the German Fleet . . . for which the Imperial Government has been constantly pressing.'

Sunday, February 12th, 1905.

My young friend and colleague, René de Chérisey, who is in charge of the legation at Tangier whilst his chief is at Fez, has just had a curious conversation with the German Chargé d'Affaires, Baron von Kühlmann.

In the course of a heart-to-heart talk about the Moroccan question, they naturally discussed it from the German Foreign Office's point of view.

"Since your agreement with England," Kühlmann said, "and especially after your agreement with Spain, we have been expecting you to keep us posted about this new situation. But we couldn't help seeing that you are systematically ignoring us in your Moroccan policy. We have shaped our own policy accordingly. Count

von Bülow has informed me that, as the Imperial Government
was not consulted in your agreements with London and Madrid,
it does not consider itself in any way bound by their stipulations."

These words are a bad omen for us. It looks as if Germany were
preparing to put a spoke in our wheel in Morocco, on the pretext
that we did not inform her of our agreements with London and
Madrid. Delcassé realized the situation at once. He rapped out:

"Do you know Chérisey personally? Can we trust what he
says? . . . Don't you think he may have taken mere tittle-tattle too
seriously? . . . If what Kühlmann said to him is true, there's
trouble brewing."

I assured him that Chérisey was not only truthful but cautious,
discreet and level-headed, in fact one of our best officers. Delcassé
kept on repeating:

"There's trouble brewing. . . . To save time, I'm going to instruct Bihourd to draw Bülow's attention to Kühlmann's remarks
and refute his charges in the strongest terms. The Germans have
no right to say that I didn't advise them of our agreements with
London and Madrid. I told them in good time and quite politely.
If they deny it, it means they're trying to pick a quarrel with us."

Monday, February 13th, 1905.

The International Commission of Enquiry into the Dogger
Bank incident held its first public sitting today, in the banqueting
hall of the Ministry of Foreign Affairs.

At the far end, the five admirals, Admiral Fournier presiding,
sit on a dais at a table spread with a red velvet cloth with a gold
fringe.

The English and Russian delegates face each other, on opposite
sides of the tribunal.

The room was crowded; at least three hundred people; the Diplomatic Corps in force; many senators and deputies; a great many
foreigners; numbers of well-dressed women—it might have been
a reception at the Académie Française.

The sitting did not last long, the time being taken up by reading
the reports in which each side sets out its arguments.

The contrast between the two representatives, who read in turn,
was striking and characteristic. The British Government's delegate,
O'Beirne, was quiet, lucid and practical. All his statements were

emphatic and to the point. He might have been reading an extract from a law book or a court document. The Russian Government's representative, Nekludoff, followed and got tied up in vague explanations and obscure, long-winded phrases. His stumbling delivery, barely audible, made his arguments seem even weaker than they actually were. The effect of his performance on the public was disastrous.

As we were leaving, I had a few words with Countess von Hohenfelsen:

"*Mon Dieu!* The agony I went through while Nekludoff was speaking. . . . And how rude O'Beirne was to us!"

Tuesday, February 14th, 1905.

The Director of Political Affairs received me in his bedroom, to which he is confined by influenza.

We resumed our discussion of the urgent reasons which, in my opinion, make it imperative for Russia to make peace.

Georges Louis agrees with me that the Russians have lost the game in the Far East and that revolution is threatening at home. But he does not think that any intervention on our part, however discreet, would induce the Tsar to negotiate:

"We should be asking for a rebuff: *What right have you to interfere in a matter which is my business and no one else's?*"

"If the Emperor gave us that sort of answer, I shouldn't hesitate to retort: '*What right have we! . . . Our right as an ally and a creditor. As your ally, we are justified in reminding you that if the war goes on you will be unable to meet your obligations to us for many years. As a creditor, our anxiety about our twelve milliards justifies us in giving you some sound advice.*'"

Georges Louis remains convinced that it would at least be premature for us to intervene.

Wednesday, February 15th, 1905.

When the Civil Lord of the British Admiralty recently alluded to the possibility of a naval trial of strength between England and Germany, he was touching one of William II's most sensitive points and the Emperor has been furious ever since.

The moment he knew the exact wording of this famous speech, he sent for the British Ambassador, Sir Francis Lascelles, and for nearly an hour bawled and stormed at him, striding and stamping round the room.

Lascelles, with his unruffled calm and charming courtesy, ultimately managed to soothe the infuriated monarch. But this vicious dressing-down illustrates the accuracy of a recent remark of King Edward to his old friend, the Marquis de Breteuil—who repeated it to me—"You may be quite certain that my nephew William fears nothing so much as a duel with England."

Thursday, February 16th, 1905.

Our ambassador in Berlin, Bihourd, has been to the Secretary of State to deny the statements attributed to Kühlmann to the effect that the Imperial Government was not informed of our agreements with London and Madrid on the subject of Morocco —and therefore entitled to consider itself as in no way bound by them.

He only succeeded in getting an ambiguous answer out of Mühlberg, though it clearly showed that Germany intends to reserve her entire freedom of action at the Court of Fez.

Friday, February 17th, 1905.

At about three o'clock this afternoon (one o'clock in Paris) as the Grand Duke Sergei, Governor-General of Moscow, was crossing the Kremlin, a terrorist threw a bomb at him and blew him to pieces.

The moment the news reached the Quai d'Orsay (five o'clock), the minister instructed me to break the news to the Grand Duke Paul.

I found both him and Madame von Hohenfelsen overcome and in tears. The Grand Duke had just received a wire from the Emperor telling him about the tragedy at the Kremlin. The telegram ended as follows: *I need you at my side in our trouble. Come at once.*

The Grand Duke is leaving this very evening for St. Petersburg. As Countess von Hohenfelsen was not mentioned in the Tsar's wire, and is not allowed to go back to Russia, she will accompany her husband only as far as Wirballen, on the frontier, and will then return straight to Paris.

"How shall I find things over there?" said the Grand Duke with a deep sigh. . . . "Where will the effrontery of these anarchists end? . . . Heaven protect the Emperor! Pray God he may be spared my father's fate." [1]

In the course of our discussion of the assassination in Moscow, the Grand Duke made a very sound observation:

"My brother's assassination is the terrorists' reply to the shooting on January 22nd. . . . Why, why didn't the Emperor receive the workmen's deputation that day!"

The Grand Duke Paul's words were nearer the mark than he realized, for I have just learned that his brother, the Grand Duke Vladimir, Military Governor of St. Petersburg, was solely responsible, morally and politically, for 'Red Sunday.' The Tsar had at first announced his intention of receiving the workmen's deputation, but his uncle Vladimir, who has always advocated the strong hand, was so violently opposed to the idea that the weak Tsar soon gave in.

Delcassé was to have given an important diplomatic banquet, followed by a reception, tomorrow. He has cancelled them, 'owing to the sudden bereavement of the Russian imperial family.'

Saturday, February 18th, 1905.

I dined with Prince and Princess von Radolin at Comtesse Jean de Castellane's. There were some ten guests, all of whom had a sound mixture of liberal and conservative elements in their outlook.

I was struck by the indifference, not to say complacency, shown in their comments on the Moscow drama. In the interests of decency they denounced the 'hateful wickedness of the terrorists,' but, under their breath, they admitted that, all things considered, the Grand Duke Sergei had deserved his fate. They thought it only natural that, in a state of society in which the government rules with the rifle, the opposition should reply with the bomb.[2]

---

[1] The Emperor Alexander II was assassinated at St. Petersburg on March 13th, 1881.

[2] The Court of Berlin's opinion of the Moscow drama was similar. In his letter of condolence (dated February 22nd) to the Tsar, William II did not hesitate to remind him of the insane shooting of January 22nd, and reproach him for not having addressed the strikers paternally (from the balcony of the Winter Palace), and thus avoided bloodshed. Then—and with equal reason—he went on to upbraid him for having neglected Moscow so much since the beginning of the war: 'In the old days, your ancestors always went to Moscow before they departed for a war; they prayed in the old churches, summoned the nobles to the Kremlin and the people to the

Sunday, February 19th, 1905.

The assassination of the Grand Duke Sergei is the latest achievement of that terrible revolutionary organization known as the *Fighting Organization*, which was founded by Guerchuny and Burtzev. As in the heroic days of nihilism, in the reign of Alexander II, the same mysterious, methodical, ruthless and devastating methods are employed.

This fresh tragedy, which has stained the Kremlin with blood, continues the lamentable series which began in 1902 when the Minister of the Interior, Sipiaguin, was assassinated. In May, 1903, the Governor of Ufa, Bogdanovitch, was killed and in July, 1904, the Minister of the Interior, Plehve. In addition, there have been attempts on the life of the Procurator-General of the Holy Synod, Pobedonostzev, the Governor of Kharkov, Prince Obolensky, and more than twenty prefects, commissioners of police, governors of prisons, gendarmerie officers, etc.

On the other side, the despotic ruthlessness of the imperial government's repressive measures, the secret activities of the *Okhrana* and the official attitude of the courts of law, demonstrate the fidelity of the Russian mind to the legal theories of the Middle Ages which were so brutally personified by Ivan the Terrible. Russian civilization, one feels, has never known the rational discipline of Roman law, still less the liberal principles of Anglo-Saxon law. As despotism is the only form of government it can imagine, it has never had any respect for human rights.

Monday, February 20th, 1905.

The German Press is beginning to discuss Morocco again, with the obvious intention of inflaming public opinion against us. Things are looking dangerous for Delcassé.

Though in bed with a severe attack of influenza, I have had a visit from General Pendézec, our Chief of Staff; he has confided his fears of seeing us embark upon a policy the result of which may be that 'Germany can put us at any moment in an extremely

---

Square. That is what Moscow and Russia expected of you a year ago. But no Tsar came! It is time you got in touch with Moscow again; you must make your authority felt by some striking gesture; you must take the risk! . . .' (*Documents published by the Bolshevists.*) We know that in 1918 William might well have applied this noble advice to himself; but in the days which preceded his flight to Holland it did not occur to him that he should 'take the risk.'

dangerous position, as our Russian ally is incapable of helping us for a long time to come.'

He went on to speak of the plan of campaign which his German 'colleague,' General von Schlieffen, has adopted for a future war with France; we have known it for nearly a year, owing to the *Avenger's* mysterious revelations.

"You will remember," he said, "that the fundamental principle of this plan is to concentrate the main mass of the German armies on the Western Front and employ them in a vast enveloping movement through Belgium which will carry them to the valley of the Oise without striking a blow. . . . The official documents, which the *Avenger* had acquired and which he showed us, leaves us in no doubt of the accuracy of his statements. All the same, I've had them checked, as far as possible. In particular, I sent some of our most reliable agents to the area where the nine army corps destined for the invasion of Belgium must concentrate. According to the *Avenger*, this zone extends west of the Rhine Provinces from Malmédy to Crefeld through Aix-la-Chapelle, Gladbach and Juliers. Our agents have thoroughly explored the district. They have found that all the railway works required for the concentration of an army, i.e., platforms, engine sheds, double tracks, etc., are either completed, or in course of completion. In several places, work which seemed less urgent was begun only five or six weeks ago; it is now being speeded up. . . . In my view, the German General Staff could put its new strategic plan into operation at a moment's notice. . . . As to the connection between this programme and the defeat of our Russian ally in the Far East, you can see it as well as I can."

General Pendézec also told me a curious fact about the official documents with which the *Avenger* had supplied himself to prove the authenticity of his disclosures. Among them he produced his 'mobilization book'—the special type used for staff officers. But, as the name of the holder is written inside the cover, the traitor had ingeniously pasted, and then sealed, a piece of black paper over it so that the inscription could not be read. He even allowed our Intelligence to have the book for a few hours so that it could be quickly photographed, page by page. The *Avenger* said to Captain Lambling: *If you don't return my book, or if I see that the piece of black paper has been tampered with, you will obviously have discovered who I am; but you'll get no more information out of me. Things will stop where they are.* When his book was returned to him intact two hours later, he coolly began to display his 'titbits.' [1]

Thursday, February 23rd, 1905.

The solemn obsequies of the Grand Duke Sergei were celebrated in Moscow today in the Monastery of Miracles, oldest and most venerated of all the Kremlin monasteries; the imperial family was represented by the Grand Duke Paul and the Grand Duke Constantine.

In Paris, a memorial service was held at the Orthodox Church in the Rue Daru, under the auspices of the Russian Ambassador. My influenza kept me away.

Friday, February 24th, 1905.

For the last four days the stage has been set for a great battle twenty kilometres south of Mukden. The Russian Army, commanded by General Kuropatkin, is about 380,000 strong, whilst the Japanese, under Field-Marshal Oyama, number about 320,000.

Saturday, February 25th, 1905.

Although I have not yet recovered from my attack of influenza, I went to the ministry, as Delcassé sent for me to confer with Georges Louis and General Pendézec.

Our Chief of Staff repeated to the minister, in forcible terms, the information he gave at my bedside five days ago. Delcassé listened without saying a word. Then he turned and looked enquiringly at Georges Louis and myself. We said we agreed with Pendézec. Delcassé, scowling, his lips taut, dryly dismissed us without expressing any opinion. But when we reached the door, he suddenly became more affable and called out after us: "Please don't think I'm not very grateful to you for being so frank with me."

[1] General Count von Schlieffen was placed on the retired list on the score of ill-health in December, 1905. His successor on the General Staff in the Königsplatz was Colonel Count von Moltke, a nephew of the illustrious Field-Marshal.

Count von Schlieffen died in 1913. Up to the very last he advocated the enveloping movement through Belgium and insisted on 'the necessity for seeking a quick decision by an irresistible thrust of the right wing. It is said that his last words were: "Strengthen the right wing!" '

Sunday, February 26th, 1905.

Yesterday, the International Commission of Enquiry gave its verdict on the Dogger Bank incident. In a spirit of wisdom and accommodation, it has given something to both sides. As the Russian Admiral has persistently accepted his government's argument, the findings of the Commission are expressed as follows: *"The majority of the commissioners consider that. . . ."*

The long judgment—it comprises no less than seventeen paragraphs—sets out that 'Admiral Rojdestvensky was not justified in opening fire on the Dogger Bank trawlers as there were no enemy destroyers among them'; it adds that 'the firing continued longer than was necessary'; it also expresses regret that Admiral Rojdestvensky, after ceasing fire, rendered no assistance to the trawlers in distress. The verdict ends with a paragraph calculated to soothe the injured feelings of the unfortunate Admiral Rojdestvensky: 'The commissioners would like to add that, in their view, the criticisms in their report are not to be considered as reflecting in any way on the military efficiency or humanity of Admiral Rojdestvensky and his squadron.'

The commissioners have said nothing about the indemnity to be paid to the Dogger Bank victims. This matter is to be settled in direct negotiations between London and St. Petersburg. The Russian Government has secretly advised the Foreign Office that it will pay the figure asked.

Monday, February 27th, 1905.

The women of Moscow have just sent the following petition to the Empress Alexandra-Feodorovna:

We, Russian women—mothers, wives and sisters of the soldiers who are giving their lives for our dear country in the Far East—make our petition to Your Majesty, because we believe that you too, as a mother, feel all the horrors of this war. You will understand how we long and pray for peace.

Peace has been outraged, not only beyond our frontiers but here at home within our borders. We are horrified to see in the recent troubles the beginning of calamities which promise to overwhelm the whole of Russia, unless the Emperor unites with his people to take steps to prevent them.

Dearly beloved Sovereign, be our advocate with him. Beg the

*Emperor to listen to the voice of his country and the appeal of
the mothers. If the Emperor leads Russia into the path of
greatness, the women will do their share in the work of organizing the country by bringing up the youth, their brothers and
children, in the new way of an ordered life.*

Tuesday, February 28th, 1905.

The battle of Mukden has begun badly for the Russians as
their right wing is in danger of being turned by the Japanese.

Wednesday, March 1st, 1905.

We have not got any results at Fez for a month. Negotiations
are dragging on from conference to conference and one palaver to
another.

To evade the discussion of precise issues, the Maghzen has
thought fit to reinforce his diplomatic representatives with a motley
array of forty 'notables,' specially recruited for the occasion—
fanatical reactionaries who, on principle and from self-interest,
are violently hostile to the reforms which even the Sultan admits
to be a vital necessity.

To say the least of it, this odd procedure is bound to make the
holy city of the Almohades a hotbed of enmity and intrigue
against us.

Thursday, March 2nd, 1905.

The battle is raging round Mukden. The Russian front is still
intact, but on the extreme right the second army has been forced
to give ground extensively to avoid being surrounded.

The priest Gapon, who led the workmen's demonstration in
St. Petersburg on the fatal day of January 22nd, is said quite
recently to have written the Emperor a scathing letter which our
socialist papers are inserting. The *Okhrana* tells me it is authentic,
so I am reproducing it below, because it throws a fierce light on
the vindictive feelings fermenting in the heart of the Russian
people.

To NICHOLAS ROMANOFF,
  FORMERLY TSAR OF RUSSIA
  MURDERER OF HIS PEOPLE

*Filled with a childlike faith in you whom I looked on as the
father of his people, I walked peacefully towards your palace,*

followed by your peaceful children. Their blood was shed. Henceforth you are the murderer of your people. The moral bond between us and you is broken for ever. Bombs and dynamite, individual outrage and terrorism in bulk—they are your progeny. The soil of Russia will soon be drenched with streams of Russian blood. Through you, Russia herself may very well perish. Only one course is open to you: abdicate the throne of Russia and with your family face your trial before the Russian people.   GEORGE GAPON.

This priest Gapon is a curious character. Quite recently he was chaplain to the central gaol in St. Petersburg, the Kresty Prison. His ecclesiastical duties brought him into direct and constant touch with the working classes in the capital. He announced that he was 'the servant of Christ according to the teaching of Tolstoi,' and made it his object in life to spread 'the true gospel of pure Christianity,' i.e., unadulterated socialism, among the poor and lowly. Simultaneously, he constituted himself a secret emissary between the prisoners and their families. In this way he soon managed to inspire his 'working-class comrades' with blind and boundless confidence in him.[1]

I remember Ratchkovsky's words one day:

"Far too many of our priests are mixed up with the socialist party; the most dangerous of them are the prison and penal-settlement chaplains, because it is through them that political prisoners keep in touch with the revolutionary organizations. . . ."

Is not all this one of the keys to Tolstoi's *Resurrection!*

Saturday, March 4th, 1905.

It is obvious from the course of the operations south of Mukden that General Kuropatkin has lost the initiative and that he is being manœuvred out of position by his opponent; but the Japanese have not yet won any decisive advantage.

The Grand Duke Paul returned from St. Petersburg yesterday evening and called on me this afternoon. As I was out, he left his

[1] This mystical demagogue, 'servant of Christ according to the teaching of Tolstoi,' was to suffer the fate of—Judas. Towards the end of 1905 he entered the service of the imperial police who employed him chiefly as an *agent provocateur*. His treachery was, however, soon discovered by fellow-members of his party. On March 28th, 1906, they trapped him at Oziersky, in Finland, and strangled him.

card on which he had written: *I have just returned to Paris and want to talk to you as soon as possible. Try and come to tea tomorrow.*

Sunday, March 5th, 1905.

At half-past five I went to tea with the Grand Duke Paul. I found him alone with Madame von Hohenfelsen. He gave orders that he was not at home so that we should be undisturbed.

He told me about his talks with the Tsar. Starting with his own private affairs he said, that he had been completely pardoned; he may return to Russia whenever he likes and his possessions will be restored to him.

Unfortunately, Countess von Hohenfelsen is not included in this pardon, as her adultery was too scandalous; the Empress Alexandra-Feodorovna, who is very strict, insists on her waiting several years longer before she is forgiven. The Grand Duke Paul will therefore continue to make Paris his home, and the restoration of his apanage—several million francs a year—will enable him to live in great style.

The Emperor opened his heart to him on the political situation: "I have never seen him so confident," the Grand Duke said; "he did not try to dodge any of my questions. . . . He discussed the war with *alarming complacency*; he hasn't the slightest doubt that we shall win in the end; he said so with such emphasis that I didn't dare mention the word peace. . . . The revolutionary outbreaks hardly worry him at all; he claims that the masses are not in the least interested in them; he believes he is one with his people."

"What about the Empress Alexandra-Feodorovna? What does *she* think? . . . Has she any influence with the Emperor?"

"Since her son was born,[1] Alexandra-Feodorovna seems to have taken a great interest in politics. She seems to me quite of the Tsar's way of thinking, except that she wants him to be more resolute and autocratic. On that point, I quite agree with her. Autocracy has always been the very backbone of Russia, my dear Paléologue; Russians need to feel the *knout* over their heads."

"And what about your great friend, Her Majesty the Dowager-Empress Marie-Feodorovna?"

[1] The Tsarevitch Alexis, born August 12th, 1904.

"Oh, Marie-Feodorovna! That's another matter . . . As a matter of fact, it was about her that I wanted to talk to you."

He told me that she is extremely pessimistic about the future:

"She has several times said to me: *We've lost our last chance of winning in the Far East; we're beaten already; we ought to make peace at once; otherwise there'll be a revolution.* . . . When I asked her if she had advised the Emperor accordingly, she replied: *I tell him so every day, but he won't listen to me; he doesn't realize our military situation any better than the position at home. He can't see that he's leading Russia into disaster.* Her last words were: *I know only one man who can open Nicholas's eyes and that's M. Delcassé. He's the best friend we have in Europe; he has immense influence in every country. So tell him from me that he will be doing us a signal service if he will offer to mediate for us.* . . . Those are the Dowager-Empress's very words. . . . You'll repeat them to M. Delcassé, won't you?"

"I'll give him her message word for word."

What the Grand Duke went on to tell me about the internal state of Russia, justifies the apprehensions of the Empress Marie-Feodorovna only too plainly. Tsarism is visibly crumbling. And what strikes me most is the muddle-headedness, lack of resolution and vigour displayed by the authorities in coping with the audacity of the revolutionaries.

Monday, March 6th, 1905.

This morning, I reported my conversation with the Grand Duke Paul to Delcassé. He started when I repeated the words of the Empress Marie-Feodorovna:

"Oh! . . . Russia must be decidedly worse than I thought."

He did not dismiss out of hand the idea of offering his services to the Russian Government with a view to peace, but he was doubtful whether the right moment had yet come for such a step. He questioned me for a long time about the operations in Manchuria and asked me what our military attachés and officer observers thought of the prospects of the great battle which has just begun outside Mukden. My pessimistic outlook made a great impression on him:

"Look here," he said. . . . "Supposing I agree to do what the Dowager Empress asks, how shall I set about it?"

"The first alternative which springs to mind is a letter from you to Lamsdorf; but that course would necessarily make your action seem official and, say what you may, would look rather like uninvited pressure. I think it would be better for you to get in touch with the Empress Marie-Feodorovna direct, as it was she who asked you to mediate."

He hesitated for a second and then said sharply:

"No! . . . I'd prefer to write direct to the Tsar. I would remind him that, during my negotiations in 1899, he himself asked me to write to him at any really serious moment. My intervention would thus remain private and personal—just a piece of friendly advice."

I entirely approved. But he frowned again and cautiously added:

"Before I decide, I'll wait and see who wins at Mukden. . . . I'll tell you what I mean. I've come round to your view that, at this stage, a peace is bound to be very humiliating for the Russians. They need it so badly at the moment that they would bless me if I could get it for them. But once they have it, they'll lay all the responsibility for their humiliation at my door. They'll make me their scapegoat. At the same time, the French nationalists will accuse me of having robbed our ally of certain victory, sacrificing them to England and selling them to Japan. Won't there be an uproar."

As he dismissed me, he said:

"Draft me a letter to the Emperor Nicholas; I want to be prepared for anything."

Tuesday, March 7th, 1905.

There is still no decision in the battle of Mukden. But the progress of the Japanese on the west is seriously threatening the lines of communication of the Russian armies, which seem engaged in the preliminaries of a retreat all along the line.

When I went to see Delcassé this afternoon, he asked me:

"Have the Russians a chance, even the silghtest chance, of pulling things round?"

"According to General Pendézec, they've lost the battle and their defeat will leave them in such a state of exhaustion and disorganization that they'll be incapable of any operation for several months."

He made no comment on this opinion of our Chief of Staff, but remarked:

"Have you drafted the letter to the Emperor Nicholas?"
I handed him the draft I wrote last night. He read it aloud, dwelling on every word:

Sire,

The first time Your Majesty did me the honour of receiving me in 1899, you deigned to say that I had your permission to write to you direct in any serious situation. Since then, Your Majesty has shown your confidence in me so frequently that I feel emboldened to take further advantage of this gracious favour.

Your Majesty knows how sympathetically the whole of France has followed Russia's heroic efforts for the past year in the Far East. You know, too, how eagerly I have seized every opportunity of serving the interests of Russia in accordance with the general spirit of the alliance between the two countries.

It is because of my heartfelt desire to continue this work that I think it my duty to offer Your Majesty certain observations which the course of recent events has suggested to me.

It seemed to me that, if I wrote privately direct to Your Majesty, I should prove once again the sincerity of my intentions.

The information I have received during the last few months, more particularly from some of Russia's best friends, has convinced me that every day the war continues makes it more difficult for Your Majesty's Government to secure a peace which it can regard as acceptable.

Of course, if the Imperial armies in Manchuria could count on a respite of several months in which to wait for the necessary reinforcements, their gallantry would be rewarded by victory. But meanwhile, would not the diplomatic situation—the only one on which I am qualified to express an opinion—have become less favourable for an equitable settlement? Might there not be reason to regret that an opportunity had not been accepted?

I venture to hope that Your Majesty will weigh these serious considerations and understand the spirit which has prompted me to bring them to your notice.

I have the honour to be, Sire, etc.

When Delcassé had read this draft, he said:

"Good. I don't think any alterations are required. . . . Now let's wait and see what happens."

Wednesday, March 8th, 1905.

The position of the Russians outside Mukden is becoming more and more precarious. The left wing of the Japanese armies is continuing its enveloping movement and is only five kilometres from the Trans-Siberian Railway at She-ni-tun. General Kuropatkin is accelerating the pace of his retreat.

Thursday, March 9th, 1905.

The Japanese have pressed on north-west of Mukden. The position of the Russians is desperate, as the Trans-Siberian Railway may be cut at any moment.

Friday, March 10th, 1905.

The Mukden drama has been going on for fifteen days and has now reached the last act. The Russian front was broken on the Huhn-ho yesterday.

Saturday, March 11th, 1905.

The Japanese entered Mukden yesterday; the entire Russian army is retiring hastily towards Tie-ling.

General Pendézec has been to see me to look at our latest telegrams. As he left, he said:

"This Mukden battle, disastrous as it is for the Russians, ought to be a great lesson to us. The vast extension of the fronts, the extraordinary duration of the action and the colossal weight of fire probably makes it the prototype of future battles. It will be as well to remember it."

As I was leaving my office at seven o'clock this evening, Delcassé sent for me.

He looked very dejected:

"Well?" he said.

I waited for the rest, but he merely repeated his exclamation: "Well?"

Then I told him in plain terms that the hour had come for him to persuade the Tsar to make peace; for the twentieth time I recapitulated my main reasons: (1) We must at all costs safeguard our alliance, which will become valueless or even non-existent if Russia collapses in a domestic upheaval; (2) We ought also to safeguard the twelve milliard francs of French savings which are invested in Russian loans or industries; (3) We must not forget that Admiral Rojdestvensky's squadron is still at Madagascar and his continued use of French waters exposes us to an ultimatum, if not some affront, from Japan; (4) If Russian power is paralysed by a revolutionary crisis, Germany is sure to take advantage of it to pick a quarrel with us over Morocco.

Delcassé gave me a sullen, hostile stare, and then said suddenly: "Very well. I've come round. . . . Write me out a telegram for Bompard at once; tell him about the Dowager-Empress's conversation with the Grand Duke Paul and ask him what he thinks about my intervening on the lines you advise."

A few minutes later, I took the telegram to the minister. He approved of it in general, but slightly modified the conclusion:

The Dowager-Empress's conversation with the Grand Duke Paul was prior to the battle of Mukden. Do you know exactly what effect this military event has had on the mind of the Emperor Nicholas? Do you consider that the position is such as enables me—without being misunderstood—to remind him that, as a true friend of Russia and devoted to the common interests of the two allied nations, I am prepared to help the Imperial Government to give effect to the decisions at which in its wisdom it may arrive.

Sunday, March 12th, 1905.

The brilliant victory of the Japanese at Mukden has given our extreme parties a fresh opportunity of attacking Delcassé's pro-Russian policy and blaming him for the 'interminable stay of the Russian squadron in Madagascan waters.' The socialists accuse him of 'exposing France to the legitimate resentment of Japan, if not the risk of a naval action in French waters, against which we should have no right to protest.' These are the very words used by Motono the day before yesterday when he was talking to Delcassé; the coincidence is odd, to say the least of it. . . .

This morning, the official socialist paper, *l'Humanité*, publishes an article which concludes as follows:

> *M. Delcassé needs—and badly needs—to be reminded that the first and most sacred of his obligations is to observe neutrality both in spirit and letter. He should be told very clearly that the France of the Revolution cannot, either directly or indirectly, lend assistance to the Tsarist autocracy, nor can the France of 1905 intervene diplomatically to save the Russia of Nicholas II from the appalling consequences of its criminal folly. What France can and must do is to cooperate with the other democratic powers to bring pressure to bear on Petersburg to accept a peace for which Russia will have to pay a very high price; every day's delay will make it higher.*

Tuesday, March 14th, 1905.

Delcassé has been telling me of a conversation he had this afternoon with the Russian Ambassador:

"Nelidov volunteered that the internal troubles in Russia and the Mukden disaster ought to convince the Emperor that he must make peace at once. He has just written to Lamsdorf to suggest that he should avail himself of my services in approaching Japan. . . . I confined myself to replying that, if the Imperial Government did ask me to make representations to Tokyo, I should certainly not refuse."

This evening I dined at Scherer's. Among those present were Salomon Reinach, Paul Janet, Dr. Pozzie, Emile Dürkheim, Gustave Lanson, Gaston Deschamps, Vidal-Lablache, Lévy-Bruhl, etc. . . .

Wholesale onslaught on Russia and the Russian alliance. Interesting point: the bitterest reproach my fellow-guests level against the Russian autocracy is its contempt for intellectuals and things of the mind. "The Grand Duke Sergei," Salomon Reinach told us, "didn't even pretend to take any interest in the Moscow Archæological Society!" These diatribes (Dürkheim's fulminations reached heights of positively biblical eloquence) help me to understand the Renaissance humanists' dislike of Paul III, Farnese, who was not as lavish as he might have been with gifts and flattery.

Lanson, who was one of the tutors to the Tsar Nicholas, was

very guarded in what he said about him: "He was a shy young man, full of good intentions, easily influenced and without personal reactions."

The description is brief, but none the less accurate.

Thursday, March 16th, 1905.

At the last court dinner in Berlin, Admiral von Senden-Bibran, the Emperor's aide-de-camp, said to our naval attaché, Captain de Sugny: "The Emperor is going to call at *your* Tangier on his approaching cruise. . . ."

The admiral's remark was apparently free from any trace of the spirit of guile or mischief. But Delcassé is none the less horrified to hear that his august adversary, and personal enemy, William II, is daring to throw down the gauntlet at Tangier— Tangier of all places!

Our ambassador at St. Petersburg has just replied to the minister's recent enquiry; he considers that intervention on the lines desired by the Empress Marie-Feodorovna would be premature, to say the least of it. His argument is odd: "The Russians are only just beginning to realize what their defeat at Mukden means; but, far from being downhearted, they are insisting upon revenge. Many who were decidedly pacifist a week ago are now in the most bellicose mood. . . ." Bompard is anticipating a *volte-face* in the near future, "when the humiliation of defeat will have given place to a recalculation of chances."

Re-reading our ambassador's reply word by word, the minister indulged in a prolonged monologue in which he carefully weighed the pros and cons of all the possible alternatives. "If I write to the Emperor. . . . If I don't write to the Emperor. . . . Have I any right to deprive the Russians of any chance of their revenge? Is it for me, their friend and ally, to say to them: *You're beaten, hopelessly beaten; you've no choice but to go down on your knees to Japan.* . . . But if revolution breaks out in Russia, what a trump card for Germany! . . ."

Then he asked me to bring out the letter to the Tsar which I had drafted. I had it with me in my dispatch-case. He read it again, quite slowly, staring hard at it as if he were trying to pierce the secrets of the future under my handwriting. . . . Suddenly his face cleared; he had come to a decision.

"No! I'm not going to send this letter. . . . All your arguments are sound and I can't think of an answer to them; but I just feel I shouldn't do it."

"In that case I should certainly advise you not to write to the Emperor. Don't take any step you instinctively feel to be wrong. You would certainly fail and you haven't the right to fail."

General Kuropatkin thought he could end his retreat at the Tie-ling line, eighty kilometres from Mukden. But, under pressure from the Japanese, he has been forced back one hundred and fifty kilometres further north in the direction of Shin-pin-gai.

Chapter XII

Friday, March 17th, 1905.

THE Russian squadron left Passandaya Bay at two o'clock yesterday afternoon, heading north-east for the western extremity of
Sumatra.

Admiral Rojdestvensky decided on this course himself; we have
not influenced him at all. What is more, it is through us that the
Imperial Admiralty has learned of his departure; so much so that
as late as this morning I was handed a telegram from St. Petersburg addressed to Passandaya.

At the present moment, the Russian squadron is thus plough-
ing the waters of the Indian Ocean, with the intention of entering the China Seas through the Straits of Malacca. It has a tiresome and arduous voyage before it—3,800 nautical miles without
a harbour or any possibility of assistance. Twice at least it will
have to coal at sea! . . .

Admiral Rojdestvensky had the choice of several routes to the
Pacific Ocean. Captain de Freycinet had suggested five. The first
passes through the Straits of Lumbok and the Celebes Sea; the
second by the Sea of Timor and the Torres Straits; the third by the
south of Australia and the Coral Sea. These three routes are long,
but each offers the great advantage of keeping the Japanese in
complete ignorance of the direction from which their enemy will
appear in the Yellow Sea. The fourth and fifth routes are far
shorter; one passes through the Sunda Strait, between Java and
Sumatra, and the other by Achin and the Straits of Malacca.

Admiral Rojdestvensky's choice has fallen on the last alternative. Strategically it is the worst, for from Achin to Singapore—
a distance of 400 miles—it is a sort of corridor, with British Malaya
on one side. The Japanese will thus be able to follow the approach
of the Russian Squadron hour by hour. From the French point of
view, Admiral Rojdestvensky's decision is just as embarrassing;
there is no doubt that once the 2nd Squadron has rounded the

Singapore Peninsula, it will want to shelter on the coast of Annam before seeking its fate in the Yellow Sea. Must we not expect that the protracted stay of the Russian *Armada* in Madagascan waters has exhausted Japan's patience with us? . . .

But, from the navigational point of view, the Malacca route is unquestionably the safest, and that consideration has been uppermost in Admiral Rojdestvensky's mind.

Saturday, March 18th, 1905.

The recent Russian disaster at Mukden has provoked two lines of thought in Germany; they are worth noting. The Germans began by paying tribute in the most flamboyant terms to the amazing courage and endurance shown by the Russian troops during this long battle, and deploring the fact that so many sacrifices in the cause of Christian civilization should have been made in vain. Then national egotism immediately asserted itself, and there is open rejoicing at the prospect of the military power of the Russian colossus being destroyed for ten, or perhaps twenty, years to come. . . . Some newspapers which go even further and take their cue from the Wilhelmstrasse, have not stopped at printing a remark like this: "It is the knell of the Franco-Russian alliance. All the hopes of revenge which the French had so naively based on our eastern neighbour, have now disappeared. Germany can breathe freely once more!"

I suspect that university circles familiar with Horace are quoting the dithyrambs on the death of Cleopatra:

Nunc est bibendem, nunc pedo libero
Pulsanda tellus. . . .

Sunday, March 19th, 1905.

Last Thursday, the Chancellor, Bülow, speaking in the Reichstag, gave the German Socialists a lecture, pointing out the absurdity and impropriety of the insults to Russia with which their press fills its columns every day.

The *Temps* is right in thinking that the French Socialists would do well to reflect on Bülow's sermon. *They also should be told, and in no uncertain voice, that however unfavourable to Russia the result of the war may be she will remain what she has always been, a great power, an alliance with whom is an historic necessity to our country. If there are any Frenchmen who forget that no defeat is irretrievable and recovery never impossible, we can only pity them their short memories.*

Monday, March 20th, 1905.

Our naval attaché in Russia, Captain de Saint-Pair, who has just come back from St. Petersburg, called on me this morning.

He is far more pessimistic than I myself; he thinks that the whole Russian edifice is about to collapse. What worries him most about the present crisis is that he sees no one with sufficient authority to assume power and carry through the necessary reforms. The bureaucracy is effete and rotten to the core. Apart from the bureaucracy, there is nothing but a crowd of schemers, adventurers, visionaries and revolutionaries.

He confirmed all his official correspondence had taught me as to the confusion and incompetence prevailing in the Imperial Navy. When Admiral Rojdestvensky left Libau for Madagascar, calling at Dakar, Libreville, Mossamedes and Angra-Pequena, he had no chart of the African coast. The Admiralty in St. Petersburg did not possess one either. . . .

Tuesday, March 21st, 1905.

The debate on the disestablishment of the Church, a controversy of enormous spiritual and political importance to the future of our country, began in the Chamber today.

Judging by the firm attitude of the Left, there is no doubt as to the ultimate result.

The Bishop of Perpignan has just addressed a letter to the clergy of his diocese in which he stigmatizes the 'Separation' bill as 'a hideous crime and ignominious apostasy.'

I dined with the Duc and Duchesse de Rohan and met the Grand Duke Paul, Countess von Hohenfelsen, Countess Brévern de la Gardie and the Marcel Prévosts. A family party and 'Morning dress, owing to H.I.H. the Grand Duke's recent bereavement' as the invitation card puts it.

As soon as Madame von Hohenfelsen entered the room, she said to me:

"We've come feeling like whipped curs. We're down to the very dregs!"

Dinner was a very depressing affair.

When we left the table, Countess Brévern, whose husband is in the Russian Diplomatic Service, took me into a corner where we were immediately joined by Madame von Hohenfelsen. They both begged me to use my influence with Delcassé to persuade the Emperor to make peace.

"He must write to the young Empress Alexandra-Feodorovna!" said Countess Brévern imperiously.

"Oh, no!" said Madame von Hohenfelsen in her caressing voice. "It would be better for him to write to the Dowager Empress, Marie-Feodorovna!"

The Grand Duke came up to us. It was his turn to belabour me.

"I'm just down and out tonight. If God doesn't help us soon, we're lost! . . . Yet M. Delcassé could still save us. He alone can spare us the humiliating peace we seem to be in for, and which will inevitably mean revolution! . . . He must write to the Emperor! . . . My dear Paléologue, do insist on his writing to the Emperor!"

"But I don't know what M. Delcassé could write to the Emperor, except to say he would do *anything* for him. Do you think the Emperor doesn't know that already?"

Wednesday, March 22nd, 1905.

Delcassé is in the clouds because the new English Ambassador, Sir Francis Bertie, has just sent him the following note:

"I am instructed to inform Your Excellency that His Britannic Majesty and his Government would be extremely pleased to see part of the French fleet at Spithead next August, when His Majesty proposes to be at Cowes for Regatta Week. . . . I am also instructed to enquire of Your Excellency whether it would be agreeable to the French Government for a detachment of the Atlantic Fleet to pay a courtesy visit to Brest about the middle of July."

Delcassé immediately accepted both the British Government's offers.

Thursday, March 23rd, 1905.

The German Chargé d'Affaires has sent us an official list of the ports of call in the Emperor William's itinerary: Tangier is included.

Why send us this document if it is true that Germany knows nothing about the Anglo-French agreement of April 8th, 1904, and does not acknowledge our special status in Morocco? The German Chancery does not as a rule notify us of the calls to be made by the imperial yacht in foreign ports! . . .

General Pendézec has just been going into an important question with me: "If war broke out between France and Germany, how far would our secret agreements with Italy entitle us to denude the Alpine frontier in order to reinforce our armies in the north-east and thus make up more or less for the devaluation of the Russian alliance? . . ." I did not hesitate to assure him that, if there was a great European war, Italy could not remain neutral; her national ambitions, geographical position, all the romance of her past and the current of her historical evolution, would drive her to attack Austria.

Friday, March 24th, 1905.

Public opinion in Germany is beginning to get heated. The Pan-Germans are talking war: the *Magdeburger Zeitung* is threatening France with invasion.

With his usual eye for effect, William II is seeking some really resounding triumph. Or is it only bluff? Our former ambassador in London and Berlin, Baron de Courcel, with whom I was dining last week, thinks it is bluff, as he regards William as "a mountebank and coward, who, at the critical moment, always runs away from the consequences of his own actions."

Saturday, March 25th, 1905.

The decisive results of the battle of Mukden are now being felt. The situation cannot be restored in favour of the Russians in the absence of most unlikely contingencies, such as an overwhelming naval victory for Rojdestvensky, or some crazy operation *à la* Charles XII into which the Japanese might let themselves be drawn out of sheer megalomania.

Thus the Tsar can have only two reasons for continuing to send reinforcements to the Far East: (1) the *arrière-pensée* of having an imposing force in hand when the moment for diplomatic negotiations arrives; (2) fear that too humiliating a peace treaty may prove a great peril to Tsarism.

Monday, March 27th, 1905.

The Berlin *Lokal Anzeiger* writes: "If France will not make overtures to the German Empire, the latter should not negotiate with her over Morocco; that is why the Emperor did not say a word about Moroccan affairs when he dined at the French Embassy recently."

The inhabitants of Tangier are getting very excited over the approaching visit of the Emperor William. On instructions from Fez, the local authorities are preparing to give him a brilliant reception; they are displaying a degree of enthusiasm and energy which belies their reputation for lethargy. Morocco obviously looks on William II's visit as the advent of her saviour.

One day last week in Berlin, Holstein was spending the evening as usual at the house of his great friend, Frau von Lebbin; she is an intelligent, cultured woman, from whom the *Éminence Grise* has no secrets. A few guests, or I should say cronies—for only a few highly-favoured people are admitted to her drawing-room—completed the party.

Someone who was there has subsequently reported that the *Wirklich-Geheimrat*, who usually has little to say, laughed and joked the whole evening over what he called the coming surprise-packet in Morocco.

Tuesday, March 28th, 1905.

The Mukden disaster seems likely to have serious effects on Russia's financial credit.

On the third of this month, two Paris bankers, Hottinguer and Noetzlin, arrived in St. Petersburg to negotiate with the Imperial Government, at its special request, a loan of 600 million francs at 5 per cent. After a very heated discussion, Witte, the President of the Committee of Ministers, and the Finance Minister, Kokovtzov, had reluctantly agreed to a price of Frs. 91.25 (for the banks), whereas the last loan of April 29th, 1904, amounting to 800 million francs, had been effected at 94 francs (for the banks) and 99 francs (for the public).

But, on March 13th, when the overwhelming Japanese victory

at Mukden was reported, the French banks wired their delegates to break off the negotiations.

At the same time, the President of the Paris brokers, Verneuil, on instructions from the committee, sent Raffalovitch, the financial agent of the Russian Imperial Treasury in France, the following ultimatum: *The committee, feeling great concern about the market position of Russian bonds in Paris, has decided not to commit itself on the question of the participation of the Brokers' Association in the new loan and not to allow an official quotation unless the Russian Government places a monthly remittance of Frs. 250,000 at the disposal of the Russian Embassy for the duration of the war, to be distributed among the press as and when the Association requires.*

The Russian ministers, disgusted at such an insolent ultimatum, haughtily declined at first; but pressure of circumstances was too much for them and they had to capitulate.

To me, the dirtiest and most distasteful feature of the inner workings of the Franco-Russian alliance has been the constant blackmail by our press-lords of the Russian Imperial Treasury, with the alleged object of protecting Russian credit in the French market. And it is not only the newspaper proprietors who get their pound of flesh; politicians, some of them men of high standing in the parliamentary world, also participate.

This scandalous business, which dates from the earliest days of the Franco-Russian alliance and has become much more popular during the war in Manchuria, is in the hands of Arthur Raffalovitch, the financial agent of the Imperial Treasury, who is attached to the Russian Embassy. He is admittedly a remarkably clever man, with a great knowledge of economics, Corresponding Member of the Institute, etc. . . . He always leaves any particularly delicate or unpleasant negotiations to the *Okhrana* agents. The celebrated Ratchovsky used to be an expert at this sort of thing. He left good pupils behind him in Rataiev, Akim, Effront, Achelking and Manuilov.

There are times when the thought of all this dirty work—of which I cannot help knowing, though it is quite outside my control—makes me feel quite sick; but I console myself with the reflection that the greatest and noblest enterprises in history have always had to throw a sop to human greed. The Crusades were not inspired solely by religious idealism.

Thursday, March 30th, 1905.

The most striking feature of the fierce duel in progress in Russia between terrorism and the Imperial Government is the futility of police activities.

In spite of the formidable organization of the gendarmerie and the *Okhrana,* uncontrolled repressive methods, the frequency of capital sentences, the atrocious paraphernalia of prisons and penal settlements, the revolutionary party is growing in numbers and becoming more stubborn, fanatical and audacious every day. In the first place, it is recruiting members from ever wider circles. Its disciples are found in all ranks of society—not, as formerly, among the intellectuals and middle class only, but among workmen, peasants and soldiers. It has even made converts among the nobility and clergy. By its intensive propaganda it has created all over the Empire a vast network of secret committees of which the most enterprising and formidable are to be found in St. Petersburg, Moscow, Vilna, Ekaterinoslav, Kieff, Saratov, Nijni-Novgorod, Riazan, Kharkov, Tiflis, Tomsk and Irkutsk.

The heart and soul of the movement used to be a young Kiev chemist, Gregory Andreivitich Guerchuny. After organizing, in person, several attempts at assassination, he was arrested towards the end of 1903. He is now in the penal settlement at Nertschinski in Siberia. The present leaders of the party are Vladimir Lvovitch Burtzev—who came officially under my notice a few months ago —Evno Azev and Boris Savinkov, both of whom had a hand in the recent assassination of the Grand Duke Sergei but succeeded in escaping abroad, and two young women—regular furies— Tatiana Leontiev and Dora Brylliant. From a philosophical point of view, Russian terrorism seems to me to be a curious case of collective psychosis and mental infection. The whole history of the Russians reveals their extreme susceptibility to mass suggestion. In no other country do psychic waves diffuse so easily and in no other country are the masses so rapidly infected by faiths, hopes, enthusiasms, passions, fears and hatreds. Conversely, no country is less accessible to the force of pure reasoning.

I am forced to the conclusion that Russian terrorism, with its veneer of noble-mindedness, the audacity of its crimes, the secrecy of its workings, the astounding courage of its actors, the ruthless severity of the punishments they bring down upon themselves, its whole paraphernalia of mystery and horror, is enormously exciting to the melodramatic Russian imagination.

Eugene-Melchior de Vogüé, with whom I was recently discussing this fascinating question, quoted a passage he thought he had read in Dostoievsky's *The Idiots*; it seems to confirm my argument: "Our statesmen wear themselves out wondering where our nihilism has come from. It has not come from anywhere! The reason why nihilism has taken root among us is because we are all nihilists at heart. . . ."

Friday, March 31st, 1905.

This morning the *Hamburg*, with the Emperor William on board, anchored in Tangier harbour at nine o'clock.

The Kaiser landed about half-past eleven.

After listening to the address of welcome made to him by an envoy in the name of the Sultan, he rode on horseback to the German Legation where about twenty members of the German colony were awaiting him. On arrival, he drew himself up to his full height and said: "It gives me great pleasure to greet you as the gallant pioneers of German commerce who are helping me to maintain and develop the interests of the Fatherland *in a free country.*"

The foreign diplomats, ministers and chargés d'affaires were then admitted one by one to pay their respects to him.

The duty of representing us in this act of international courtesy devolved on Count René de Chérisey, Second Secretary of our legation, who performed it with his usual tact and composure. After a few polite commonplaces, the Emperor clicked his heels and thundered out, emphasizing every word: "Yes, Monsieur, Morocco is a very fine country, especially from the commercial point of view. So I hope that the nations of Europe will know how to safeguard their economic interests here. Speaking personally, I am determined to see that German commercial interests are respected." On this, he bade Chérisey farewell.

The official programme of the imperial visit comprised various items, the most important of which was a reception at the Kasbah. But for some reason which we do not know at the moment, William returned straight to the quay from his legation and went on board immediately. A few minutes later the *Hamburg* sailed for Gibraltar.

Saturday, April 1st, 1905.

Great agitation in Paris. Even the most intelligent people, men like Francis Charmes, are very uneasy in their minds. The opposition is indulging in alarmist language.

How will Delcassé handle it all? Will there be a German Fashoda? My faith in his skill remains unshaken.

If nothing fresh crops up, the situation will gradually improve. But, with an impulsive creature like the Kaiser, anything may happen. He is so highly strung, so apt to say something which our honour cannot let us ignore, or to do something which suddenly faces us with the irreparable.

Sunday, April 2nd, 1905.

Delcassé's composure in this crisis is admirable. As always on such occasions, he retires into his shell, takes refuge in stubborn silence, cancels all his appointments, shuts himself up in his flat and practically refuses to see anyone.

But, on the rare occasions when I have been able to get near him, I have found him perfectly calm but equally determined.

In fact, he sounded positively cheerful as he said: "All things considered, I'm not sorry about William's trumpet-blast at Tangier. Nothing could have a more salutary effect on the English. . . . If William had showed his annoyance with us by some tirade at Metz or Strasburg, the English would have taken no notice. But for a German ship to come and fly the Hohenzollern standard off the Moroccan coast, right opposite Gibraltar—do you think the English can stand that? You can be quite certain that many of them are turning their eyes towards France now! . . ."

Monday, April 3rd, 1905.

During the last few days, the papers have been publishing the announcement of the Franco-British naval demonstration which the British Government suggested on March 22nd.

The public here has received the news with indifference or apprehension.

Tuesday, April 4th, 1905.

The situation is still dangerous. But I see one favourable omen—

the fact that the Emperor William, during his short stay in Tangier, seemed to have realized the seriousness of his action.

The programme arranged with the Maghzen provided that the Emperor should land from the *Hamburg* at 7.30 in the morning and go to the German Legation to meet the Diplomatic Corps and receive an address of welcome from the German colony. The Sultan's envoy was then to give a luncheon in his honour at the Kasbah, overlooking the town. He was to spend the afternoon watching a brilliant gymkhana by Moroccan *caids* and re-embark at five. . . . A few furlongs from where the *Hamburg* was anchored, a French cruiser, the *Du Chayla*, has been moored for several months. In accordance with the rules of maritime etiquette, the commander of this vessel, Captain Debon, immediately went on board the *Hamburg* to pay his respects to the Emperor. After giving him a friendly welcome, the Kaiser asked him:

"Do you know Tangier harbour well?"

"Yes, Sire. I've been stationed here for over three months."

"Well then, tell me honestly, from one sailor to another,—do you think it's dangerous for me to land?"

"Oh no, Sire. Not at all. It's a little choppy, but not rough and there isn't much wind."

The Kaiser did not answer for a moment; then, with an absorbed air, he turned the conversation to technical naval matters. But suddenly he renewed his question:

"So you honestly think there's no danger in my landing?"

Captain Debon, somewhat taken aback at his persistence, firmly repeated:

"Not the slightest, Sire; the harbour's pretty calm today."

"What will it be like when I have to return at five?"

"Oh! Sire; I can't say eight hours ahead! I can only tell Your Majesty that at the moment I have no reason to think the weather will get worse."

After thanking him, the Emperor dismissed him. . . . Such a positive assurance should have made him decide to land at once, with the idea of reembarking earlier if the sea became rough. But he wasted two and a half hours hesitating and issuing contradictory orders. He ultimately landed at a quarter to twelve. A company of Moroccan soldiers, commanded by a French officer, formed a guard of honour on the quay. At the head of these men was the famous Caid Maclean, an English deserter, who has constituted himself our enemy. The Emperor, without waiting for the *sala-malecs,* quickly mounted his horse and rode to the German Legation. His face was sallow and he looked worried. While he was climbing the steep road which winds through the town, a few hooligans who had mingled with his escort began to cheer. William II leaned over to the Caid Maclean, who was walking beside his horse, and snapped out:

"Silence those people. My nerves are on edge."

At the legation, he made a pompous speech to the colony, solemnly avowing his determination to *'preserve the rights and interests of Germany in a free Morocco.'* When he reappeared, everyone noticed how his face had changed. At the same time, a great fuss and flurry was observed among his escort; officers hurried here and there; the Caid Maclean changed the formation of his troops and sent off messengers. Everyone was dumbfounded when it was learned that the Emperor would attend neither the luncheon at the Kasbah nor the display on the Marshan. Amidst a mournful silence, the procession hastily returned to the quay. William II embarked at once. Half an hour later, the *Hamburg* set sail.

Once again, William II has failed to follow up his actions to their logical conclusion.[1]

Wednesday, April 5th, 1905.

Radolin returned from Monte Carlo yesterday and put in an appearance at Delcassé's diplomatic audience. A few minutes earlier, he had received from his friend Holstein a wire in code warning him to be *extremely* cautious in all his dealings with Delcassé. By the way, a Berlin paper has recently written: "Prince von Radolin is no match for M. Delcassé. To keep him in Paris is simply thrusting the lamb into the wolf's jaws!"

---

[1] The same mental and physiological 'reflex' was observed on August 1st, 1914, directly after William II had declared war on the Emperor Nicholas. Six hours after his ambassador had solemnly made the fatal pronouncement, William made an incomprehensible appeal to the Tsar's love of peace—as if he had suddenly realized the irrevocability of his action and still hoped to save the situation by this message *in extremis.*

Admiral von Tirpitz, Secretary of State of the Imperial Navy, is another witness to the physical and moral depression of William whenever he had to make vital decisions: "I have never seen such a haggard, tragic face as the Emperor's at that time. . . ." Field-Marshal Waldersee had foretold this years before, when he wrote: "God preserve us from war so long as William II is on the throne, for his nerves will fail him at once."

Radolin looked worried and his face was drawn, but neither he nor Delcassé breathed a word about Morocco.

Thursday, April 6th, 1905.

Edward VII, on his way to Marseilles to join Queen Alexandra, met the President of the Republic between Pierrefitte-Stains and the Gare de Lyon. Delcassé was not present at their interview.

The King and the President conversed alone for half an hour. Speaking of the Moroccan affair, Edward VII said:

"My nephew's attitude is quite inexplicable. He doesn't know what he's doing or what he wants; as a matter of fact, his ministers entirely disagree with him . . . the crisis you're passing through is only a storm and it will blow over."

"Yes," replied the President, "but it may do a great deal of damage while it's blowing over."

No specific, practical question was discussed.

Friday, April 7th, 1905.

After taking three weeks to cross the Indian Ocean, Admiral Rojdestvensky's squadron, comprising forty-eight vessels, has just rounded the western extremity of Sumatra; it passed Malacca yesterday, will be off Singapore tomorrow, and, a few hours later, will enter the China Seas. These particulars were supplied to me by Captain Malo-Lefebvre,[1] who added:

"I imagine that after such a lengthy voyage, which must have been pretty trying at times, the squadron will need a prolonged rest. It's obviously the coast of Annam that they're making for, so we're going to be faced with some nice little problems from the neutrality point of view. . . . But that, my dear sir, is not my department, but yours."

When I told Delcassé that the Russian *Armada* would reach the China Seas tomorrow and would doubtless stop on the Annam coast, he almost jumped out of his skin:

"Why is it going to stop on the coast of Annam?"

"Geographically, it can shelter nowhere else before it enters the zone of operations."

---

[1] Captain Malo-Lefebvre had taken Captain de Freycinet's place on the Secret War Committee some time previously.

He started again, recovered his composure and summed up the situation quite unemotionally:

"Now that the theater of war is so near, can we possibly go on offering the Russian squadron hospitality in French waters without flagrantly violating international law? In the case of Gaboon and Madagascar, our complacence might be excused at a pinch; but isn't it quite unthinkable in the case of Annam? . . . Won't Japan answer with an ultimatum? What a howl the socialists would set up! We mustn't forget that French sentiment is not at all pro-Russian at the moment. . . . But what can I do? Refuse Admiral Rojdestvensky an anchorage and thus rob him of any chance of taking in supplies, waiting for his reinforcements and fitting his squadron out for the critical encounter? It would be as good as driving him to a catastrophe for which the Russian people would certainly hold us exclusively responsible?"

I agreed, and he continued:

"After all, I don't know *officially* where the Russian Squadron is. I read in the papers that it is reported off Malacca. Where is it going? I've not the slightest idea. . . . You tell me it is going to put in at the coast of Annam. You may be right—but *you* don't know anything either . . . *officially*. If, in the next few days, I get an *official* telegram from Saigon or Hué, advising me that Russian ships are anchored in such and such a bay on the coast of Annam, well! I shall do what international law requires —order them to sail away within the regulation twenty-four hours. But I've an idea that it will take at least a week to fix things up between Paris and Indo-China by telegram, establish the truth of the information and dispatch the necessary order to Admiral Rojdestvensky—possibly even longer. So the Russian squadron will have plenty of time to take in fresh supplies before we compel it to leave our waters. . . . You understand, don't you?"

And there our conversation suddenly ended.

Saturday, April 8th, 1905.

I lunched with the Grand Duke Paul and Countess von Hohenfelsen: no other guests.

We talked about the position in Russia. My host and hostess said they were more optimistic. Since the disaster at Mukden, there has been a great improvement in the national *morale*. All eyes and hopes are now fixed on Rojdestvensky's squadron; no one doubts that by a great naval victory it can still deprive Japan of the command of the sea—the sole reason for her superiority—after which the Russian armies will soon take a brilliant revenge. The Emperor too is as determined as ever to continue the war. . . . The position at home is also improving. The ministers are beginning to have a better idea of their task—to apply the strong hand, and ruthlessly. Ratchkovsky, restored to favour, is doing wonders. That's the way to handle Russia!

"So M. Delcassé's instinct was right last month when he refused to intervene and advise the Emperor to make peace?"

He replied with good grace:

"Yes," he frankly admitted. "M. Delcassé was wiser than I . . . But you mustn't forget that I had specific instructions from the Empress Marie-Feodorovna."

He asked me about Admiral Rojdestvensky's squadron:

"It was reported in the Straits of Malacca yesterday," I replied, "so I assume that it is now rounding the Singapore Peninsula and will enter the China Seas tomorrow. . . . The decisive hour won't be long."

The Grand Duke and Madame von Hohenfelsen crossed themselves several times.

"*Gospodi pomilui!* Lord have mercy on us!"

Monday, April 10th, 1905.

Bihourd has dined with Bülow; but our piteous ambassador was unable either to find or create an opportunity for discussing the Moroccan question.

Relations between France and Germany are becoming more strained every day.

Delcassé's plan is to defer any discussion with Germany on the subject of Morocco until the suggestion of a conference has finally fallen through. He thinks that he could then open serious negotiations with Berlin without losing face.

But the question is whether public opinion—which is getting out of hand—will give him time to indulge in such slow and risky tactics?

Tuesday, April 11th, 1905.

Paul Cambon has just arrived from London and came to see me this morning. He shares my anxieties and has promised to see Delcassé tomorrow before his diplomatic audience and advise him to broach the question of Morocco quite frankly with Radolin.

One of our secret agents, who has sources of information in the Wilhelmstrasse, has advised us that the visit of the Emperor William to Tangier was not merely suggested to him, but positively insisted upon, by the Chancellor, Bülow, under continuous pressure from the mysterious Holstein.

The Kaiser is said to have resisted for quite a long time, because he realized instinctively that such a step might have serious consequences. But, as usual, he gave way in the end. Thus, once again, the imperial puppet's antics have been inspired by the acrimonious temper and inflexible will of the *Éminence Grise*.[1]

Friday, April 14th, 1905.

Delcassé dined at the German Embassy last night.

Under pressure from the President of the Council, he has decided to discuss Morocco with Radolin.

"I can't understand," he said, "why your Press is so angry with us about Morocco. How on earth can they profess to believe the statement that Germany knew nothing about the Anglo-French and Franco-Spanish Agreements of 1904? You will remember that I gave you the main outline of those arrangements."

"Yes, I know," replied the ambassador, "and I certainly did not fail to report what you told me to Berlin. But what the German papers are denying is that there was any *official* communication."

Delcassé insisted that he had been perfectly open in the explanations he volunteered to the Imperial Chancery both through Radolin in March, 1904 and through Bihourd in April and October of the same year. He concluded:

"I find myself compelled to ask you this question: Is there really a misunderstanding? If so, you already know from my last speech in the Chamber that I am only too anxious to clear it up."

[1] Prince von Bülow admits in his *Memoirs* (Vol. II, p. 135), that he had to bring great pressure to bear on the Emperor before he could induce him to accept the suggestion of calling at Tangier. Four months later, when William was having a dispute with his Chancellor, he wrote: "Do not forget that it was you who staged my Tangier visit, quite against my wishes and in order to bring off a *coup* in your Moroccan policy. . . ."

Radolin looked very embarrassed and stammered that he had no instructions to enable him to answer that question; he would refer it to Berlin.

Sunday, April 16th, 1905.

Radovitz, the German Ambassador at Madrid, is moving heaven and earth to persuade Alfonso to abandon his idea of visiting Paris in the near future. In his conversations with his foreign colleagues, Spanish journalists and the Premier, Maura, he affects to be highly apprehensive about the risks to which the young King will be exposed in France—outrages from the socialists, the daggers and bombs of anarchists, etc. . . . He even went so far as to communicate his fears to the Queen-Mother, appealing to her feelings as a mother and her pride as an ex-queen. But the courageous Dona Maria-Christina assumed her haughtiest air and promptly changed the subject.

Monday, April 17th, 1905.

From one of our officers employed at the Diégo-Suarez naval base, and who was sent on some commission to Passandaya Bay, Captain Malo-Lefebvre has received some curious and depressing news of the attitude and outlook of the Russian officers and men a few days before they sailed for the China Seas.

Staffs and subordinates were animated by the same feeling—resignation to the inevitable, with a conviction that it would be in vain.

But this fatalistic submission to an unhappy fate did not conflict with a grim determination to make a fight of it. They were involved in a futile adventure from which there was no issue; but they would go through with it, though they knew they would never return; they would all perish and their families and Russia would never see them again! . . . If only they could get it over quickly! . . .

Among the staffs these gloomy forebodings were mingled with bitter criticisms and furious diatribes against the Admiralty at St. Petersburg, "the imbeciles and traitors who would have to answer to God some day for this ill-fated expedition."

But, high above the officers and men, there stood out a lofty and noble figure—Admiral Rojdestvensky. Always calm and collected, keeping the secrets of his loneliness and gnawing anxieties locked up in his own bosom, he was the very incarnation of courage, energy and determination—the living embodiment of the stimulating words he addressed quite recently to his squadron: "Do not forget that the Emperor and Russia always have their eyes fixed on us!"

Tuesday, April 18th, 1905.

There is no lack of prophets who profess to understand present-day Russia and foretell the vast, obscure, social tragedy for which the scene is being set among the masses, behind the superb *décor* and Byzantine paraphernalia of Tsarism. Among those who seem the most far-sighted, or at any rate have made the greatest impression on me, I should mention Bakunin, Herzen, Prince Kropotkin, Tolstoi, Dostoievsky and—first of the line and their master in the art of intuitive divination—Joseph de Maistre.

Let me quote what the author of the *Soirées de St. Petersburg* wrote on August 27th, 1811:

> *Everything conspires to convince me that governments of our pattern are not suited to Russia . . . if the Russian nation came to understand and acquire a taste for our insidious, new-fangled notions, if some scholarly Pugatchev were to found a sect and the masses, shaken in their beliefs, started a revolution in the European style, I have no words to describe what we might well apprehend:*
>
> *. . . Bella, horrida bella*
> *Et multo Nevam spumantem sanguine cerno.*

Wednesday, April 19th, 1905.

At the Palais Bourbon, this morning, Jaurès violently attacked Delcassé on his Moroccan policy. His main charge was that he had refused to talk to Germany. The minister's reply was a series of brief, inconsistent and evasive sentences. The Chamber gave them a very chilly reception. As there was no resolution, no vote was taken; but after the sitting, members of all parties were going about saying: "Delcassé is finished."

On April 14th, the Russian squadron anchored off the coast of Annam, in Kam-ranh Bay, 200 miles north of Saigon. It was immediately joined by four *Hamburg-Amerika colliers*.

As I was reporting this news to Delcassé, he swiftly interrupted me:

"You say the Russian ships were at Kam-ranh yesterday. Are they still there now? I don't know, neither do you. . . . Anyhow, where's Kam-ranh? I've never heard of it; but I should be very surprised to hear that there are any French officials there."

"As a matter of fact, there are no French authorities in Kam-ranh Bay; that's just why the Russian ships have chosen it. But it's common knowledge that they are in our waters. If there aren't any French officials at Kam-ranh, there are French cruisers at Saigon; we can't pretend we are unable to police our coasts. To-morrow, if not today, you may be handed an insolent summons by the Japanese Minister, Motono. The socialists will promptly interpolate you, and then . . ."

"Well, what are we to do?"

"Wire to Saigon for one of our cruisers to find Admiral Rojdestvensky immediately and request him to put to sea again within twenty-four hours . . . of course, we needn't be inquisitive about where the Russian squadron is going next. If it anchors in another bay on the coast of Annam after leaving Kam-ranh, we will again dispatch a cruiser to ask it to leave. In that way we shall be respecting the letter, if not the spirit, of international law and giving Admiral Rojdestvensky time to join up with the battleships which Admiral Nebogatoff is bringing him by the Suez Canal route.

"When are these battleships due to arrive?"

"Not for a fortnight."

"I shall never be able to keep public opinion quiet for as long as that! . . . And what a rumpus the English public will make! . . . It's too risky! . . . The Russian Squadron must leave Indo-China as soon as possible and never come back!"

"Obviously you have the right to forbid Admiral Rojdestvensky to put in anywhere else on the coast of Indo-China; you are even entitled to have him followed by French cruisers until he has gone north. But, if he goes off to meet the enemy without getting all his supplies and joining up with his reinforcements, he is heading straight for a catastrophe for which Russia will hold us exclusively responsible."

"Very well. I've decided what I'm going to do. Go to the Ministry of Marine and ask them to cable instructions to Saigon to send a cruiser to request Admiral Rojdestvensky, as tactfully as possible, to put to sea again within twenty-four hours. Having done so, the cruiser is to return to Saigon without worrying about where the Russian squadron is going next."

"We might give this ticklish job to the commander of our Indo-China division, Admiral de Jonquières. I know him slightly. He's a man of great ingenuity and tact."

"That's a good idea. Send Admiral de Jonquières himself; it's my personal wish. . . . When you've finished with the Ministry of Marine, go straight to the Japanese Legation and tell M. Motono from me what I've just decided. Don't lose a minute."

At the Ministry I soon fixed up with Captain Malo-Lefebvre the instructions to be issued to Admiral de Jonquières.

At the Japanese Legation I was received by Motono, whose politeness was more frigid, and his expression more inscrutable, than ever. I told him that we did not know exactly where the Russian squadron was; that it was extremely difficult for us to police the long, rocky and almost uninhabited coast between Touran and Saigon, but we should none the less make every effort to carry out our international obligations. I wound up by telling him of the instructions we had just issued to Admiral de Jonquières.

Motono heard me out without a word of comment. When I had finished he fixed me with his stern, cynical eyes:

"I shall take the liberty of asking you in the near future what steps the Government of the Republic has taken to carry on its administrative functions on the coast of Annam. Please remind M. Delcassé of what I said yesterday: *An exceptionally critical time is coming for my country*."

Thursday, April 20th, 1905.

Delcassé seems to be inclined to resign; the article published in the *Temps*, this evening, makes him feel that he can no longer rely even on the support of the moderates.

The public and the Chamber are making their usual mistake; they blindly accept the German side of the story—inconsistent and fallacious though it is—and refuse to see the strong points of the French argument.

Georges Louis and I have been chatting about Delcassé's possible resignation. Our view is that, if he only had his own interests to consider, Delcassé should retire at once, as he no longer has sufficient backing to emerge with honour from the Franco-German dispute. . . . But, from the point of view of the national interest, he should stay where he is; we have no other statesman so well qualified to play the subtle, supple game which is called for if we are gradually to entice Germany into the necessary arrangements. We have plenty more good trumps in our hands!

Friday, April 21st, 1905.

The Russian squadrons' call at Kam-ranh has raised a tremendous storm in Japan against France. Every day, our tenderness towards the 'national enemy' is denounced at innumerable meetings. The English Press echoes the cry and is calling on the Balfour Cabinet to address a forcible protest to the French Government. The *Standard* even goes so far as to write: "The situation is becoming critical."

We assume that Admiral Rojdestvensky will raise anchor tomorrow.

Chapter XIII

April 22nd—May 29th, 1905

Saturday, April 22nd, 1905.

As HE warned me last night, Delcassé handed his resignation to the President of the Republic this morning.

M. Loubet 'put the greatest pressure on him' to retain his portfolio. Rouvier was present at the time and spoke to the same effect. Delcassé has therefore withdrawn his resignation.

The minister sent for me at five o'clock. He told me briefly what occurred at the Élysée this morning, and then said with considerable feeling:

"I want you, as a personal favour, to leave for Berlin tonight. You will inform Bihourd of the position. . . . There was a spasm of weakness in the Chamber and among the public, but they have recovered. We are re-forming our front against Germany and will continue our tactics. . . . After my conversation with Radolin on April 13th, I think I cannot make any more advances to Germany. If she doesn't wish to negotiate, so much the worse; I shall go my own way just the same. . . . But I am anxious one day to be able to prove to the cabinets of Europe and public opinion in France that the assertion that I kept Germany entirely in the dark regarding my Morocco policy is fundamentally untrue. I am therefore going to prepare a Yellow Book for publication. You will settle with Bihourd what corrections or omissions should be made in the dispatches I received from him. . . . Lastly, I want you to study on the spot what measures and combinations are still open to me; so stay in Berlin as long as you think necessary. . . . If you can possibly see X . . . without compromising yourself, question him thoroughly. Try to find out what Bülow's object is and how far he's influenced by Holstein. . . . You know my ideas and intentions. I can only say; do your best . . . and thank you!"

I left Paris at ten p.m.

Easter Sunday, April 23rd, 1905.
I crossed Germany from Aix-la-Chapelle to Berlin, *via* Hildes-
heim and Magdeburg.

A dull morning. A layer of snow had fallen and covered the
slopes of the Hartz Mountains as high as Gosslaw. Afternoon
sunny.

The whole population in Sunday best—like the beginning of
Faust. Every moment I was struck by the prosperity of the country.
The thought occurred to me: "Surely a country which looks so
wealthy and contented must be pacific? Would the Morocco dispute be enough to rouse the nation's warlike instincts?"

I arrived at the Potsdam Station at Berlin at six in the evening.

Bihourd was waiting for me on the platform. I was dumbfounded when he greeted me with the words:

"Well, have you brought me instructions to give way? If we
continue Delcassé's policy, it means war! . . . Yes, war! . . .
And then we're lost!"

"Come, come!" I said to calm him.

But he went on, his voice quivering:

"The way we're going, war is inevitable! . . . You've no idea
of Germany's strength! . . . We cannot . . . I repeat: if we don't
give in at once, it means war and we shall be done for!"

All this was said—very loudly—on the station platform, in the
midst of 300 people and only two paces from the footman with his
tricolour cockade which made us conspicuous!

In the carriage, Bihourd harped back again to his pathetic refrain. He is obsessed by the memories of July, 1870, terrified and
stupefied by the haughty disdain of the German Government.
Bülow can do what he likes with him.

He is really not responsible for his actions. His hands shake, his
breathing is short, his conversation jerky. He blinks his eyelids the
whole time and looks worried. All this shows only too clearly that
his hypersensitivity is caused by cardiac-neurosis. As soon as we
arrived at the Embassy, he did not give me a moment's rest but
took me to his study and bombarded me with questions.

"The best way of avoiding war," I told him, "is to look as if one
was not afraid of it. Of course the memories of July, 1870, must
be particularly vivid here, in the *Pariser Platz* Embassy, but still
you must face them with quiet calm, and a more open mind."

He came back to his refrain once more:

"The French Government ought to agree to an international conference; otherwise it means war."

"There can no longer be any question of a conference, as Delcassé has torpedoed the idea."

"Then the German Government will persist in its claims. Nothing will stop it, not even the prospect of a war."

"And do you think Germany will also like the idea of finding England against her?"

"England? . . . She's against us, she won't support us!"

"No, you're wrong. She isn't against us but on our side. The British Government has definitely told us that in the present crisis Germany's success would mean nothing less than admission of her supremacy and it is determined to oppose it."

"No, no," said Bihourd, in great agitation, "no, the prospect of having to fight England would not deter Germany. We must negotiate without delay, otherwise war is inevitable, inevitable!"

I ultimately told the ambassador the special object of my visit —the Yellow Book—and asked him:

"Isn't there some roundabout way of starting conversations? I know that over the main entrance in the Wilhelmstrasse the words, 'French Government not admitted here,' are written. But surely there are some side-doors, hidden doors?"

"No—none . . . You can't imagine how difficult my work is. The Emperor has boycotted me. The Chancellor and Secretary of State have given me the cold shoulder and nothing will make them change their tactics."

"Can't you talk to some financier, like Friedländer, Schwabach or Mendelssohn, or with politicians?"

"No, it's hopeless."

"Yet if Prince von Donnersmarck had been in Paris I should have gone to see him and I swear he would have talked to me."

I feel pretty confident that even in the days of the terrible Bismarck, the Saint Valliers, the Courcels and the Herbettes found ways of talking to people. But Bihourd is completely paralysed by the frigid inflexibility of Bülow and Richthofen.

The ambassador had an engagement, made several days earlier, to dine in town and left me to the care of the Counsellor, Prinet. I spent the evening with him.

He discussed the situation quite reasonably and unemotionally.
His opinion may be summed up as follows:

"The Berlin Cabinet is adamant over the Morocco question.
They are extremely exasperated by the failure of the conference
suggestion and by Delcassé's remaining in office. They won't stop
at war . . . unless we show a more conciliatory attitude."

Monday, April 24th, 1905.
I talked to the ambassador again this morning. He is even more
frantic than yesterday.

As the St. Petersburg courier leaves at noon for Paris, I am
sending Georges Louis a few lines to let him know my first impressions: I ended: 'Of course I understand that the *Pariser Platz*
Embassy has particularly vivid memories of July, 1870, but I do
wish it would look at them with greater calm, resolution and a
more open mind.'

In the afternoon I went for a walk in Berlin. Everyone was out
of doors as it is Easter Monday. Since January, 1899, the last time
I was here, there is a marked increase of wealth—lush, cosy wealth,
all very bourgeois—no elegance or refinement.

At five o'clock I worked with Bihourd and tried in vain to revive him. He refuses to hand Mühlberg, the Under-Secretary of
State, (whom he is seeing tomorrow), our file of diplomatic correspondence which we propose to incorporate in a Yellow Book:

"He won't accept them," he said. "The German Government
considers that the question whether it has been properly notified
of the Anglo-French and Franco-Spanish Agreements is closed.
When I last talked to Mühlberg, he asked me for the record of
the conversation between Delcassé and Radolin on April 13th, 1905;
I'm going to send it him by letter. Tomorrow I shall try to hand
him personally the text of the agreement of March 23, 1904—but
nothing more."

In the evening I dined at the Embassy with my young colleagues.

Tuesday, April 25th, 1905.
I have had a talk with Commandant de Sugny, the naval attaché,
and Major de Laguiche, the military attaché. Both of them are
serious-minded, level-headed and well informed. Sugny is *persona*

gratissima with the Emperor, who talks to him a good deal. Laguiche, a son-in-law of Prince Augustus von Arenberg, owes his
excellent reception by Berlin society to his advantages of family
and wealth. He spent a long time in Vienna before coming here—
an experience which has given him a host of connections and a
vast field of observation.

I questioned these two officers separately, but both gave me the
same answer:

Germany is not seeking war, but she will not hesitate to go to
war if she sees no other means of safeguarding her rights and
interests in Morocco. The armed intervention of England will not
stop her. Public opinion is placid enough at the moment, but
within a week the government could rouse it to the degree required.
In military circles it is thought that this is a favourable moment
for a fight with France. Roon and Moltke would undoubtedly be
of that opinion. If a Crown Council were held today Schlieffen
would not take a different view. . . . The rulers of the secondary
states would be neither consulted nor listened to if the Emperor
decided on war. The order for mobilization would be carried out
on the nail all over the Empire.

Sugny confirmed my view that the Tangier affair had greatly
exceeded the Emperor's anticipations. Admiral von Senden-Bibran
had mentioned the visit to him in terms which simply emphasized
the Emperor's desire to remind us—but with no element of challenge—that the matter had not been settled with Germany.

Bihourd, returning from the secretariat, said to me:

"I've seen Mühlberg and tried to give him the text of the conversation between Delcassé and Radolin on March 23rd, 1904: I
insisted that this document was referred to in the conversation of
April 13th, 1905, and was therefore complementary to it. Mühlberg assumed his chilliest manner and replied that the Imperial
Government was sufficiently apprised of the conversation of 1904
through the report made by Radolin at that time. He abruptly
switched off to the Cretan insurrection. . . . You can see that
they are refusing even to discuss Morocco."

At six o'clock I had a call from X . . . He is a man of few
words, but they are to the point:

"The influence of Holstein," he said, "is greater than ever. The
temperament of both the Emperor and the Chancellor is such

that, if left to themselves, they would favour a *rapprochement* with France. But the terrible *Éminence Grise* is tireless in stirring them up and, whenever they look like resisting him, the Chief of the General Staff immediately comes to the rescue. . . ."

I left Berlin at 11 p.m.

Wednesday, April 26th, 1905.

I reached Paris at 4 p.m. and was received by Delcassé at five o'clock.

I gave him an account of my mission, concluding as follows:

"From a practical point of view, this is the result I've arrived at: (1) for reasons referable partly to the organization of the Imperial Chancery and partly to the personality of our ambassador, you must expect nothing from the French Embassy in Berlin if there is to be diplomatic action; (2) in the position in which you are, you cannot hope for success against Germany as she will not stop at war and French public opinion will not follow you. You must therefore find some means of opening negotiations—not directly, as Germany declines, but indirectly through the instrumentality of some third power, Russia, England or Italy."

Delcassé nearly jumped out of his skin and burst out:

"Take the initiative in opening negotiations, even indirect—not I! I made an advance to Germany on April 13th when I tried to start a conversation with Radolin. . . . I shan't try again. . . . Anyhow, I've got the best cards to play. The German Government's suggestion of a conference hasn't found an echo anywhere. Rome, Madrid, Vienna, Washington; it's failed everywhere. All Europe is on my side. England is backing me through thick and thin. She won't stop at war either. . . . No, indeed, it's not for me to open up negotiations. . . . I'm in a splendid position. You've no idea of the congratulations I've received on remaining in power. . . ."

He went on in the same strain for some time, patently intoxicated by the pleasure shown at the withdrawal of his resignation.

I resumed:

"Let me talk to you frankly; the situation is serious. It may well be that from the diplomatic point of view you have a real chance of success. But Germany can bring to bear one formidable argument which is outside diplomacy—war. You remind me of a very skilful chess player who would certainly win the game if his opponent was not quite prepared to bring his fist down on the board and scatter the pieces the moment he saw the game was lost. Your policy will be victorious *in theory*, but *in practice* we shall be beaten."

"Germany can't want war. Her present attitude is only bluff; she knows quite well that she'll have England against her. As I told you before, England will back us through thick and thin and she won't sign peace without us. . . . Do you really think that the Emperor William can calmly face the prospect of seeing his navy destroyed, his merchant marine ruined and his ports bombarded by the English Fleet?"

"The Emperor William certainly can't be indifferent to such a possibility. But the critical scene of action won't be the Baltic or the North Sea; the decisive front is from the Sambre to the Vosges. Thus the German Army will have plenty of time to crush us before England has time to send us even 20,000 men. . . . One last word, Minister. When I awoke near Cologne this morning, I thought of the nine army corps which would concentrate there with the object of reaching the valleys of the Aisne and Oise *via* Belgian territory, out-flanking our North-Eastern Army and marching straight on Paris. You remember the revelations of the *Avenger*. . . . As my train sped along the banks of the Meuse, I couldn't help thinking that German columns would pass that way. The gloomy reflections which have been haunting me make it my duty not to mince my words, and I'm not doing so."

"What is your conclusion?"

"I've just told you my conclusion. Try to ease the strained relations between France and Germany by indirect negotiations. Apply to Russia, England or Italy. Ask them to talk officially to Berlin and thus find a perfectly honourable way of enabling you to exchange explanations with Germany. If such tactics fail, through Germany's *intransigeance*, you will have at least proved the conciliatory spirit of your policy before the eyes of the world. Simultaneously, you'll get French public opinion behind you. At the moment it holds aloof, because it doesn't understand you and is swayed by agitation against you."

"Thank you. I'll think it over; come and see me tomorrow morning."

At that moment, a secretary came in to tell him that the

President of the Council, Rouvier, wanted to speak to him on the telephone.

Delcassé went into the next room, where the telephone was. A few minutes later he came back:

"The President of the Council is dining at the German Embassy tonight. He asked me if I had any new suggestion to make in case Prince Radolin mentions Morocco. . . . M. Rouvier and I now see eye to eye. This little incident will show you."

Yesterday evening, Delcassé sent our ambassador in Russia the following telegram:

> *The Emperor Nicholas has sent M. de Nelidov to convey to me his extreme satisfaction that I have found myself able to withdraw my resignation, 'because he knows that I am a tried and trusted friend of the allied nation of France.'*
>
> *When King Edward VII also learned of my resignation, he expressed his great anxiety to see me retain my office, owing to the frank and friendly relations he has with me. When he heard of my decision, he sent his congratulations.*

Thursday, April 27th, 1905.

I was with Delcassé at midday.

"I've just seen Paul Cambon," he said, "and told him of our conversation yesterday. He doesn't share your opinion; he's still convinced that Germany is bluffing."

Then, in the same breath:

"I've been thinking about indirect negotiations; I can't decide between the King of Italy and the Emperor of Russia as go-between. What's your idea?"

"I strongly favour the King of Italy. The Emperor of Russia is far from intelligent, unapproachable and has a strong dislike for England. Victor Emmanuel, on the other hand, is most intelligent and anyone can get at him any day. There is no one better than he to play the English card, which is the best trump in your game."

Delcassé then showed me the note which Sir Francis Bertie handed him on April 25th, a note in which the British Government states that it regards Germany's policy as 'unreasonable' and promises the French Government its firm support.

This afternoon our cypher department deciphered a telegram from Radolin to Bülow in which he recounts the conversation he had with Rouvier yesterday evening:

The President of the Council told me that he had a warm admiration for our Emperor. Twice running, he said that France wanted peace at any price and no longer harboured any idea of revenge. He asked me if an agreement on the subject of Morocco could not be arrived at between us by direct negotiations between the cabinets, in the form of a circular, etc. . . .

A few minutes before dinner, one of M. Rouvier's confidantes had called upon me. He assured me that the President of the Council would only be too willing to let Delcassé go.

Here is another deciphered telegram from Radolin, which gives us the key to the article published on April 26th on the front page of a great Paris newspaper:

M. de X——, an ex-officer, called on me to say: "The governing director of the great paper for which I write from time to time is all-powerful; he makes and unmakes ministers. He regards the policy of M. Delcassé as bad and is ready to overthrow him in order to pave the way for a rapprochement with Germany. Do you think you could get me an audience with the Emperor William with a view to a sensational article?"

Only two days ago I realized the strength of the government of the Reich's defences, and how closely its approaches are guarded. . . . And look what I find here!

Friday, April 28th, 1905.

The day before yesterday, Geoffray, our chargé d'affaires in London, received from Sir Thomas Sanderson, the Permanent Under-Secretary of State, a private letter which ended thus: *I am certain that Lord Lansdowne will learn with great satisfaction that M. Delcassé is to retain his post. His retirement would have been a European calamity.*

Our cypher department has brought me an odd telegram from Berlin. Bülow, greatly preoccupied with the imminent visit of the King of England to the President of the Republic, has sent the following instructions to Radolin:

If the King of England mentions Morocco, you will reply:
"He has not been able to appreciate how England, in treating
with France in the matter of Morocco, could dispose of Ger-
many's interests in that country. The German Government is
proposing a conference at which all the powers can insist upon
their rights."

I have discussed this telegram with Delcassé. I begged him to
draw the King's attention to the fact that our present dispute with
Germany is only an episode in a long premeditated plan; by way
of reminder I summarized the indices, the landmarks, by which
this plan has been gradually revealed to us:

(1) The strange warning given by the Emperor William to the
King of the Belgians (January 28th, 1904).
(2) Suggestive confidences of a German diplomat (February
4th, 1904).
(3) The underhand activities of the Emperor William, at
Tokyo no less than St. Petersburg, to provoke the outbreak
of war between Russia and Japan with a view to paralysing
the Franco-Russian alliance.
(4) The revelations of the *Avenger* (April 15th, 1904) which
shows that the German General Staff has prepared a great
offensive against France, a vast enveloping movement
which will drive everything before it as it develops on
Belgian territory astride the Meuse and sweeps down to
the valley of the Oise, thus turning our system of fortifications in the East.
(5) The intrigues of the Emperor William with the Emperor
Nicholas against England and Prince Radolin's confidential
remark to the Spanish Ambassador, Marquis del Muni
(November 2nd, 1904).
(6) The Emperor William's theatrical behaviour at Tangier
(March 31st, 1905).

I added:
"If war broke out in the next month, what a weight of responsibility would be yours if you had not done everything possible to
avert a catastrophe which had been heralded by such obvious
signs!"

Delcassé's only reply was a gloomy silence. But, as I was leaving, his eyes suddenly flashed and he burst out with cutting contempt:

"You read Rouvier's conversation with the German Ambassador yesterday, didn't you? . . . Monstrous! Infamous! That man would sell France for a gamble on the Stock Exchange!"

Saturday, April 29th, 1905.

The *Éminence Grise* of the Wilhelmstrasse, the policeman-diplomat, Baron von Holstein, has telegraphed to Radolin to prepare him for any talk he may have with the King of England, who arrives tomorrow.

We will not give way. We can agree only to a conference, i.e., a discussion with all the powers and not with France. I believe that England is forcing France into a conflict with Germany, a conflict in which she will have everything to gain in the way of extending her interests in the Far East and elsewhere. I know from a reliable source, though at second-hand, that England will not go beyond diplomatic support to France. France has let herself tread on our toes. If we allow it, she will do it again at once. So we shall not give way.

Sunday, April 30th, 1905.

After leaving the bay of Kam-ranh on April 22nd, the Russian squadron has put out to sea, steering north-east, while the *Descartes* was returning to Saigon.

But, a few hours later, Admiral Rojdestvensky made all his ships put about and proceed to anchor in the bay of Van-fong, fifty miles to the north of Kam-ranh.

The moment the news was received in Paris, a telegram from the Minister of Marine started a repetition of the other day's performance. For the second time, Admiral de Jonquières will invite the Russian squadron to leave our shores.

At the ministerial council, the resumption of this ingenious scenario led to a hot debate. Rouvier, the President of the Council, was furious at 'the impertinence of this Russian Fleet in using our coast as a base of operations.' He thumped his fist on the table and burst out:

"We've had enough this time. I insist upon the Minister for

Foreign Affairs making strong representations to St. Petersburg to insure that Admiral Rojdestvensky shall receive immediate orders to leave Indo-China and not come back!"

As usually happens when his colleagues venture to question him, 'the Minister for Foreign Affairs' took refuge in a surly silence. But he none the less sent me to Nelidov "to beg him to draw the Emperor's immediate attention to the risks to which we are exposing ourselves by our connivance at the actions of the Russian Fleet."

Monday, May 1st, 1905.

When calling at Palermo, the Emperor William said to his friend, the Duke of Andria:

"So my trip to Tangier has made France grind her teeth, has it? Germany can't be treated like a snail. . . . We shall make a private treaty with Morocco and in it I shall preserve our rights. . . ."

The news we are getting from Fez confirms this threat in every way.

On the one hand, the Sultan and his ministers, egged on by the German Consul, have just announced that they desire to submit to a European conference our demand that they shall carry out the reforms.

In addition, Count von Tattenbach, formerly German envoy to Portugal, a crony of the famous Holstein and recently accredited to Mulai Abd-el-Aziz, is very shortly going to the Court of the Sharif.

Tuesday, May 2nd, 1905.

On April 30th there was a banquet at the Élysée in honour of the King of England.

The King talked to Radolin for thirty-five minutes after dinner. Several times he was seen to shake his head in response to something said by the ambassador. We know nothing definite about the conversation.

Delcassé himself had long talks with the King on Sunday and Monday. He says that he is 'very satisfied' with the statements Edward VII has made to him; but he is singularly reticent about the nature and details of those statements—from which I conclude that the King has strongly advised him to do everything he can to try to bring about better relations with Germany.

Thursday, May 4th, 1905.

Delcassé lunched with Edward VII yesterday at the house of the Marquise de Breteuil. The King kept him for an hour's talk.

This conversation has relieved his nerves and restored his composure. At any rate it would appear so, judging by his instructions, drafted *manu propria*, to Saint-René Taillandier. He begins by saying: "Point out to the *Maghzen* that the present crisis is temporary; that in future, as now, Morocco will have France for neighbour and must therefore always reckon with her. . . ." Such words are as wise as they are beyond criticism. But in the first glow of writing, the minister had added: "Tell the *Maghzen* that, if he yields to the dangerous counsels of Germany, we will make him feel the weight of our arm on the Algerian frontier. . . ." A gentle protest from Georges Louis was enough to make him cut this imprudent phrase out of his telegram.

Yesterday evening, there was a concert at the house of the Marquise de Pracomtal. The German Embassy was there in force —Radolin and the Princess, Flotow, Lucius and his wife, Mercy, the Bavarian Chargé d'Affaires, and his wife who is Radolin's daughter. The coolness of their reception made a great impression on them. After twenty minutes, Radolin, realizing that the company meant to keep them in quarantine, nodded to the Princess and went home.

Friday, May 5th, 1905.

Right up to yesterday, Delcassé seemed as resolute and confident as ever, but today he has that worried look that betokens bad times. Since Edward VII went back he is left to his own resources; single-handed he must face his ministerial colleagues who loath him and lobby against him in the Chambers.

When Georges Louis went to get his signature to various documents this evening, he found him sullen, dejected, concealing his thoughts. The minister hardly spoke save to storm at the vast network of conspiracy, intrigue and treachery he sees about him. So Louis advised me to find some excuse to call on him and cheer him up.

But I would rather not see him today; what I should have to tell him is anything but cheering.

At four o'clock I had a visit from our Chief of Staff. He came to tell me that he must leave tomorrow for a tour of inspection in the Alps; he wanted to know whether he had not better postpone his journey in view of the present situation. As he will only be away a week, I replied that I did not anticipate that anything serious would happen in that short time. Then we went on to talk of the position in which France would find herself in face of a sudden attack by Germany.

I suddenly realized that this was really what General Pendézec wanted to discuss with me. In a trembling voice, he said:

"A sudden attack by Germany! We couldn't resist it! It would be worse than 1870! Our defeat would be even more rapid and complete! Just think a minute, my friend: in the first place, not a vestige of help from Russia! What should we have with which to meet the 1,500,000 men of the German Army? 900,000 at the outside—of which 100,000, possibly 200,000, would refuse to take the field. You've read what Hervé said at the last socialist meeting: *Our reply to the mobilization order will be the reservists' strike.* . . . And look at the high command! It's much worse still! The generalissimo, General Brugère, has resigned and there has been no fresh appointment. Of our Eastern armies, two are without commanders. And all this thanks to the insufferable conceit of Brugère, who wants to be an unchallenged leader in war because he thinks he's another Napoleon. . . . That's the present situation in a nutshell! Isn't it ghastly?"

He passed his hand across his fat face, which was damp with sweat and tears.

I burst out in indignation:

"What's this? Here we are on the fifth of May, 1905, faced with the peril of a war with Germany, and you, the Chief of Staff, tell me that we have no C. in C. and that two of our armies are without commanders!"

"I say so because it's true!"

"And in these circumstances you accept the responsibility of preparing for war!"

"I've completely covered myself by writing personally to the Minister to emphasize the immense dangers of the situation. Berteaux showed my letter to the President of the Republic, who

confined himself to the single remark: *'That letter's very extreme!*
And that's how things were left. . . . My God, what a shame!' "

Just as Pendézec was leaving, General Moulin was announced.
He has just come back from St. Petersburg.

When I was left alone with Moulin, I asked him:

"If Germany attacks us in the near future, what help would
our Russian ally be able to give us?"

"We couldn't hope for any help from our Russian ally for
three years at least. And I think those three years will stretch to
eight, ten, or fifteen years if, as I very much fear, the disastrous end
of the war in the Far East leads to the utter collapse of Tsarism."

His diagnosis of the internal condition of Russia is far worse
than anything I imagined. He foretells a general revolt of the
Russian people; Zemstky Sobors forming themselves into regional
conventions; mob fury venting itself in terrible violence; all the
Jews massacred; Poland, Finland and the Baltic Provinces ravaged
with fire and sword; the mujiks egged on by their priests and
demanding the partition of land; famine, anarchy and a tornado
of atrocities such as has not been seen since the times of Boris
Godunov and Pugacheff.

Georges Louis and I have been discussing the views—only too
well-founded, alas!—expressed by General Pendézec and General
Moulin. The conclusion at which we have arrived is as follows:

We cannot doubt that there is a good deal of 'bluff' in the
menacing attitude of Germany. But even less doubtful is the
inferiority of our position from a military point of view. Yet, however obvious the possibility of a German attack may be, we still
have some excellent cards to play—particularly the English card.
These cards may prove decisive and Delcassé is the only man
capable of playing them like a master. It is thus essential, and
essential now, that he should work in concert with London in
finding some means of persuading Germany to abandon her
hectoring tactics. What is equally important is that he should
be more open with his fellow ministers about the difficulties of
his task, get them to back him up and, if necessary, arrange for
someone to interpellate him in the Chamber. In the last resort,
he must make the country his judge.

Sunday, May 7th, 1905.

The Baron de Courcel (formerly our ambassador in Berlin

and London) who has had two talks with Edward VII—at the
Élysée and the house of the Marquise de Jaucourt—tells me
privately that the King made a very sensible suggestion: "You
must settle this Moroccan business quickly. Sponge it off. . . .
Schwamm darüber! . . . Schwamm darüber!"

Monday, May 8th, 1905.

For the third time, the Russian squadron has taken refuge in
the territorial waters of Annam; it does not want to leave before
it is joined by Admiral Nebogatov's Division which left Libau on
February 16th.

Five days ago, Admiral de Jonquières, who came from Saigon
on the *Guichen,* courteously requested Admiral Rojdestvensky to
leave Van-fong within twenty-four hours. The next day, all the
ships raised anchor and appeared to be making for the Straits of
Formosa. But the *Guichen* was barely out of sight before they
turned about and came back to their previous anchorage in the
bay of Van-fong.

Tuesday, May 9th, 1905.

Prince von Donnersmarck is passing through Paris. I should very
much have liked to resume the talk I had with him last year
(May 2nd, 1904); it seems wiser to keep away.

But Francis Charmes met him yesterday at the house of Pallain,
Governor of the Banque de France, and he wrote to me at once to
say that he would come this afternoon to report his conversation.

As I am under the impression that he will ask me for news for
his article of May 15th in the *Revue des Deux Mondes,* I went
to the minister for instructions.

Delcassé gave me a jovial reception—in marked contrast to
his bloodshot eyes and haggard face. He professed entire confidence in the approaching success of the course on which he has
decided; he repeated several times:

"Germany is committing fault after fault, one folly after another,
in her tactics. Anyone can see that William and his diplomats are
anything but formidable. . . ."

He declined point blank when I suggested taking Francis
Charmes to him so that he could question him about his conversation with Donnersmarck:

"I know all about what Herr von Donnersmarck said and am

fully aware of the purpose for which this ex-spy of Bismarck has come to Paris. He's come for help—and got it! I even know where he's got it from! How shameful, how humiliating it all is!"

I then discovered what is at the back of his mind, and all the bitterness and righteous anger which are making his blood boil. He was too excited to remain seated and began to stride up and down. He began a furious diatribe against the President of the Council in a voice which was quite beyond control:

"This wretched Rouvier, who approves all I do to my face and then tries to knife me the moment my back's turned. . . . He's the traitor who had the audacity to say to the German Ambassador: *I don't care a damn about Alsace and Lorraine. Would you like me to sacrifice Delcassé?* The Frankfurt and Berlin stock exchanges must be mighty pleased with him. . . . Herr von Donnersmarck can't say enough in his praise. You'll soon see that these two villains are up to some game against me."

Exhaustion brought him to a stop.

At half-past three I received Francis Charmes.

"Yesterday," he said, "Prince von Donnersmarck, whom I've known a long time, talked to me in his usual frank, unguarded way. Our conversation lasted nearly an hour."

This is a summary of what the Prince told Francis Charmes: "The Moroccan question, taken by itself, could be settled in five minutes; the plans of France and the interests of Germany in no way conflict in Morocco. . . . But the present dispute is something much bigger than Morocco. The real issue is the general relations between France and Germany. We are tired of your treating us as if we did not exist. You talk familiarly with all the powers; you never want to talk to us. You receive all the foreign sovereigns in Paris—the only exception is the Emperor William. In all the great capitals you are represented by ambassadors who are men of high distinction; but your representative in Berlin is a dull-witted puppet with whom any conversation is impossible. . . . You've got to change all that. What we want from you is not merely less strained relations, but friendship—real friendship. If we don't become real friends, you'll make an alliance with England. . . . We won't tolerate an Anglo-French alliance at any price—*at any price*. We've let you have your Franco-Russian alliance. But not another!"

Francis Charmes wittily replied to Donnersmarck:

"You've a very odd way of persuading us into the friendship you want."

"If we hadn't hit hard, you would never have understood," the Prince answered.

After a pause, he concluded with a remark which was half warning and half threat:

"The present incident will be critical. When it's over, the relations between our two countries will be either cordial or damaged beyond repair."

As Prince von Donnersmarck was leaving the Banque de France with Charmes, he added:

"I saw M. Rouvier, yesterday. . . . There's a real statesman for you! He really has a business head!"

Francis Charmes makes no secret of the fact that he is much upset by this conversation:

"We can't go on ignoring Germany," he said; "we must draw closer to her. Delcassé's remaining in office is a national danger. Ponder Donnersmarck's words. Speaking personally, I summarize them in the formula: *Friendship or war*. . . . For goodness' sake, get Delcassé to resign voluntarily."

"I certainly shan't advise Delcassé to retire voluntarily. If the breach between him and his colleagues widens, I would sooner advise him to bring the matter up in the Chamber; the least he can do is to make the country his judge."

Wednesday, May 10th, 1905.

Delcassé was exultant when I saw him this morning and reported the conversation between Francis Charmes and Prince von Donnersmarck:

"What you're saying is the best justification of my policy; it has been my stock retort to people who begged me to be more communicative and friendly with Germany. . . . Francis Charmes' summary of Donnersmarck's words is very accurate; the Emperor William is offering us *friendship or war*! What sort of friendship can you imagine between France and Germany while the gulf of Alsace-Lorraine lies between us? At any rate, friendship is possible today on one condition and one condition only—that the French nation brings itself to tell the German nation what the President of the Council told His Excellency Prince von Radolin: *I don't care a damn about Alsace and Lorraine! Let's forget the past and embrace!* France hasn't yet fallen quite so low! William is mistaken. . . ."

We have at length managed to get the Russian squadron away from the coast of Annam; it will not return. It intends to cruise off Cape Varella until it is joined, very shortly, by Admiral Nebogatov's Division. The junction will be effected in the open sea.

Thursday, May 11th, 1905.

I lunched at the Comtesse d'Haussonville's with Gustave Schlumberger and Pierre de Nolhac. They were all equally worried. D'Haussonville said to me:

"I'm haunted by memories of 1870; I can't sleep. . . ."

During the day, I had a call from Barrère, who has arrived from Rome and has just had a conference with Delcassé.

He is very annoyed—and rightly—with the 'idiotic pessimism' he finds everywhere, even among those like Francis Charmes whom he regarded as really stable and sensible. His own view is that there is nothing tragic about the situation.

"William II's arrogance," he said, "is nothing but bluff. The Germans may be stupid, but they are not stupid enough to quarrel with France over a question which interests them as little as the Morocco business."

"It's quite likely that William II's arrogance is only bluff—but it isn't a certainty."

I then told Barrère of the alarming indications we have had from Germany during the last year, since Russia has been at grips with Japan. I laid particular stress on the revelations of the *Avenger:*

"After such warnings," I said, "we have no right to deceive ourselves about Germany's designs against us. What is at stake is nothing less than our national existence."

"Take my word for it," Barrère continued, "the danger exists in the imagination of Paris rather than Berlin. If public opinion here had behaved itself better, Germany would have moderated her tone."

"Yes, but public opinion here would have been less fainthearted if Delcassé had not been continuously attacked by his

colleagues in the Cabinet, particularly the President of the Council.
. . . I believe you know Rouvier?"

"I knew him in Gambetta's time. Gambetta had a high opinion
of his fine intellect and strength of character."

"Go and see him and try to open his eyes."

"I'll call on him tomorrow."

Friday, May 12th, 1905.

Yielding to the fervid entreaties of Barrère, Georges Louis and
myself, Delcassé has instructed Paul Cambon to put the plain question to Lansdowne: "If Germany, using the Moroccan business as
a pretext, attacks France, can we count on England to come to our
support with all her forces?"

The fact that the Russian squadron has lingered so long on the
coast of Annam, has caused a howl of rage in Japan and irritated
public opinion in England. *The Times* writes—with a great show of
truth: *What would France say if, in the course of a war in which
her national future was at stake, the fleet of her enemies found
asylum in English harbours. Monsieur Delcassé must find a speedy
way out of this dangerous situation, which could soon assume a
most critical and lamentable character.*

This article has made a very strong impression on Delcassé; when
I entered his room today, he burst out:

"What on earth is this Russian squadron waiting for? . . .
Surely they don't want us to kick them out? . . ."

I calmed him down at once:

"Don't worry, Minister; I think I can assure you that Admiral
Rojdestvensky's squadron has at last been joined by the ships of
Admiral Nebogatov; the junction was effected outside our territorial
waters, off Cape Padaran. . . . We assume that the fleet is now
proceeding towards Formosa. So we need not bother about it any
more."

"How long do you think it will be before it meets the Japanese
fleet?"

"Commander Malo-Lefebvre thinks the meeting cannot take
place for twelve days or so. But of course we are in complete ignorance as to Admiral Togo's intentions."

Saturday, May 13th, 1905.

During the last few days, an odd, anxious note has crept into the German press—as if they were beginning to appreciate the gravity of the crisis created by the provocative demonstration of the Emperor William at Tangier.

The *Berliner Tageblatt* and *Vossische Zeitung,* for instance, are already anticipating the failure of Tattenbach's mission: "We have embarked on this business rashly. . . . Thanks to the proximity of her Algerian possessions, France has *an unassailable position* in Morocco. . . . A direct understanding between Paris and Berlin would have been much better. . . ."

The *Hamburger Nachrichten,* Bismarck's old organ, in a prophetic vein sounds an even more critical note:

In the opinion of our government, we must achieve a success in Morocco at any price. Otherwise the prestige of the Empire will be seriously damaged, as Germany will have suffered a humiliating reverse the first time she showed her teeth since Bismarck's day.

This means that Germany must be rushed into war to make good the shortcomings of her diplomacy. The German nation does not share that view; it does not consider the question of Morocco of sufficient importance to justify a war which would be a great misfortune, whatever its outcome.

And what would happen, if, despite all our optimistic anticipations, Germany were beaten? Who would shoulder this appalling responsibility?

The government has forgotten that, in all diplomatic operations, if one has no intention of ultimately drawing the sword, it is essential to avoid being faced with the alternative of either retracing one's steps or mobilizing an army. As it is impossible to go to war over Morocco, it would have been better for us to avoid committing ourselves deeply by the Emperor's visit to Tangier, and to confine ourselves to diplomatic negotiations.

What will actually happen if France persists in damaging our interests by her peaceful penetration? We shall be faced with the alternative of either yielding or declaring war on her. We shall then realize what a mistake we have made.

Monday, May 15th, 1905.

I had Barrère, Georges Louis, Francis Charmes and Commander de Sugny to lunch with me today.

Our naval attaché is returning to Berlin this evening. As he will be seeing Admiral Von Senden-Bibran (a confidante to whom the Emperor William pays more attention than to anyone else) immediately on his arrival, we gave him our candid opinion, which can be summed up in the following conclusions:

(1) Our military situation and Russia's distress compel us to improve our relations with Germany.
(2) Delcassé now realizes that this is essential.
(3) It is a matter of relaxing the tension, and no more.
(4) Anglo-French friendship and the Franco-Russian alliance must remain the basis of our foreign policy.

Lord Lansdowne, who is anxious about the possibilities of war which are hovering over Europe, has recently sounded our ambassador in London 'about concluding a general *entente* between Great Britain and France in preparation for all eventualities.'

The matter was discussed this morning at the Élysée, at a council which was attended by President Loubet, Rouvier, Delcassé, Barrère and Paul Cambon.

After a short discussion, Rouvier emphatically opposed the opening of negotiations on any such lines. Several times he repeated to Paul Cambon:

"For heaven's sake, go no further with negotiations of that kind; if the Germans come to hear of them, they'll attack us at once."

Barrère, angry and disgusted, remarked to me very justly:

"Rouvier's chicken-heartedness will cost France dear! Every policy has its drawbacks; but a policy of fear is the most dangerous of all!"

"I agree. . . . To reject England's help at the present moment is sheer lunacy!"

Tuesday, May 16th, 1905.

The Russian *Armada* of fifty-nine ships (eight battleships, fourteen cruisers, three guardships, nine destroyers, sixteen transports, two hospital ships and seven auxiliary vessels) is now proceeding in a north-easterly direction, with the object of reaching Vladivostok by the Korean Straits.

We calculate that today it should be due off Cape Bojeador, the most northerly point of the Philippines.

Wednesday, May 17th, 1905.

Delcassé has started on a campaign of courtesy towards Germany.

The Government of the Republic is accordingly sending a special mission for the approaching marriage of the Crown Prince with Duchess Cecily of Mecklenburg-Schwerin.

As head of this mission, the choice lay between a civilian (perhaps the Baron de Courcel or Prince Auguste d'Arenberg) or one of our high military officers. A decision has been given in favour of the latter and General de Lacroix, Governor of Lyons and Commander of the XIVth Corps, has been selected. He is a friend of mine: a fine man with good brains and aristocratic manners—in a word the highest type of French officer. I suggested his name to Delcassé when I returned from Berlin last month.

Will politeness be enough to satisfy Germany? . . . No. She will regard it merely as a preamble, a first success for her, a first capitulation on our part. Before long we shall really have to get down to the dispute.

Saturday, May 20th, 1905.

I dined at the house of the Marquis de Breteuil with Sir Francis Bertie, the English Ambassador, Lady Feodorovna Bertie, the Duchess of Manchester, the Marquis and Marquise de Jaucourt, the Comtesse Joachim Murat, the Comtesse Jacques de Pourtalès, the Baron de Courcel, Admiral Duperré, the Comte de Kerjégu, etc.

In the smoking-room, Sir Francis Bertie, jovial and impulsive as ever, suddenly remarked to Courcel and myself:

"It's not enough to have created the *entente cordiale;* we must give it muscles and the wherewithal to show its strength. We shall never save the cause of peace until the brawlers and trouble-makers in Berlin are afraid of us. . . ."

I took the master of the house into a corner to question him about King Edward's recent conversations with Delcassé.

The British Sovereign and the Marquis de Breteuil have been

close friends for over twenty-five years. They were boon companions in their youth and since then their friendship has always had its serious side. I know from a reliable source that Edward has a very high opinion of his French friend, whom he regards as possessing all those qualities—courage, honour, conscience, a cool head, tact and natural nobility—which in his eyes form the make-up of the perfect gentleman. I had thus little doubt that he had reported, in broad outline at least, his conversations with Delcassé.

"Yes," Breteuil said to me, "the King told me the general sense of his observations to your minister. He added: *I authorize you to make such use of them as you may think necessary, but be very discreet.* You, my dear Paléologue, are the first and only person to whom I shall repeat Edward VII's statements, as in case of need it will be your task to clarify or confirm M. Delcassé's recollection. . . . The King finally said to him: *Your Moroccan policy is beyond reproach from the point of view of international law. So carry on with it resolutely, on your present lines. But at the same time, use all your skill to improve your relations with Germany a bit; my government will give you every assistance in its power. . . . Otherwise, France might suddenly find herself in a serious position.* These words of the King seem to me the essence of wisdom. Don't you agree?"

"Indeed, they are. . . . But didn't the King go on to say what England would do if France, as the result of German provocation, found herself compelled to resort to arms? Monsieur Delcassé struck me as having returned from his conversation with Edward VII with a feeling of perfect certainty that in such an eventuality Britain would come to our help with all her forces."

"I'm morally certain that that is King Edward's private opinion, but, in view of his habitual caution and sense of propriety, I find it hard to believe that he said anything which his ministers alone have the right to say. I have always known him very anxious not to exceed his constitutional functions." [1]

---

[1] By way of illustrating the affectionate intimacy between the Marquis de Breteuil and the royal family of England, let me record that in March, 1912, King George V asked him, 'as a personal favour,' to have the Prince of Wales, who was then seventeen and a half, at his home in Paris 'for four or five months,' and 'teach him all about France.' A few days later, the young prince took up residence at the Hotel Breteuil, in the Avenue du Bois-de-Boulogne, and led the same life as his host's sons—in accordance with the express wish of his father.

Sunday, May 21st, 1905.

I lunched with Eugène-Melchior de Vogüé; only his wife and son were present.

"You know," he said, "that I went through the 1870 campaign. During the last few weeks, I have been haunted by evil memories of those days. I can already see our armies beaten, Paris in the grip of revolution, France dismembered."

"Your imagination is running away with you! My own doesn't work so fast and is certainly less lugubrious."

"But, between ourselves, *cher ami* (I swear I won't repeat what you say), do you think we might wake up one morning and find ourselves at war with Germany?"

"Any morning. . . . You're going too fast again. Sticking to facts and probable contingencies, I consider that the aggressive policy of the Emperor William may well result in such relations between France and Germany that a single 'incident' may ignite the powder. But, honestly, I am not under the impression that a Franco-German war is inevitable from this day forward."

Monday, May 22nd, 1905.

I have often admired Delcassé's genius for getting accurate information of all the intrigues in progress against him in the lobbies of the Senate, the Chamber and the leading organs of the press. He personally instructs and directs his informers—at least two of whom I know—and rewards them generously. *Arcana impera.* . . . This morning he remarked to me:

"You haven't the slightest idea of the disgusting and disloyal campaign which the President of the Council is conducting against me in Parliament. . . . He is going from group to group, denouncing me as a patriot-monomaniac, a self-deceiving germanophobe whose reasoning powers are out of control and leading the country to disaster. So his hearers are begging him to save France and get rid of me as soon as possible. Clemenceau, of course, backs him through thick and thin. . . . What a beastly business it all is. . . ."

From 3 to 6 p.m. I was in the chair at the meeting of the committee for preparations for war.

Whilst we were engaged in our usual discussion of all the complex and detailed problems before us, in view of the prospect of a great European war, I could not keep my thoughts away from the recent statements of Prince von Donnersmarck which Francis Charmes summarized only too well in the phrase: "The only choice which Germany now leaves us is *friendship or war*."

Tuesday, May 23rd, 1905.

The young King of Spain (he is only nineteen)[1] will be our guest in a few days; he has, in fact, decided that Paris shall be his first place of call in the round of ceremonial visits he is to pay to the great foreign capitals.

Alfonso XIII has often given us proof of his friendly feeling towards France; we have had another just lately. In a recent conversation with our ambassador, Jules Cambon, he said:

"I ascertained, quite casually but from an absolutely certain source, that Germany is actively expanding her armaments. She has ordered from Krupps 3,000 guns of a pattern very similar to yours. To keep this order a secret and prevent it from being debated in the Reichstag, 200,000,000 marks will be taken from the war funds."

I immediately reported this piece of information to General Pendézec:

"The King's confidential communication is only too accurate. We know that since April 15th last the Krupp works have received an order for 1,600 65 mm. guns of a pattern which undoubtedly resemble ours very strongly, and that Krupps have taken on 5,000 men to carry out the job at once. The Ehrhardt Works also have received an order for 1,400 guns and have taken on 3,000 hands. I assume that the entire replacement of the German artillery will be complete within twelve months. The Spring of 1906 will thus be a critical moment for relations between France and Germany. We've only just time to manufacture the field howitzers we lack; the German Army is particularly well off for them—twenty-four 125 mm. howitzers per army corps. It will cost us twenty-two million francs. . . ."

Thursday, May 25th, 1905.

Count von Tattenbach opened fire against us the moment he arrived at the court of the Sharif on the twelfth of this month.

---

[1] Born at Madrid on May 17th, 1886. Son of Alfonso XIII and Maria Cristina, Archduchess of Austria.

I learn from a reliable source that his text in his conversations with the Sultan and his ministers and notables, is as follows: "The Maghzen must not allow itself to be intimidated by the demands of the French plenipotentiaries. Monsieur Delcassé's Moroccan policy is personal to himself. It is meeting with strong opposition in the Chambers and even in the government, because France, which has lost her old military virtues, is resolved at any price not to embark upon an adventure which might very well end in a war with her powerful neighbour. . . . So the Sultan need not be afraid of asserting his right to unfettered sovereignty. Germany is ready to defend him. If he temporarily requires administrative or financial help, she will gladly supply it. All she asks in return is that he shall appeal to the powers to undertake the protection and guarantee of his independence. . . . The illustrious Morocco must not become simply a French department, like Tunis. . . ."

The Sultan's government seems to have been won over already by this insidious argument.

Discussing the above news with Delcassé, I added:

"Why Tattenbach's words seem particularly serious is because he is the confidante and henchman of Holstein; so I have no doubt that they were inspired by the *Éminence Grise* of the Wilhelmstrasse. Moreover, it is odd to see that the German Minister was accompanied to Fez by his wife, Countess von Tattenbach, and her sister, Countess von Schlippenbach. This Countess von Schlippenbach is Holstein's friend—almost the only friend he has. You know how he hates society, gets out of all court functions, and even the Emperor's personal invitations, and leads a solitary hermit existence, like a wild boar in its lair. To this churlish manner of life there are only two exceptions—Madame von Lebbin and Madame von Schlippenbach; these are the only friendships, or even feminine acquaintances, that he has."

Friday, May 26th, 1905.

After passing between Formosa and the Lin-Kin Islands, Admiral Rojdestvensky's squadron entered Japanese waters this morning. At any moment now, we may hear of the great naval battle on which Russia sets her last hopes.

Sunday, May 28th, 1905.

According to a telegram from Tokyo, the Japanese Fleet, commanded by Admiral Togo, is blocking the path of Admiral Rojdestvensky's squadron in the Korean Straits off the island of Tsu-shima. There is no news of the result of the battle.

Monday, May 29th, 1905.

The '2nd Squadron of the Pacific Ocean' has ceased to exist.

In the great and furious battle which took place on May 27th off the island of Tsu-shima, all the Russian ships were sunk or captured. The *Suvorov*, flying the broad pennant of Admiral Rojdestvensky, foundered and the Admiral, who was seriously wounded, was transferred at the last moment to another ship which had to strike its flag shortly afterwards. The 'Invincible Armada,' which Philip II launched against England to avenge the death of Mary Stuart and nip British naval power in the bud, did not suffer a more complete disaster off Gravelines. It has been said that the battle of July 29th, 1588 marked the end of Spanish predominance in Europe; history will no doubt record that the battle of May 27th, 1905, marks the end of Russian domination in Asia.

Commander de Freycinet has been in to give me some technical information. We felt sad as we talked of this unfortunate squadron which has given us so much work and trouble. We could not help realizing that its very defects, the patent absurdity of its adventure, the tragic destiny of which it was the prey, and conscious prey, the heroism it has none the less displayed even in its pessimism and resignation—all these things had brought it very close to our hearts.

Speaking of Admiral Togo's strategy, Commander Freycinet said: "We don't yet know enough about the various phases of the battle to be able to express an opinion. But the remarkable feature is the position selected by Admiral Togo and his plan of operations. He resisted the temptation to seek out the enemy at the corner of Singapore or off the coast of Annam or the Philippines, though public opinion in Japan, nerve-wracked and panic-stricken, implored him to do so. On the contrary, he placed his whole fleet in the Strait of Tsu-shima from which, using the Tuner Sea, he could promptly have caught up with the Russian squadron if the latter had tried to make Vladivostok by the Northern Straits. Lurking

THE BATTLE OF TSU-SHIMA, MAY 27TH, 1905

unseen in a region perfectly familiar to his ships, he has suddenly struck the great blow." [1]

[1] In September, 1905, our naval attaché in Japan, Commander Martini, went to see Admiral Rojdestvensky, who was interned as a prisoner of war at Kyoto.

Speaking of the strategy he had adopted to reach Vladivostok, the admiral frankly admitted that 'he did not expect to find the whole Japanese Fleet in the Strait of Tsu-shima: he thought that Admiral Togo had distributed his forces over the various channels leading to the Sea of Japan.'

Chapter XIV

MAY 30TH—JUNE 6TH, 1905

Tuesday, May 30th, 1905.

PUNCTUALLY at three o'clock, the King of Spain arrived at the Porte Dauphine Station, where he was met by the President of the Republic and the ministers.

A perfect day, with the sky as bright and clear as at midsummer.

All along the route, through the Avenue du Bois-de-Boulogne and the Avenue des Champs-Élysées, the crowd, promptly charmed by the bright and honest face of the young monarch, gave him a most vociferous welcome. Not a single discordant note. The socialists, who were proposing to boo 'the murderer' of their Spanish brothers, abstained from any demonstration.

At 3.30 the cavalcade stopped at the residence of the Minister for Foreign Affairs, which is the "palais royal" for the occasion.

After the President of the Republic had gone, Jules Cambon showed the King through the apartments prepared for him; only the *major domo*, the Duke of Sotomayor, was with them.

When they entered the bedroom, Alfonso XIII flung his arms round Jules Cambon's neck and embraced him fervently:

"I'm a very lucky man!" he cried. . . . "I shall never forget coming down the Champs-Élysées with the Paris crowd cheering me."

Then the ambassador showed him the furniture in the room and told him something about it. The pieces have been brought from Versailles, Compiègne and Fontainebleau and all are of historical interest, but the King paid most attention to those associated with Napoleon I. By way of concluding his observations, Jules Cambon pointed out a superb gilded bronze inkstand which once stood on the Emperor's table at the Tuileries:

"Admittedly, Napoleon I has left bitter memories behind him in Spain," he said. "But what does it matter now? He was a great captain and a great sovereign. You need not hesitate to dip your pen in his inkpot, sire."

The Duke of Sotomayor interrupted:

237

"Yes, sir, dip your pen in it without fear, and as often as possible. But may it never be to sign your abdication!"

There was a banquet at the Élysée Palace at eight o'clock.

Both coming and going, a huge and delighted crowd never stopped cheering the royal carriages. I have never seen the Paris crowd so pleased and excited since the great days of the Russian alliance and the memorable visit of Nicholas II in 1896. What a contrast to the outrageous demonstration to which Alfonso XII was treated in 1883.[1] As a matter of fact, one can never foretell the attitude of the Paris public. It is very impressionable, capricious, hyper-emotional and susceptible to the effects of mental contagion and mass suggestion.

Wednesday, May 31st, 1905.

While the King of Spain was making his entry into Paris yesterday, a very important dispatch came in from London. In it, Paul Cambon tells us that on the previous day, May 29th, Lord Lansdowne had sent him a letter inviting the French Government to discuss in advance with the British Government the complications to be apprehended during the somewhat anxious period through which we are at present passing.[2] In forwarding this document, the ambassador added: "The wording of this letter appears carefully studied; it has certainly received the approval of the Prime Minister, and perhaps the King, before being sent to me. It follows that Lord Lansdowne is realizing that he has spontaneously invited me to discuss in advance the measures to be taken to meet all eventualities."

[1] *In September, 1883, Alfonso XII, who was then at Berlin, received from William I the title of 'Honorary Colonel of the 15th Regiment of Prussian Uhlans,' stationed at Strasburg.*

A few days later, he came officially to Paris on a formal visit to the President of the Republic, Jules Grévy. From the moment of his arrival at the Gare du Nord, and all along the route to his Embassy, he was subjected to noisy insults and hostile demonstrations organized by the League of Patriots. His first thought was to return to Spain at once; but the President of the Republic called 'in the name of France' and made a very dignified appeal to him 'not to take a handful of scoundrels for the French nation. . . .' Touched by these words, Alfonso deferred his departure until the next day; he even accepted an invitation to dine at the Élysée.

[2] *I am not sure that I succeeded in making quite clear to you that there should be full and confidential discussion between the two governments, not so much in consequence of some act of unprovoked aggression on the part of another Power as in anticipation of any complications to be apprehended during the somewhat anxious period through which we are at present passing.*

Delcassé has immediately replied to Paul Cambon:

"Tell Lord Lansdowne that I also am of opinion that the two governments should show complete confidence in each other and that I am ready to join him in examining all the aspects of a situation which is undoubtedly somewhat anxious."

This morning, Delcassé instructed me, in view of his discussion with the President of the Council and the President of the Republic, to draw up a detailed memorandum on the problems with which we are faced as the result of Lord Lansdowne's approaches.

After a day taken up by receptions and celebrations, the King of Spain went to the Opera where Saint-Saëns' *Samson et Dalila* was given.

The theatre, with its galaxy of ladies and masses of flowers, presented a dazzling scene, a demonstration of the supreme refinement of Parisian luxury and taste.

From my box I had a good look at Alfonso XIII. He is very young and boyish; he seems thoroughly wide awake and looks eager and nice; his manner is free and easy. He was obviously entertained by all he was seeing and the fact that he himself was giving others something to look at; he could not keep still; his glass roved incessantly and he never stopped questioning the paternal President Loubet, who all but slumbered at his side. What would his ancestors, Charles V, Louis XIV, Philip V, Charles III, Ferdinand VII, say, if they could look down from heaven and see him celebrating his accession by beginning a round of visits under the aegis of the President of a Republic!

The performance finished with a ballet, *la Maladetta*. Alfonso had his opera-glasses fixed on the stage throughout.

I had hardly got home before a most unpleasant message came through on the telephone. As the royal carriages were turning the corner of the Rue de Rohan and the Rue de Rivoli, an anarchist threw a bomb under the vehicle in which Alfonso and President Loubet were riding. Neither was touched, but there were several casualties among the escort and the crowd.

Thursday, June 1st, 1905. Ascension.

Ascensit Dominus in cœlos cœlorum ad orientem. Alleluia!

By way of celebrating this holiest of holy days, I have not left the office, my time having been fully occupied with the following matters:

(1) The attempt on the life of the King of Spain (conference with a Commissioner from the *Sûreté Générale*);

(2) Germany's secret armaments (conference with the Director of War Intelligence).

(3) The overtures which England has just made to us with a view to an alliance (draft memorandum for Paul Cambon).

The police have discovered the author (and his accomplices) of the plot against Alfonso XIII to which he nearly fell a victim yesterday. Their arrest is imminent; they are all Spaniards. What a piece of luck for us that they are not French!

When the bomb exploded against the carriage, slightly damaging one of the wheels, the young King did not even tremble.

"I thought someone had let off some fireworks," he remarked to Loubet with a smile.

But, at that moment, the footman on the box turned round, looking very frightened:

"The horse Nero is wounded, *Monsieur le Président.*"

Then several of the cuirassiers' horses to right and left reared up or fell. But the colonel commanding the escort rapped out an order:

"Drive on! Drive on! Fast as you can go!" The King simply said to Loubet:

"*Monsieur le Président,* I shall never forget that I received my baptism of fire among the French cuirassiers."

As a matter of historical interest, I note that the intersection of the Rue de Rohan and the Rue de Rivoli is the exact scene of the 'infernal machine' affair on the 5th *Nivôse,* Year IX.

This morning, June 1st, notwithstanding the strain and excitement of yesterday, Alfonso XIII was up at seven o'clock to attend mass in a chapel of the church of Sainte Clotilde.

At eight o'clock he left the Gare de l'Est for the Camp of Châlons, to be present at the great artillery manœuvres.

This evening he dines at the Élysée.

At the court circle yesterday evening, the Emperor William sent for our naval attaché, Commander de Sugny, and, 'in a state of great excitement,' fired off questions about the 'overwhelming disaster to the Russian Fleet at Tsu-shima.' He then resumed his old 'gag' about the 'Yellow Peril.' Raising his voice and striking an attitude, he concluded with the remark: "All this should teach you to look after your navy. But not a bit of it! For ten years your Foreign Minister has refused to listen to anyone! Mark my word; it's better to be my friend than my enemy. . . . Tell them *that* at home!" Thereupon he departed with a theatrical gesture.

Friday, June 2nd, 1905.

Alfonso XIII spent the day at Saint-Cyr and Versailles.

The police are profitably pursuing their enquiries into the attempted assassination: they have already arrested four accomplices, all Spaniards; the prime culprit, a Catalan named Alexandro Farraz, will be caught before long.

Our Moroccan policy has just suffered a serious reverse; it is not difficult to see the hand of Germany in it.

Mulai Abd-el-Aziz has officially informed Saint-René Taillandier that, under pressure from the notables, he is reserving his decision about the reforms we have proposed on the ground that he intends first to submit them to those Powers which are diplomatically represented at his court.

The *Sharif* and his viziers and notables have thus become the tools of Germany.

Saturday, June 3rd, 1905.

Alfonso XIII's gay and open manner, and his warm-heartedness, accessibility and ready wit, are continuing to endear him to everyone he meets. He knows exactly how a crowned head should behave. What a contrast to poor Nicholas II who proved himself so *gauche* and mediocre and cut such a pitiable figure on his visits in 1896 and 1901!

Paul Cambon, fearing that Delcassé at bay may let himself be drawn into some risky adventure, has just sent him a 'private and personal letter' which is another monument to the sagacity of our ambassador. *Ex abundantia cautelæ* he sent this letter under cover of a note to myself, so that I can make a copy for the secret files in my keeping. Here is the letter:

London, June 1, 1905.

I have not yet spoken to Lord Lansdowne about his letter on the subject of a general understanding between our two governments.

. . . A conversation of this kind cannot be started before we have envisaged all its consequences or without M. Rouvier's consent.

You remember his last words as we left the Élysée:[1] "Above all, no negotiations!"

Unless he has completely changed his mind, it seems to me that it is difficult for you to assume the responsibility of replying to approaches which will lead us to an alliance.

What are we to reply to Lord Lansdowne if he suggests that, in view of the formidable possibilities, the Chiefs-of-Staff of our armies and navies shall meet?

This is the sort of proposal we shall get if we accept the idea of a general discussion too readily.

Your Cabinet colleagues and public opinion certainly would not follow you and you would be accused of bringing war on us.

So I think it is wiser to reply in terms cordial enough not to throw cold water on Lord Lansdowne's good intentions but vague enough to discourage any suggestion of immediate co-operation. . . .

PAUL CAMBON.

Sunday, June 4th, 1905.

Alfonso XIII has to leave Paris for Cherbourg this evening. The programme for his last day includes attendance at Auteuil Races and, by way of finale, a banquet followed by a reception at the Ministry for Foreign Affairs.

Just before a quarter to twelve, while the orchestra was playing the Spanish national anthem as the King was leaving, an officer of the cypher department, Béguin-Billecoq, sidled up to me and handed me "an urgent telegram, very serious, despatched from Rome at 8.45 p.m. this evening; the minister should no doubt know of it at once."

[1] After the Council Meeting at the Élysée on May 15th (Loubet, Rouvier, Delcassé, Paul Cambon and Barrère).

I beckoned Georges Louis and we read it together in a window recess; it informed us that the German Ambassador, Graf von Monts, had made the following declaration to the Foreign Minister, Tittoni:

The German Government has reason to believe that M. Saint-René Taillandier, now at Fez, has threatened the Sultan with the military occupation of certain points in Morocco with the object of compelling him to refuse Germany's demands. If the French troops carry out that threat by crossing the Moroccan frontier, the German troops will immediately cross the French frontier.

The moment the King had left, we read Barrère's telegram to Delcassé, who at once took Georges Louis and myself into his room. He was not in the least excited.

"This declaration is absurd! I have never delivered any sort of ultimatum to the Sultan of Morocco and Saint-René Taillandier is not the man to do a thing like that on his own initiative. . . . Germany's gone mad because she feels herself lost. . . . Anyhow, this telegram will make my task at the Cabinet meeting even more difficult. . . . Let's sleep on it!"

Monday, June 5th, 1905.

This morning, Delcassé communicated to the President of the Council yesterday's telegram in which our ambassador in Rome recorded Count von Monts' declaration to Tittoni.

Rouvier went straight to the Élysée where he said to the President of the Republic: "M. Delcassé is leading us into war. We can't work together any longer. Tomorrow morning I shall make the Council of Ministers choose between his policy and mine; this time tomorrow, one of us will be out of office."

It was Loubet himself who repeated this conversation to Delcassé; he went on to implore him to make some attempt at a *rapprochement* with Germany. Delcassé replied to the President of the Republic: "Tomorrow morning I also will make the Council of Ministers choose between M. Rouvier's policy and mine; this time tomorrow, one of us will be out of office."

I asked Delcassé:

"Are you really thinking of resigning after the Cabinet meeting? I thought you had decided to resign only after a full-dress debate in the Chambers—a bold course which I admit appealed to me greatly."

"Yes, I'd decided that way, but I've changed my mind. Rouvier has worked Parliament up against me so well that I would not be allowed to speak; I'd be hissed and rushed off the Tribune. Besides, I couldn't use my best argument—the English offer of an alliance— in a public debate. Don't worry; if I'm out of office tomorrow evening, I shall have only too speedy an opportunity of saying what I think *urbi et orbi*. . . . Let's forget it. I've an urgent job for you."

He then told me that 'from information received from a very reliable source,' the President of the Council will attack him about the English offer of an alliance and recommend that this offer should be declined. He went on:

"Rouvier recently had a call from an emissary of Bülow, who said: *The German Chancery knows for certain that Delcassé is negotiating a military and naval alliance with England. If that alliance is concluded, Germany will immediately declare war on France. . . . Before the British Fleet has time to do us any serious harm, we shall have shattered the French armies and the way to Paris will be at our mercy. In any event, France is rich enough to indemnify us by the terms of peace for all losses inflicted on our trade and shipping by the British Fleet. . . .* This emissary (I don't know his name) is a financier, duly accredited by Bülow. Simultaneously, Rouvier has received from Miquel, the First Secretary at the German Embassy, a note in which all the Emperor William's grievances against me are set forth."

Delcassé wound up by asking me to produce a score of documents he wants to re-read this evening, as he needs them to support his arguments at the Council meeting. I took them to him an hour later; I did not fail to include Paul Cambon's letter of June 1st.

As I was about to give him a word or two of explanation, he cut me short with a sardonic laugh:

"I have just learned the name of this important emissary who conveyed Germany's orders to the head of the French Government; it is Isaac R——; he's a dirty . . . . broker who deals in something or other in the lobbies of the Bourse. . . . Who can deny that Count von Bülow has made an excellent choice for the post of ambassador extraordinary to be accredited to Monsieur Rouvier. . . . And I can tell you something else I've just heard: When

Miquel handed the President of the Council his list of grievances, he remarked: *The Chancellor of the German Empire wants to have no further dealings with M. Delcassé. . . .* Don't forget those words, my dear Paléologue I'd like to have them on my tombstone! I couldn't wish for a better epitaph!"

Tuesday, June 6th, 1905.

At the close of the Cabinet meeting this morning, Delcassé announced his resignation; the President of the Republic accepted it at once.

He sent for me, and at two o'clock, I entered his room to collect the confidential or secret documents I gave him yesterday evening.

He did not hide his emotion; as a matter of fact, it brought the tears to his eyes. But of complaint, recrimination or invective there was none, and not a single bitter or hurtful word did he utter: his grief was calm and noble. This painful emotion revealed to me the very depths of his soul—something I had never seen before. It is not in his pride or his ambition that he is hurt—but in his patriotism, which is his whole religion.

I was equally moved myself. For seven years I have been living in daily contact with this minister, whom history will certainly class among the great servants of France and to whom I owe the best moments of my career.

He described the discussion which took place this morning at the official residence of the President of the Republic:

"I gave my colleagues a summary of the argument with which you are familiar. Germany, I told them, is threatening us. I consider that the threat is only bluff. We should therefore resist it. . . . Now, here is England offering us her alliance; I think we should accept it at once. Of two things, one; either Germany is bluffing—in which case she will be less likely to keep it up if she sees that England is ready to defend us—or else, contrary to my anticipations, she really means war—in which case the cooperation of the British Fleet is of vital importance to us. I wound up:

"*Consider very carefully the decision you are about to take, gentlemen. Today, England is boldly espousing our cause. But tomorrow, if she sees you weakening, trembling before the insolent bluster of William, she will lose all faith in you. Turning her batteries, she will soon arrange a reconciliation with Berlin, and our colonial empire will pay for it. . . .* The President and ministers heard me out without a single interruption; but I had only to look at them to realize that I was beating the air; they had made up their minds and condemned me even before hearing me. . . . Rouvier replied: *You must not think that Germany is bluffing. She is both worried and humiliated by the isolation in which you are keeping her and the ring you have forged around her. In our dispute with Morocco she sees an excellent opportunity of breaking this blockade, and to break it she will, if necessary, stop at nothing. . . . On the other hand, she knows that England has recently offered us a military and naval alliance* . . . I interrupted: *How comes Germany to know of an offer which is a dead secret? In London there are only three people in the know—the King, Balfour and Lansdowne; in this country, I haven't breathed a word except to the President of the Republic and yourself.* He blushed, knowing only too well what was in my mind; then he continued: *All I can tell you is that Germany knows of the English offer. . . . A few days ago, Chancellor Bülow sent one of his friends to tell me that, if we accept the British Government's proposal, Germany will hear of it at once and declare war on us. . . .* He dare not give the name of the filthy little outside broker, Isaac R——, who is the 'friend' in question. In a melodramatic voice he continued his discourse before the panic-stricken ministers: *Are we in a state to face a war with Germany? No! A thousand times no! Even with the help of the English Fleet we should walk into a catastrophe worse than 1870. . . . We should be criminals to plunge into such an adventure; France would never recover. . . .* I expected that the President of the Republic would at least make some pretence of supporting my argument: not a word. It only remained to close the discussion. The Council was unanimous against me."

I thanked him once again for the absolute confidence he had always shown in me:

"May I come and talk to you from time to time?"

"With pleasure! . . . I'll tell you what we'll soon be talking about—the enormous disillusionment in store for M. Rouvier in the Cabinet I'm just leaving. The Germans will make him pay dearly for his victory today."

Chapter XV

JUNE 7TH—JULY 8TH, 1905

Wednesday, June 7th, 1905.

MY NEW minister, Maurice Rouvier, sent for me this morning to show him some of the special files in my keeping (Franco-Russian alliance, pourparlers with the British Government, German military plans, etc.). Eyes sparkling, and speaking in his rapid, concise way, he gave me a warm welcome:

"I know all about your particular duties and how ably you discharge them. We must work well together. There's only one thing I ask: always be candid with me. Don't be afraid of hurting my feelings. You have my confidence straight away. . . . Let's go through those papers."

Then he changed his mind:

"Leave them with me until tomorrow. I'll read them at my leisure this evening. I've too much to do at the moment."

Before I left, I asked him how and when he wished me to keep him in touch with my special work.

"Don't let's tie ourselves down to routine," he said roguishly. "I shan't be here long . . . two or three weeks at the outside. As soon as I have improved our relations with Germany, I shall go back to the Ministry of Finance; I'm only a stop-gap here; I'm no diplomat; the money-bag is my job. . . . So if you want to talk to me or show me something, come along whenever you like; I can fit you in between two appointments. As regards your special duties, please carry on just as if M. Delcassé were still here; I shall be only too grateful."

I had Princess Lucien Murat, Comte and Comtesse Stanislas de Castellane, Jules Cambon and others to dine with me this evening. All my guests, except the judicious Cambon, think war is imminent. Stanislas de Castellane, who is a deputy, said:

"There is terrific excitement in the Chamber: they're oozing funk; everyone's anxiously wondering whether the sacrifice of Delcassé will be enough to assuage Germany's wrath."

247

I pointed out that the Chamber might have thought of that a little sooner, and helped myself to Delcassé's parting words to me:

"The Germans will make M. Rouvier pay dearly for the victory he has just won."

At half-past ten, we all went on to Comtesse Jean de Castellane's in the Rue Brignole, where a brilliant company had gathered—a savoury blend of politics and high life. The Duchesse de Dino, Talleyrand's last fount of inspiration, gazing down from the remote fastness of her portrait with her eager, nervous face, a battleground of passions and visions, seemed the presiding genius of the place.

Here and there guests collected in groups to argue, orate or get excited, while mysterious confabulations and grave asides went on in quiet corners. The same emotion was reflected in every face—anxiety, as if everyone had at last appreciated all the humiliation of the moment and the menace of the days to come.

Francis Charmes, with a face as long as a fiddle, drew me towards a window:

"Well," I said, "I hope you're satisfied! . . . Delcassé's gone."

"Anything but! I've just been reading a summary of the German Press in the *Journal des Débats*. There's a note of swagger and boasting in their comments which bodes ill for the future. . . . Yet Delcassé couldn't have hung on. Germany refused to deal with him any longer: Bülow told Rouvier so in confidence."

I continued:

"If M. Rouvier had had enough political and national sense, he ought to have extricated us from the crisis by the resignation of the whole Cabinet. By sacrificing his Foreign Minister at Germany's bidding, he has got into her clutches; he'll soon find out."

Thursday, June 8th, 1905.

Jules Cambon called on me on his return from a long talk with the President of the Council.

Rouvier told him about 'the secret warning' he received a few days ago from Bülow through a confidential emissary: *I know that the British Government is offering its alliance to the French Government. If the French Government accept—and I shall hear of it at once—we shall immediately declare war on France.* The President of the Council continued:

"My course of action has been dictated by this terrible warning. In spite of the great services rendered by M. Delcassé, I realized that it was impossible for me to continue working with him. Germany refuses to have any further dealings with him. They cannot, and never will, forgive him the humiliation he has inflicted upon them in trying to isolate them in the world. . . .

"As for England, you must know how I feel about her. I used to be a great personal friend of Gambetta; I'm still his fervent disciple—which is tantamount to saying that I'm a strong advocate of Franco-British friendship. But I won't go so far as an alliance. . . . No, thank you! No alliance, and no military and naval arrangements! I'm absolutely certain that Germany would fall upon us at once. And we shouldn't be in a position to resist her. We'd be down and out within three weeks."

The President of the Council concluded by telling Jules Cambon that he had no intention of remaining at the Foreign Office:

"As soon as I have improved our relations with Germany—and I don't think it will take long—I shall go back to the Ministry of Finance, which is my real job."

The Imperial Chancellor, Bernhardt, Count von Bülow, has not had to wait long for the reward for his share in Delcassé's resignation. He has been created 'Prince von Bülow' and is entitled to be addressed as 'Serene Highness.' Of course the German Press is showering magniloquent eulogies upon him.

Friday, June 9th, 1905.

General Pendézec has just been to tell me of the discussion the day before yesterday at the meeting of the Conseil Supérieur de la Guerre, with Berteaux presiding. The only business on the agenda was a brief revision of all the tasks facing the army leaders in case of general mobilization.

As regards the concentration, no change has been made in *Plan XV*. Brugère, the generalissimo, still declines to admit the possibility of a vast German offensive starting from Aix-la-Chapelle and developing astride the Meuse in the direction of Namur and Maubeuge. So our extreme wing is still placed at Bar-le-Duc.

I put a question to General Pendézec:

"What are General Brugère's reasons for disregarding the threat of a great German offensive through Belgium, seeing that our Intelligence has discovered every indication of a vast concentration in the Aix-la-Chapelle–Crefeld–Malmédy area?"

"General Brugère," he replied, "doesn't believe, that the potential effectives of the German Army are adequate to carry out an operation on such a scale. He thinks Germany is not capable of mobilizing enough combatant units at the outset to envelop the massed French armies from the north and east."

To this I retorted that we did not know too much about the potential numerical strength of the German armies. We may well get a nasty surprise over the *Ersatz* and reserve corps. To me, the really striking feature of the *Avenger's* disclosures is that they tally exactly with the present tendencies of German strategy. We happen to be very well informed on that subject: we have been able to lay hands on some most significant documents dealing with what is being taught at the General Staff conferences. Our enemies are never tired of preaching the virtues of vast enveloping movements as the only way of destroying one's adversary quickly. The idea of attacking France through Belgium is completely in accordance with that doctrine.

Saturday, June 10th, 1905.

The veil has been lifted. Germany has just shown her hand.

Rouvier made an appointment with Prince von Radolin today to discuss the Morocco question officially. He imagined that the conversation would be brief, simple, straightforward and friendly. He thought he saw the ambassador coming forward with outstretched hand and smiling face and fondly believed that agreement would be a matter of moments.

Quite the contrary! In his chilliest manner, Radolin dryly resumed the arguments he had used to Delcassé:

"The Imperial Government wishes the Morocco question to be brought before a European Conference."

"It would be far better for France and Germany to settle their Morocco dispute direct," the astounded Rouvier replied. "It would not take us two long to come to terms; a conference would then be superfluous."

"No, the Imperial Government absolutely insists on a conference," Radolin repeated, even more frigidly.

Rouvier, unable to conceal his extreme agitation, then endeavoured to prove that if the Moroccan question were brought before an international tribunal before France and Germany had come to a preliminary agreement, the dispute might become a very serious matter. He wound up with some heat:

"Believe me, Prince; in the interests of both our countries we must try to reach an agreement direct. No conference."

"Very well," said the ambassador and rose to go. "Very well! If there's to be no conference, we shall insist that no change is made in the *status quo* in Morocco."

As he reached the doorway, he added:

"It is also my duty to tell you, Monsieur le Président, that if France were to attempt to modify the *status quo* in Morocco in any way *Germany would be behind the Sultan Moulai Abd-el-Aziz with all her forces.*"

A few minutes after Prince von Radolin had left, Rouvier's private secretary, the faithful Combalat, assuming from the silence that the visitor had gone, opened the door a trifle; he had been told to bring in the financier, Henri Bousquet (who had an urgent message from Baron Jacques de Gunzbourg), as soon as possible and show him up by the back way. The pair entered the *Sanctus sanctorum* and saw the minister hunched over his desk (Vergennes' desk!), his elbows on the table, his chin cupped in his hands and a haggard, hopeless look in his eyes.

Combalat and Bousquet were themselves nonplussed and hesitated. Rouvier, however, beckoned to them to come closer and, in a quivering voice, related the conversation I have just recorded, concluding with the words:

"And what do you think the ambassador actually had the impertinence to say—there, just by the door, as I was seeing him out: *Don't forget, Monsieur le President, that Germany will henceforth be behind the Sultan of Morocco with all her forces.* . . . He actually had the impertinence to say that to me. . . . me, the head of the French Government! . . . *Nom de Dieu! Nom de Dieu! Nom de Dieu! . . .*"

His great frame was suddenly shaken with fury and he brought his fist down on the table with such a terrific thump that he sent the lid of the inkpot flying.

Monday, June 12th, 1905.

Paul Cambon has arrived from London and was seen by the Minister immediately. He came straight on to me:

"France seems to me to have gone mad," he said. "Out of sheer funk we've fallen into all the traps Germany set for us. The prophets in the Wilhelmstrasse must be having a good laugh among themselves. I reckon that at least ninety per cent of their arrogance and insolence towards us is pure bluff. . . . We must pull ourselves together, get our common sense back and lift up our heads again. I told Rouvier that England has her eye on us about the conference and, if we strike our flag to Germany, it's all up with the *Entente Cordiale. . . . But what can I do?*" he replied helplessly. "*Germany is set on the conference and won't give way.*"

"*You have only to refuse, politely but firmly, and stick to your offer to settling the Moroccan dispute with them direct. . . . You can be quite certain that the Emperor doesn't really care a rap about Morocco in this business; he simply sees a chance of showing the world the futility of the Franco-Russian alliance and the Anglo-French entente. His main object is to gratify his pride. If you grant him that indulgence now, he'll want more and go on and on until you have humbly admitted German hegemony in Europe just as in Bismarck's time.*" The Minister seemed to be very impressed by my last remark. I wonder if I have convinced him? I don't know."

Tuesday, June 13th, 1905.

I have had a talk with General de Lacroix, the Military Governor of Lyons, who returned from Berlin yesterday after representing France at the Crown Prince's wedding.[1] His impressions are more or less as follows:

The Emperor received him very graciously and treated him with the most engaging and marked politeness.

All the arrangements for the reception of our representatives at the wedding and the court festivities, were most considerate and in good taste.

As soon as the wedding was over, William II made a dead set for General de Lacroix, whose aristocratic manners and air of distinction were bound to be to his liking.

For the next three days, the 7th, 8th and 9th June, he kept him at his side at Dobritz Camp on the Brandenburg Plain, where the guards' manœuvres were in progress. He took a lot of trouble to

[1] On June 6th, 1905, William, Imperial Prince of Germany and Royal Prince of Prussia (born May 6th, 1882), married Cecile, Duchess of Mecklenburg (born September 20th, 1886).

explain everything and constantly invited his opinion. He also engaged him in long *tête-à-tête* and plied him with questions on outstanding military subjects, such as the campaigns of 1809 and 1814, the war of 1870 and the present war in Manchuria.

On the morning of June 7th, the Emperor sent for General de Lacroix. "So Delcassé has resigned," he exclaimed. "You may take it from me, General, that his resignation is a very good thing for France. I can assure you that Delcassé was leading your country to disaster. . . . *Disaster!* I say." His eyes flashed. He lapsed into solemn silence and then resumed: "In France you don't sufficiently appreciate the grave effect of the war in Manchuria on the power of Russia. . . . The battle of Mukden is a historic event which will have incalculable results. It is a fearful threat to Christian civilization. . . . In future the world will listen to me when I talk about the Yellow Peril!"

Thursday, June 15th, 1905.

This evening, Boni de Castellane, the Magnificent, gave a housewarming party in the superb *salons* of his mansion, which is at the corner of the Avenue du Bois-de-Boulogne and the Avenue Malakoff. Dazzling splendour, characterized by picturesque originality and perfect taste. It was like a scene at Versailles or the Trianon, with *décor* by Lebrun and Tiepolo.

But there was a singular lack of gaiety. Apprehension was visible on every face. The moment Comtesse de P. came in, she took my arm:

"Have a good look round, *cher ami*," she said gravely. "This may be the last party under peace conditions and therefore the last of this social *régime*. For a whole week I've been reviving my memories of July, 1870."

Eugène-Melchior de Vogüé, d'Haussonville, Denys Cochin, Prince Murat, Bréteuil, the Marquis de Ségur, and Etienne Lavisse, all obsessed by the same haunting fear, buttonholed me in succession and put the same question, almost in the same terms: "Things are very bad, aren't they? . . . It means war, doesn't it?"

Then Prince von Radolin arrived. He soon noticed that everyone was avoiding him. Seeing me the centre of a group, he beckoned to me with his most friendly smile. We moved off to a deserted sofa, a wonderful Gobelin of the Louis XVI period. There we sat talking.

As we seemed quite absorbed in our conversation, the other guests could not take their eyes off us.

The ambassador's face looked very drawn and he spoke slowly and wearily:

"There's a storm in the air tonight and I've got a fearful headache. But, to prevent comment, I thought I ought to turn up. I am misunderstood enough already."

"If it's only a question of misunderstandings, why haven't they been cleared up already?"

"You must know that I'm doing my best. But Paris ought to try and realize the situation and how it affects our honour. Things can't go on as they were under M. Delcassé. . . . I won't conceal from you, dear Monsieur Paléologue, that my last talks with M. Rouvier reduced me to despair. . . . You have a great deal of influence at the Quai d'Orsay. As I've been lucky enough to meet you here tonight, I won't hesitate to tell you that the relations between France and Germany have got to change for the better. If they don't, what's going to happen? Good God! What's going to happen? . . ."

I confined myself to replying:

"As regards the Morocco business, I can assure you that M. Rouvier is determined to go as far as possible in the way of compromise and conciliation. As regards a fresh orientation of Franco-German relations, this is such a serious question and raises such delicate and ticklish problems that I must ask you to excuse me from going into it with you."

He nodded assent in his own courtly fashion and rose. In any event, had he not told me all he had to say—or all I could have guessed? . . . Germany's game has not varied in the last two months; epitomized, it consists of using the prospect of war to compel us to range ourselves with the other satellites of the Teutonic powers.

Friday, June 16th, 1905.

Something new and unexpected has happened—something which seems to presage important developments in world politics. For the first time in its history, the United States of America is intervening in European affairs. Hitherto it has regarded a studied aloofness from the problems of the old continent, 'European entanglements,' as a national dogma. This dogma had indestructible foundations—Washington's will and the Monroe Doctrine.

At the request of William II, President Roosevelt is now considering what he can do to compose the grave differences which have arisen between France and Germany over the Moroccan question. He sent for our ambassador, Jusserand, and told him: "The Emperor William has just written me a personal letter in which he says that he is demanding a conference to settle his dispute with France, and *that the refusal of his request involves the risk of war.* He tells me that your English friends are inciting you to resist, and further that you have made a defensive and offensive alliance with England. He has asked me to make representations in London with the object of persuading the British Government to withdraw their opposition to the conference. That I decline to do; it would be an unfriendly act towards you; it would look as if I were trying to break up the Anglo-French Entente. . . . On the other hand, I don't really believe that the Emperor William's ideas are as bellicose as they sound in his letter, though it is possible. So much is at stake that we can't be too careful. . . . I find it extraordinarily difficult to advise you, but I'm wondering if you wouldn't choose the lesser of two evils by agreeing to the conference."

Saturday, June 17th, 1905.

The German Ambassador yesterday handed us a note which begins as follows: *The Imperial Government cannot discuss the programme of the conference with France until the Government of the Republic has formally accepted the invitation to be represented at it.*

Rouvier was bowled over by the tone of this note—neither more nor less than an ultimatum—and said to Georges Louis:

"This makes me believe what the Emperor said in his letter to Roosevelt—if we don't agree to the conference, war will be inevitable."

In a state of great agitation, he instructed the Political Director to draw up a memorandum 'this very night' on the arrangements to be made by the Ministry of Foreign Affairs if Germany's bellicose attitude suddenly precipitated a war.

One result was that I was working until 2 a.m. in Georges Louis' flat, writing the memorandum required by the Minister. We then studied the scheme formulated in the *Instructions de Guerre,* i.e., the directions to our diplomatic and consular agents in case of hostilities becoming imminent. Then I sent letters in code to Raindre, our ambassador in Switzerland, and Gérard and Denant, our ministers in Belgium and Luxemburg, asking them to proceed forthwith with their secret arrangements for watching the German frontiers at those points where signs of a German mobilization could not be concealed.

In the afternoon I saw General Pendézec to tell him the latest developments. I found him increasingly pessimistic.

"We'll fight if we have to fight," he said. "But what a ghastly risk, my dear chap. France may easily perish altogether. The German armies, 1,500,000 strong, will sweep over us in one great flood. Except for Verdun, not one of our fortresses is in a state to resist them. There are works on the front north of Toul which a squadron of Uhlans could carry. It's the Chamber's fault for perpetually cutting down the army estimates. Messieurs Combes and Jaurès have much to answer for these last few years. . . ."

I asked him if the *Conseil Supérieur de la Guerre* had discussed the theory of a German invasion astride the Meuse at their meeting on June 7th.

"No," he told me, "*Plan XV* still remains unchanged."

Sunday, June 18th, 1905.

Rouvier saw Prince von Radolin yesterday. The latter obstinately stood his ground. Rouvier then conferred with Paul Cambon who had just arrived from London.

Our ambassador came to see me this morning:

"We've blundered so badly and made such fools of ourselves all along during the last few weeks," he said. "The Minister has been so incompetent, clumsy and, worst of all, cowardly in his negotiations with Radolin that I consider we've lost the game. So we shall have to submit to a conference. I'm off to prepare Lansdowne for it: it will be extremely humiliating. . . ."

Rouvier confided to Paul Cambon his increasing dislike for diplomacy and told him how anxious he was, as soon as circumstances permitted, to give up the formidable portfolio he has taken on so rashly. He finds Delcassé's mantle a shirt of Nessus. He remarked to his friend, Baron Jacques de Gunzbourg, the day before yesterday:

"I feel suffocated here. Why the devil did I take it on? . . . The worst of it is that I don't see how I can get out of it. . . ."

The Grand Duke Alexis-Alexandrovitch, the Emperor's uncle, Admiral-General and C.-in-C. of the Fleet, has just been relieved of his important naval duties 'at his own request.'

Public opinion in Russia unanimously attributes to him the successive naval reverses in the Far East. The appalling disaster at Tsu-shima has released the torrent of national fury and the Emperor has seen that he must be ruthless.

Impressive as it sounds, the sentence is really extremely mild, for there is no doubt that the system of lies and evasion practised by the admiral's staff did very seriouly compromise the efficiency and fighting power of the Russian fleet.

The other evening, I walked back from the Grand Duke Paul's with one of his former aides-de-camp, who had recently returned from Russia. We were gloomily discussing the Tsu-shima disaster, which led the general to tell me about a lovely creature who is extremely popular with the gay set in St. Petersburg and the object of unremitting attention from a certain gentleman in high circles.

The general continued, in acid tones:

"I saw her recently in evening dress; she was a more delightful vision than ever and positively dripping with jewellery. I couldn't help fuming to myself: 'That diamond aigrette, that sapphire bracelet, that pearl necklace, that emerald clasp, all those superb gems—the *Kniaz Suvoroff*, the *Bogatyr*, the *Alexander I*, and the *Borodino* paid for them, no doubt.' And that's why those fine ships are now at the bottom of the sea."

Monday, June 19th, 1905.

Yesterday, our ambassador in Washington, Jusserand, dined with President Roosevelt, who told him:

"France ought to adopt a conciliatory attitude towards Germany. You must know that I'm not the sort of man to yield to threats. But there are many concessions to be made, without loss of honour, to avoid a war. I would not hesitate if I were in your place. You'll have to give some sort of sop to the Emperor William's unbounded vanity."

National feeling is decidedly reviving in France: let me quote from an article which Georges Clemenceau (Delcassé's most stubborn and virulent foe, and a man who would stop at nothing to accomplish his downfall), has just published in his paper, *l'Aurore:*

> *Nothing less than the fate of France is today the stake of battle.To be or not to be; that is the problem with which, for the first time since the Hundred Years' War, we are faced as the result of ruthless competition for supremacy. . . . We owe it to ourselves, we owe it to our fathers and our children, to do everything in our power to preserve the treasure of French life which we have received from those who have gone before and for which we shall have to account to those who come after us.*

Tuesday, June 20th, 1905.

President Roosevelt, who decidedly appears to be setting up as universal arbiter, has just offered Russia and Japan his good offices to put an end to hostilities. Both in St. Petersburg and Tokyo, his proposals, framed with a bluntness quite American, have produced so marked an impression that the two governments have agreed to nominate plenipotentiaries to consider possible terms of peace.

Unfortunately, it is still very doubtful whether the negotiations now about to start will succeed. On the one hand, the Japanese want to exploit to the full their brilliant victory at Tsu-shima and are making preparations to capture the great island of Saghalien, the possession of which would give them control of the seas up to Kamskatka. On the other hand, the Emperor Nicholas would like to have one last throw in the military field before coming to terms with 'the dirty little Yellows'; in this design he has been encouraged by a moving appeal which all the generals in Manchuria have sent him: *The respective positions of the belligerent armies in no wise compel us to make peace. Our enemies, flushed with their successes, will want to impose conditions incompatible with the honour of Russia; we are not yet reduced to that extremity. The Tsu-shima disaster is deplorable; but it does not affect the morale of our brave troops who are determined to fight on until the Almighty has gloriously crowned their efforts. . . .*

The Russian Army in Manchuria numbers 400,000 men at the present time. Including the drafts on the way, it will be 500,000 strong by August 1st. The war could thus be prolonged for several months—if the throne of the Romanovs and the whole autocratic *régime* were not liable to be swept away by a revolutionary tornado one fine day.

Tuesday, June 20th, 1905.

This morning, the Minister invited the Political Director and myself to discuss the following question: "If war broke out to-morrow, how much help would Russia still be able to give us? Is it not time to remind our allies of the heavy obligations towards France which the agreement of 1894 imposes upon her?

At the conclusion of the discussion, Rouvier instructed me to draft a telegram on the following lines for our ambassador at St. Petersburg: "Henceforth we are compelled to envisage an attack by Germany. What would Russia do in that eventuality? Of course we are aware that at the present moment our ally is in no condition to give the help stipulated for in the military conventions. But, if it is not in her power to meet all her obligations, it should be a matter of honour for her to do what she can, in some form or other. We therefore think that it would be very helpful if the Tsar made strong personal representations to the Emperor William. Our ambassador is invited to speak to Count Lamsdorf in that sense."

Friday, June 23rd, 1905.

I have been to see Delcassé at his little town house in the Boulevard de Clichy. I have called on him twice—without finding him in—since he left the Quai d'Orsay.

I arrived at the moment he came in from riding; he seemed very well; his eyes were bright and his face had lost its worried look. He gave me a warm welcome.

He spoke without bitterness of his recent fall, but with a certain fierce pride repeated Miquel's insolent remark to Rouvier: *The Chancellor of the German Empire wants to have no further dealings with M. Delcassé.* He also repeated:

"That's what you must put on my tombstone, my dear Paléologue. I couldn't wish for a finer epitaph!"

He then started a long discussion of the present situation:

"I still think that there's only one line to take—make an alliance with England. And I'll guarantee that Germany won't budge."

"Yes, we must steer a course for the English alliance. But I don't think it will remove the danger of war. According to you, the Kaiser's attitude is just bluff. You may be right. But if so, he has become the prisoner of that attitude; he has cut himself off from the road to reconciliation and the possibility of retreat. That's where the danger lies, I think. William has us tied up in an *impasse*; but he has tied himself up too. An additional reason for making an alliance with England as soon as possible."

In an attempt to reconcile our points of view, I suggested a working formula which he accepted; *the alliance with England will not guarantee us against attack by Germany, but it will enable us to resist it.*

Saturday, June 24th, 1905.

This morning Rouvier had a long conference with our future generalissimo, General Brugère. Then he asked me to get him information, 'as accurate as possible,' about the military aid which Russia is still in a position to give us.

General Pendézec, whom I questioned on the matter, gave me the following answer:

"I think that, in spite of the disasters in the Far East, Russia would still be capable of concentrating 350,000 men on her western frontier; but that army would only have old artillery—all the new guns are in Manchuria. The military effort of our ally would thus be almost nil. In the direction of the Vistula and the Niemen, Germany would find 50,000 regulars and a few landwehr divisions sufficient cover. There would be nothing to prevent the Austrian Army from invading Poland, the Ukraine and Volhynia; it would thus find an open road to Moscow."

"What about help from England?"

"In my opinion, the help of England at the present time would not be of any value to us. I put it at nil. I should much prefer an alliance with Switzerland, in which case we could use her territory and attack Germany through Bavaria and Swabia, as Moreau did in 1800."

Sunday, June 25th, 1905.

There is no improvement in the situation in Berlin.

Prince von Bülow has said to Bihourd:

"Your government's last note has both surprised and disappointed me. I can't accept its conclusions. Take a bit of friendly advice from me: *Settle up this Moroccan business as soon as possible; the more I think about it, the worse it seems; it's a very bad business. So don't waste any time. . . . Don't dawdle along a road which is bordered with precipices.*"

Monday, June 26th, 1905.

This evening, the new British Ambassador, Sir Francis Bertie, gave his *ricevimento*.

There was quite a crowd at the embassy in the Faubourg St. Honoré, once the residence of Pauline Borghese: all the ministers, the whole diplomatic corps, many parliamentary representatives and generals, etc., were there. Illuminations in the garden; strings of coloured lights from tree to tree. A warm, bright night which attracted most of the guests out of doors. A bevy of smartly and expensively-dressed women.

I talked with the Minister of War, Maurice Berteaux, and then with our generalissimo, General Brugère. The former questioned me briefly about 'the dangers of the situation.' He spoke with the grim stoicism of a man who realizes the full extent of the danger and is equal, or rather resigned, to facing it bravely. Brugère pleased me even more: no bravado, but calm and cheerful confidence which had an excellent effect on everyone.

I realized that the general state of mind this evening was very different from the pessimism which made such a painful impression on me at Boni de Castellane's on June 15th. We have recovered our balance: there is no more fear or cowardice; we are not prepared to grovel before Germany any longer; we have familiarized ourselves with the idea of war.

Yet, only a few paces from Prince von Radolin, Georges Clemenceau, hand on hip and his eyes flashing, was bellowing:

"We won't give way any further. . . . If Germany wants war, well! . . . we'll fight!"

A few minutes later, d'Haussonville whispered:

"I've just heard Clemenceau holding forth. I've suddenly taken a liking to the old Jacobin. Danton must have talked like that."

Courcel, our former ambassador in Berlin and London, said to me:

"This has been a very odd evening. I've spoken to more than a score of guests, men of all ranks, countries and callings. My general impression is this: *the Franco-British alliance is now a fact.*"

Tuesday, June 27th, 1905.

Bompard, our ambassador at St. Petersburg, has made strong
representations to Count Lamsdorf and the Emperor Nicholas that
Russia should give us all the help possible in Berlin. "I find," he
writes, "that the Imperial Government is very favourably disposed
towards us. It is all the more anxious to come to our aid because it
fears that, if it were unable or unwilling to do so, it would find itself
faced with two equally unpleasant possibilities. If we were left to
the care of England, we might place ourselves wholly in her hands
and—who knows?—substitute her for Russia in our international
agreements. On the other hand, if Russia deserted us, we might
buy the advantages Germany would allow us in Morocco by concessions to her in the East, so Russia's interests no less than her
feelings guarantee us the goodwill of the Imperial Government.
. . ." Bompard has obtained a promise from Lamsdorf that the
Tsar's ambassador in Berlin, Count von Osten-Sacken, shall formally notify Prince von Bülow to the following effect: "Russia,
weakened though she is, is not indifferent to the Franco-German
quarrel, for that quarrel involves the balance of power and jeopar-
dizes peace in Europe: Russia therefore regards herself as directly
affected by the present crisis."

The Emperor Nicholas has just written personally to the Emperor
William on this theme.

Thursday, June 29th, 1905.

The day before yesterday, President Roosevelt sent for the German Ambassador, Baron von Sternburg, and made a vigorous protest against the bellicose attitude of his country:

"You've obtained the consent of the French Government to the
principle of a conference; you've thus gained your main point and
it is now your interest and duty to be accommodating about the
others. War would be madness on your part. Even with an empire
as powerful as yours, it might end in frightful catastrophes. To
begin with, you may be quite certain that you would lose your fleet
and your colonies; England would make short work of them. And
even admitting that you crushed France, what good would it do
you? The annexation of further French provinces would only increase the number of your enemies within your own frontiers. It
would be like poison in your blood. . . ."

I dined quietly this evening with Madame de Pierrebourg, who lives in the Avenue du Bois-de-Boulogne, and met Baron de Courcel, who was plied with questions about the state of our relations with Germany and the risks of war. As ever, his reply was practical and to the point:

"Since we humiliated ourselves by sacrificing M. Delcassé, public feeling has been distinctly aroused all over France. The time has gone by when the Emperor William could hope to bully and intimidate us into obedience; so it is probable that we are progressing towards better times. . . . But if Germany starts provoking us again, and if the war party definitely gets the upper hand in Berlin, I have no doubt that England will back us with might and main. . . ."

At 10.30 I left with the ambassador. The night was bright and warm. He suggested continuing our conversation while we walked home down the Avenue des Champs-Élysées. I agreed. He took my arm:

"You've seen that I don't underestimate the dangers of the Franco-German quarrel; but I'm not at all certain that the domestic crisis through which Austria-Hungary is passing is not an even greater danger to the peace of Europe. . . . The recent incidents in the Budapest Chamber seem to me extremely serious. The attacks on the Fejervary ministry, these stormy outbursts of rage and abuse and the repeated cheers for Norway, all convince me that the dual monarchy is ripe for dissolution and the Hapsburg monarchy hasn't long to live." [1]

"What do you think will prove the effective cause of that dissolution?"

"I can see at least two. The first everyone is already thinking of— the death of Francis Joseph. The second, which may materialize much sooner, would be some adventure in the Balkans."

At that moment we were crossing the Rond-Point in the Champs-Élysées; we dawdled under the trees. Courcel went on:

"It's the Balkan question which seems to me the greatest danger threatening Europe. For the last few years—and especially since

[1] The *Storthing* of Christiania had just proclaimed the complete and final severance of the constitutional ties which had linked Norway and Sweden since 1814. This Norwegian proclamation of independence had fired the imagination of the party of 'Maygar Independence'—the great national party of Andrassy, Kossuth and Apponyi.

Russia's war with Japan—the Vienna Cabinet has been hypnotized, so to speak, by the Balkans. All Austria's foreign ambitions are now concentrated on Macedonia. Austrian hegemony in the Balkan Peninsula is the last dream of the Hapsburgs, their last chance of cutting a figure in history. I assume that Germany, in view of her close associations with Austria, will now be drawn into the Balkan imbroglio. So it will no longer be a case of Austria's fate being linked with that of Germany. Germany's fate is linked with Austria's. . . . This result would have made Bismarck foam with rage. You remember how he smelt the Balkan danger—what he called *the Serbo-Bulgarian thieves'-kitchen*—as far back as 1884. He at once came to the conclusion that the Berlin-Vienna compact must have a counterpart in the shape of a Berlin-Petersburg compact. So, while trumpeting the glories of the Austro-German alliance from the housetops, he conceived the machiavellian idea of covering himself in the Russian quarter by a reinsurance treaty. Incidentally, he was the only man on earth who could have invented the euphemism 'reinsurance' as a synonym for 'rank treachery.' As for the Franco-Russian alliance and an Anglo-French *entente*—they were never out of his thoughts; they were his nightmare; he would never have allowed us time to fix them up; he'd have declared war at the first suspicion: he told me so himself one evening at Varzin, in one of those candid and highly-flavoured after-dinner conversations in which his forcible temperament found the most extraordinarily reckless expression."

"You knew all about the Germany of Bismarck's time. What do you think of the Germany of today?"

"I think that Germany today, the Germany of William II, still represents a mighty force in the world; but no one can doubt that her power and prestige are diminishing; the Hohenzollern *Reich* is patently on the wane."

Here we reached the Avenue Marigny, where our ways parted. The Ambassador, half closing his eyes as if he were trying to scrutinize his inmost thoughts, then said to me:

"I envy you, my dear Paléologue. . . . I'll tell you why. If you last out a normal lifetime, say another twenty years, you'll probably see something I shall never see;[1] you'll see Alsace and Lorraine restored to France; then you'll see the Hohenzollern dynasty dis-

[1] Here the prophet was mistaken, partially at least; he survived until June 13th, 1919.

appear, because Teutonic structures have never lasted very long; lastly, you'll see Germany faced with an interminable era of disorder and confusion—just like after the Thirty Years' War."

Thereupon we separated.

As I walked home down the Avenue Marigny, cogitating on this odd piece of prophecy, I fell to wondering whether it had not gradually taken shape in Courcel's mind as the logical and ruthless conclusion of the pregnant words of Bismarck in that conversation long ago. The 'Iron Chancellor' would seem to have given him the key to future events which, more or less rapidly, would destroy his work when he was no longer there to save it.[1]

Friday, June 30th, 1905.

The German Chancery is in no way abating its haughty demands. Only yesterday, Prince von Bülow said to Bihourd:

"You may take it that the Moroccan question is a mere trifle in the balance in which the relations between our two countries are weighed. . . . The present situation is both dangerous and nerve-wracking. Be quick and clear it up by agreeing to a conference."

These words of Bülow justify Delcassé's argument up to the hilt: the development of French influence in Morocco in no way affects the interests of Germany; what she wants, and means to have at our expense, is to recover the matchless prestige she enjoyed in Bismarck's time; the confirmation of her supremacy in Europe and a solemn warning to anyone rash enough to deny Teutonism's right to dominate the world.

The revolutionary storm has raged much more fiercely in Russia the last few days. From the Baltic provinces to the plains of the Volga, there is an endless story of disorders, risings and looting. Repression is frequently impossible, as the troops refuse to intervene.

The incidents of which Odessa has just become the theatre are even more terrifying. The crew of a cruiser, the *Kniaz Potemkin*, has not only mutinied but had the audacity to bombard the town while the populace looted and burned the warehouses. A division of 30,000 men, sent from Kharkov, is now engaged in trying to

---

[1] It is known that the last words uttered by Bismarck in his death-throes were: "Germany! Germany! Germany! Help! Help! Alas!" When he died on July 30th, 1898, William II had already been on the throne ten years.

restore order—no easy task. But the Black Sea Squadron, simultaneously despatched from Constantinople, has not succeeded in
capturing the *Kniaz Potemkin* which has put out to sea, followed
by another cruiser, the *Georgy Pobiedonozev*, the crew of which
has also mutinied.

Saturday, July 1st, 1905.

Paul Cambon has sent us the following sagacious telegram from
London: *People in Paris do not sufficiently realize the strength of
our position. The hour of panic has passed; the Emperor William's
attitude has been condemned on all sides; the statesmen in Berlin
are more embarrassed than ourselves and will make concessions to
us to get themselves out of the mess. But we must not let ourselves
seem in too much of a hurry or give the impression that we are
being hustled by public impatience in France.*

Thursday, July 6th, 1905.

Someone recently discovered in Paris the remains of one of the
heroes of the War of Independence—Admiral Paul Jones, who died
on July 18th, 1792; a naval squadron has come to Cherbourg to
take the body home.

At about eleven o'clock this morning, I saw some five hundred
marines and sailors, with twenty officers, arriving at the Gare des
Invalides. A battalion of the 103rd of the line, with their band and
standard, gave them military honours.

In the afternoon there was a funeral service at Trinity Church
in the Avenue de l'Alma. Gathered round the ambassador, Mac-
Cormick, were the whole American colony in Paris and all the
French Ministers, Rouvier at their head.

Then, amidst a vast show of troops, the coffin of Admiral Paul
Jones was escorted to the Invalides, from which it will be transferred to Cherbourg tomorrow.

As I watched the American detachment marching past my win-
dows, I admired its fine bearing, the splendid physique of the men
and the self-confidence of their officers. But I could not resist a
curious feeling: only a few days ago, the United States intervened
for the first time in the troubles of Europe. May it not be that what
I have witnessed is a symbolic harbinger of their military intervention? . . . And when America lets the old continent feel the weight
of her arms, will it be for the benefit of France? . . .

Saturday, July 8th, 1905.

Agreement with Germany has been reached after a month of negotiation. Today Rouvier and Radolin have exchanged letters which put an end to this long and acrimonious quarrel. The following is a summary of the terms:

We undertake to maintain the independence and sovereignty of the Moroccan Sharif, the integrity of his empire and freedom of trade in his States. In return, the Imperial Government recognizes the special interests of France in Morocco and 'undertakes not to attempt anything which conflicts with the rights she has derived from her treaties.' In these circumstances, the Government of the Republic "abandons its former objections to the conference and agrees to be represented."

So Germany has got what she wanted; she has forced the conference upon us. In the agreement which has just been signed, her main object has been to show the world that, in spite of our system of alliances and friendships, we have not been able to stand up against her demands and threats. But, to satisfy her pride in that way, she has had to concede us, even in the Moroccan affair, something of real value, since she has had to admit our exceptional position in the Empire of the Sharif. What is more—and equally valuable to us—the Anglo-French, Franco-Italian and Franco-Spanish compacts continue in full force; thus Delcassé's vital achievement remains intact. Lastly, with the vision of the German menace clearly before their eyes, France and England have realized as never before that a close association is a necessity.

This evening, Major von Hugo, Military Attaché at the German Embassy, telegraphed to Baron von Holstein, Berlin's *Eminence Grise*:

Entbindung glücklich erfolgt, obwohl mit Zange, nach zweistundigen Wehen. 'Successful delivery, though with forceps, after two hours' labour.'

EPILOGUE[1]

Sunday, July 9th, 1905.

IN ACCORDANCE with an old court custom, Alfonso XIII is Honorary Colonel of the 66th Regiment of Prussian Infantry and the 5th Regiment of Bavarian Artillery. He had planned to pay a visit to the Emperor of Germany towards the end of September.

During recent weeks, however, William has been pressing him, in the most indiscreet fashion, to be in Berlin by September 1st, so that he can be present next day at the great Guards' review at which the Kaiser takes the salute every year in commemoration of Sedan.

Alfonso XIII's sense of dignity, no less than his affection for France, has prompted him to refuse in no uncertain terms to play the very odd part assigned to him. He said to our ambassador, Jules Cambon:

"William II is worrying my life out to participate in the great review on the *Sedan-tag*; he wants me to ride past him and then take my place at his side, as if I were one of his vassals, like the King of Saxony, the King of Wurtemberg or the Grand Duke of Baden. I must go to Berlin, but I mean to have a personal, ceremonial reception there, and to be treated as a King of Spain should be; so they won't see me at the review on September 2nd. . . ."

Turning to the general situation in Europe, Alfonso XIII informed our ambassador that he is still very anxious. He even admitted that war is possible, and said in firm tones:

"If war breaks out, it is well understood that England, France and Spain will stick together."

Wednesday, July 12th, 1905.

My colleague, Paul Révoil, who was Deputy President-General at Tunis, minister at Tangier, then Governor-General of Algeria, and finally 'unattached,' has been recently called out of his retire-

---

[1] In this last chapter, it has not been thought necessary to preserve the day-to-day continuity of the record; all that is required is a few entries, covering a period of eighteen months, to show the historical sequel.

ment by Rouvier who appointed him for 'special duties in the minister's secretariat.' [1]

In that capacity, he was closely associated with the troublesome negotiations which culminated in the agreement of July 8th.

He was lunching with me this morning. We talked freely, as no one else was present. I have known him a long time, and always had a high opinion not only of his charming and upright character, but also of his quick, versatile and astonishingly fertile intellect. He it is, no doubt, who will be our plenipotentiary at the approaching conference.

We considered the various lines which this conference could take—though, as a matter of fact, it apparently will not assemble for several months. What will happen meanwhile? . . .

"The agreement of July doesn't really decide anything," I said. "One side is humiliated and the other disappointed. The future is as black as ever."

"That's my opinion too. The agreement of July 8th is not an adjustment of differences; it's a truce. The perilous crisis through which we have just passed will soon begin again.

"Radolin didn't give Rouvier the slightest impression that he honestly desired friendship and a reconciliation. Germany has tried to find out how far we could be squeezed; she has come up against a degree of resistance which she did not expect. Hence her present disappointment. But you may take it for certain that she hasn't renounced her aims; she's going on with her see-saw game of honeyed words and threatening attitudes.

"Unfortunately, that game has paid her too well for her to give it up. But our national pride, which is patently reviving, may suddenly get out of hand, and then nothing on earth will prevent war.

"That's what Rouvier told me himself this morning: *Germany wouldn't behave differently if she wanted to make war inevitable.*"

"Our minister is getting on. . . . Before long you'll see him come round to Delcassé's point of view.

"He's not very far away now—and the miracle is due to German diplomacy and German methods."

[1] Appointed ambassador at Berne on November 28th, 1905, then at Madrid on January 23rd, 1906. He died on April 28th, 1914.

Thursday, July 13th, 1905.

After much shilly-shallying, Nicholas II has appointed Serge Witte, an ex-Finance Minister, to represent the Imperial Government at the conferences between Russia and Japan which are about to begin on American soil.

The choice strikes me as significant. When Witte was in office, i.e., up to August, 1903, he courageously opposed the crazy and discreditable policy which led up to the war in the Far East. His sense of reality and clear-sightedness have long since convinced him of the necessity of liquidating this monstrous adventure at the earliest possible moment. It may therefore be assumed that, in carrying out his thankless task, he will bring himself to accept the inevitable conditions.

Sunday, July 16th, 1905.

An English squadron, under the command of Sir William May, has just spent five days at Brest. It had a wonderful reception.

On July 14th, the admiral and five hundred of his officers were present at the Longchamp review and afterwards lunched at the Élysée. The next day, a dinner in their honour was given at the Ministry of Marine.

The visit of an English squadron to a French port has no political significance in the ordinary way. But it is otherwise this time. On the suggestion of Edward VII, the British Government has—for Germany's benefit—deliberately given us a proof of its friendship, a demonstration to the whole world of the *entente cordiale* between the two nations. It is understood in that sense in Berlin.[1]

Friday, July 21st, 1905.

The Japanese have now captured the whole of the great island of Saghalien; the last Russian garrison has surrendered. So their naval supremacy now extends from the Yellow Sea to the Sea of Okhotsk.

---

[1] A few days later, on July 27th, the Kaiser, referring to this visit of the British squadron to Brest, advised the Tsar 'to keep a rather tighter hand over the French.' His irritation found vent in barrack-room language: "Marianne must remember that she is your wife. Her duty is to sleep with you, in your bed, with perhaps a hug or a kiss for me from time to time. But she has no right to creep away to the bed of that incorrigible intriguer, Edward VII . . ." (*Documents published by the Bolsheviks.*)

Sunday, July 23rd, 1905.

Witte, the Russian plenipotentiary at the peace conference, has spent a few hours in Paris on his way to New York.

The talks he has had with the President of the Republic have confirmed the opinion we had formed of him as a man of great energy and high intelligence, but unamiable, proud, jealous and devoured by ambition. He may very well find his defects as useful as his virtues in the thankless task ahead of him.

He has said nothing, and could say nothing, about the attitude he proposes to adopt towards the Japanese, or the lengths to which he is prepared to go in the way of concessions.

But, in his conversation with Rouvier, he did not hesitate to tackle him fairly and squarely on the most delicate, ticklish and formidable problem in European politics. With a haughty air that was almost offensive, he declared:

"I have always thought that the continental powers should band themselves together to resist the domination of the maritime powers. That necessarily implies a compact between our two countries and Germany."

Rouvier, whose eyes had lost their steely look, had no difficulty in replying:

"And how does Alsace-Lorraine fit into your arrangement, Monsieur?"

"You're right, Monsieur; I'd forgotten."

Rouvier, quickly pacified, ended the conversation with the remark:

"We're not looking for any alliance but yours; it's all we want."

Thereupon Witte took a dignified leave.

Tuesday, July 25th, 1905.

A talk I have just had with one of the heads of the Russian police abroad has given me a very gloomy insight into the internal condition of the Empire. The throne of the Romanovs has never been in such dire peril since the social war in Pugachev's time.

When I related this conversation to Rouvier, he said:

"It may well be that the crisis through which Tsarism is passing may prove beneficial by compelling it to set its house in order."

"Perhaps so . . . but disasters must come first."

In support of my prophecy I have the authority of an excellent letter which the eloquent Bolingbroke once wrote to Swift: "An extraordinary reform cannot be brought about by ordinary means; it requires those which are both a punishment and a lesson. . . . *Nothing less than a national calamity is required to cure national corruption.*"

Friday, July 28th, 1905.

Last Monday, July 24th, the Emperor Nicholas and the Emperor William met on board their yachts, the *Polar Star* and the *Hohenzollern*, off Björko in the Gulf of Finland.

This unexpected meeting between our foe and our ally was bound to make the worst possible impression in France, an impression which the enigmatic comments of the Russian Government have done nothing to remove.

What we know for certain is that the suggestion of a meeting came from William II and that the two monarchs had 'a very long talk' on the *Hohenzollern*. What is still more serious is that, at the end of the conversation, the Kaiser sent for a high official of his suite, Heinrich von Tschirsky[1] (Prussian plenipotentiary in Hamburg) and a little later Nicholas II called in his Naval Minister, Admiral Birilev. We deduce that the Emperors wanted to commit the results of their discussion *to writing;* for it is not usual in such circumstances for monarchs to turn themselves into draftsmen; they only sign. We do not know what was the precise object of this understanding, or rather compact. But we may fear the worst from Nicholas II; he has often shown us that he cannot resist the cajoling, flattery and bragging of his impetuous cousin.

Our ambassador in St. Petersburg has tried in vain to get a candid explanation out of Lamsdorf, who pretends to be attaching no importance to the Björko interview.

"I assure you that this meeting was purely unofficial; nothing but a polite visit."

But in view of the effect of the Björko mystery on public opinion in France, the Russian Government has just sent us a 'very confidential' note:

> *As erroneous accounts are in circulation with regard to the interview between the two emperors, it would appear helpful to make its real significance clear.*

[1] On January 21st, 1906, he was appointed Secretary of State for Foreign Affairs. In 1914, he was ambassador at Vienna.

The Emperor of Germany, who happened to be cruising off the Swedish coast, telegraphed to the Emperor of Russia that he would like to meet him. The Emperor Nicholas, who was pleased with the suggestion, proposed that he should meet the Emperor William at Björko.

The meeting, which was entirely informal, made an excellent impression on His Majesty.

The exchange of views which took place between the two monarchs has in fact led to the conclusion that the peace of Europe is not endangered and, in particular, that there is every chance of arriving at a friendly solution of the Moroccan question, which is France's chief anxiety.

It would certainly appear that, in bringing up this question, the Emperor is concerned less with the subject of the dispute itself than with his desire to arrest the development of the growing friendship between France and England, a friendship which he regards as highly prejudicial to German interests, particularly if it is reinforced by the participation of Russia.

Obviously, we must seek the clue to the mystery in the last paragraph. It is against an Anglo-French friendship that William II is inciting the feeble and ever vacillating Russian autocrat. But why was the amiable understanding between the two monarchs reduced to writing? Why were Tschirsky and Birilev called in at the conclusion of the discussion, if not to make a formal record of the agreement at which they had arrived? Is not what has happened on the *Hohenzollern* off Björko the practical conclusion of the 'Dear Willy' and 'Dear Nicky' correspondence—that personal and private correspondence the revelation of which caused us such great anxiety a month ago? . . .

Sunday, August 6th, 1905.

Rouvier, whose solid materialism fears the uncertain and obscure more than anything else, is extremely worried. He said to me this evening:

'What have these two emperors been up to against us? . . . William II will soon make me as rabid a Germanophobe as Delcassé.'

To his friend Révoil he has made no secret of his very great anxiety:

"Think of my responsibility to posterity if Germany destroyed the Franco-Russian alliance during my term of office!"

The Russian and Japanese plenipotentiaries met for the first time yesterday on board the presidential yacht, *Mayflower*, in Oyster Bay roads.

President Roosevelt then gave them lunch, followed by a toast in concise and vigorous terms:

> *Gentlemen, I give you a toast which I ask you to drink with me, standing, in silence and without replying. I drink to the prosperity of the two sovereigns and the two great nations whose representatives meet today on board my ship. It is my greatest desire, my fervent prayer that, in the interests not only of the two great powers but of humanity itself, a just and lasting peace will speedily be accomplished.*

Tuesday, August 15th, 1905.

The French Northern Squadron, comprising six battleships and five cruisers, under the command of Admiral Caillard, has just spent six days at Cowes and Portsmouth.

Our sailors have everywhere met with a warm, and indeed enthusiastic, reception. King Edward, the Admiralty, the ministers, the House of Lords, the House of Commons and the City of London have left no stone unturned to make the visit of our officers and their crews to English soil as pleasant as possible.

The most remarkable demonstration of goodwill was that of Edward VII himself. He has been as charming and cordial as can be in his long and frequent visits to our ships, his toasts to our navy and his talks with our officers.

Then there was the reception by the City of London, with the traditional splendour peculiar to banquets to royal guests, the Lord Mayor having the Foreign Secretary and the Lord Chancellor at his side. 'As the procession passed,' writes Paul Cambon, 'the crowds, the cheering and the street decorations combined to rouse popular enthusiasm to fever heat and give the reception the character of a national demonstration.'

The occasion concluded with a banquet given by the House of Lords and the House of Commons in Westminster Hall. This ancient edifice was built by the first Norman Kings and its very walls seem an epitome of English history. Never before had it witnessed an assembly of foreign guests. All the political parties were represented, from the Prime Minister, Arthur Balfour, to the leader of the Liberal opposition, John Morley. So the warm sympathies which the British nation now entertains for our country found very striking expression.

As Balfour said when concluding his toast: "This is one of those days on which a great nation speaks with but one voice." . . . And I would subscribe willingly to the prophecy of John Morley: "Of all the historic halls of Europe, Westminster Hall alone can evoke so many memories. But none of these memories will be as important for western civilization as the extraordinary meeting here today."

Monday, August 21st, 1905.

I returned yesterday from a short trip to the Tyrol and the Italian lakes. I found relations between France and Germany in the same state, i.e., there is not the slightest sign of any improvement.

Rouvier, who has also been away for a few days' holiday, is still obsessed by the mystery of Björko. I have just sent him a memorandum summarizing all the information we have been able to obtain about the meeting of the two emperors. The points which seem to me established are as follows:

(1) the agreement reached between the two monarchs was committed to writing;

(2) this agreement is a reply to the Anglo-Japanese treaty of August 12th last; the Emperor William, it appears, considers that the treaty in question upsets the world balance of power, as the Japanese and British fleets will henceforth be supreme in the Indian Ocean and the China Seas;

(3) the only counterweight to the predominance of the Anglo-Japanese group in the Far East is the formation of a great European alliance, with Germany and Russia at its head;

(4) this new system would absorb, but not destroy, the Franco-Russian alliance. If necessary, France would be compelled to consent. Even last autumn, William II had written to the Tsar: "I'll make France come in with us."

Tuesday, August 22nd, 1905.

I made a long call on General Brun, who has just taken General Pendézec's place as Chief of Staff. His precise and moderate language, ready wit, practical intellect and broadmindedness have made a great impression on me.

I told him all about the diplomatic situation, emphasizing the fact that, in spite of the compact of July 8th last, Germany has not ceased to make things hot for us in Morocco by inciting and supporting the Sultan against us.

"In a word," said General Brun, "you can't say that there is any improvement in our relations with Germany?"

"None."

"Anything new in the Russian quarter?"

"I think we shall soon hear that peace has been signed. President Roosevelt has taken the matter in hand quite ruthlessly. He has been so forceful and determined—not to say positively rude—in his representations to St. Petersburg that the two belligerents, who admittedly are at the end of their tether, will soon be compelled to come to terms on the basis he suggests."

We then tried to work out how long Russia will need to build up her military forces again when she finally emerges from the Manchurian hornet's nest. Our conclusion is that in the most favourable circumstances (i.e., assuming that Tsarism maintains and strengthens its position) *it will be five years at least* before the Russian army is in a position to carry out the obligations imposed upon it by the terms of our alliance.

We next discussed the practical form and real value of an alliance with England. On this subject General Brun said:

"I've had the question studied very quietly by Major Huguet, our military attaché in London. . . . At first sight, I should think that England could land 150,000 men between the fifteenth and twentieth days of mobilization. That army, after joining up with the Belgian, would attack the right flank of the German armies if, as we have every reason to think, our enemies chose the valley of the Meuse, in the direction of the Oise, as their line of advance. . . . But, from the diplomatic point of view, do you think that we shall really see this English alliance an accomplished fact some day?"

"M. Rouvier, with whom I've discussed the matter from time to time, is strongly opposed to the idea; but, even now, he is not as hostile as when he first took over: he is beginning to see through Germany's game."

Just before we parted, General Brun told me of some very curious information our espionage service has recently picked up—information to the effect that the German General Staff is studying a scheme to attack us through Swiss territory. Three army corps, debouching from Upper Alsace between Delémont and Porrentruy, would march on Vesoul with the object of turning the Belfort-Montbéliard obstacle. Germany would thus invade us through Belgium and Switzerland simultaneously. . . . Why should Swiss neutrality count for more than Belgium's in German eyes?

Tuesday, August 29th, 1905.

For several days the negotiators at Portsmouth struggled in fierce debate, knocking their heads against irreducible ultimatums. Yesterday it looked as if the *pourparlers* might be broken off at any moment; but President Roosevelt has just sent the Emperor Nicholas a telegram which has all the resonance and weight of a *quos ego!* . . .

I see that Count Lamsdorf has publicly declared that Russia will neither pay any money to Japan nor cede an inch of territory. I beg Your Majesty to reflect that there is no sense in that declaration, since Saghalien is already in the hands of the Japanese. If, as a consequence of such an attitude, the war were to continue, no one could forsee the result. But the most competent opinion considers that the prolongation of the struggle will not merely compel Russia to abandon Saghalien: it will cost her the whole of eastern Siberia. Of course, I think it would be bad for Japan to continue the war, but I believe it would be much worse for Russia. . . . I cannot too strongly express my conviction that, if peace is desirable for the whole world, it is Russia's particular interest, perhaps a vital interest, that it should be concluded as soon as possible.

Rouvier, lost in admiration of such bold and artful candour, gave me immediate instructions to draft (for signature by the President of the Republic), a telegram exhorting Nicholas II to take Roosevelt's advice.

I took him the draft half an hour later—at seven o'clock. But, however insipid my eloquence may seem compared to the style of the American President, and however far I have gone in my search for euphemisms and polite phrases, I implored Rouvier to let the matter drop—all the more so because the minister has only myself to turn to, Georges Louis being away:

"This action will at one stroke cost us all the credit the Russians give us for keeping our opinions to ourselves since the war began. May I add that the exhortations of the President of the Republic to the Emperor Nicholas will certainly influence the latter far less than the telegram of President Roosevelt. M. Loubet can't talk to him so bluntly! I think I ought also to tell you that M. Delcassé always declined to suggest to the Tsar that he should make peace. 'I know,' he once said, 'that, sooner or later, the Russians will have to submit to a humiliating peace; but they would never forgive us for having encouraged them to do so and they would tell the world that they would never have done so except under pressure from us.'"

Rouvier's face brightened at these words; he remarked cheerfully:

"I'm not a bigger fool than Delcassé . . . there's your telegram; tear it up!"

Then we philosophized over the rôle of universal arbiter which the United States of America now seems destined to play in world politics.

"Before long," said Rouvier, "European finance will be completely dominated by the Americans."

"And they'll control diplomacy through finance."

At 7.20 p.m., just as I was leaving the minister's room, a cable from New York announced that peace was signed!

Rouvier gave me a cheerful tap on the shoulder; he was positively beaming:

"Draft me three telegrams at once for the President of the Republic to sign—one for the Tsar, one for the Emperor of Japan and one for Roosevelt. Mind you're eloquent!"

A few minutes later I submitted these three telegrams, which he approved:

To His Excellency the President of the United States, Washington.

Your Excellency has just rendered humanity a service on which I congratulate you with all my heart. The French Republic is proud of the part played by her American sister in this historic event.

To His Majesty the Emperor of Russia, Tsarskoie-Selo.

I send Your Majesty my warmest congratulations in the great event which has been brought about by your wisdom. France,

Russia's ally, is glad to see a war distinguished by so many heroic deeds brought to a close by so honourable a peace.

To His Majesty the Emperor of Japan, Tokyo.

I congratulate Your Majesty on the great act of wisdom and humanity which you have just accomplished.

Tuesday, September 5th, 1905.

Bihourd, our ambassador in Berlin, had a talk yesterday with Prince von Bülow, who was passing through the capital.

The Chancellor resumed his old tactics—a blend of *badinage* and intimidation. Reverting to his previous theme, he introduced several new variations on the necessity of putting an end to Franco-German misunderstandings, treating the Emperor William properly and realizing the importance of France and Germany 'living in peace instead of quarrelling.' But, simultaneously, he went out of his way to exaggerate all the difficulties of the problem, even going so far as to revive old controversies which were thought long since closed. "I felt," writes Bihourd, "that I was suddenly being put back two months."

In a recent talk with Rouvier, Prince von Radolin did not conceal the fact that he did not approve the policy of his Government 'which can only poison relations between the two governments.' Laying his hand on his heart, he swore that he meant every word he said when he promised us heaven and earth if we would make the concessions for which he asked.

Saturday, September 9th, 1905.

Georges Louis' absence has meant that I alone have to deal with Rouvier on a very serious subject which has cropped up unexpectedly: the termination of Anglo-Russian rivalry in Asia, a *rapprochement* between England and Russia in Europe, and collaboration, if not an alliance, between the 'bear' and the 'whale.'

On August 12th, the British and Japanese Governments renewed their agreements of January 30th, 1902, with a provision that they should apply not only to eastern Asia but even to 'the region of India.' The result is that henceforth England can count on the armies of the Mikado for the defence of her Indian Empire and the adjoining countries, viz. Tibet, Afghanistan and Persia.

When informing us of this treaty a few days ago, the British Secretary of State asked us 'as a great favour' to help him in preventing the Russians from putting an undesirable construction upon it. Lord Lansdowne has been very open with Paul Cambon about it: *We are extremely anxious*, he wrote, *that the Russian Government shall not regard the new alliance as an unfriendly act towards itself. . . . I go further and say that in my opinion our compact with Japan in no way excludes the idea of a friendly understanding with Russia covering the future developments of our policy in those regions where the interests of the two powers are in contact.*

In my talk with Rouvier I supported the British request and arguments with all my might, reminding him of what has just happened at Björko, the atmosphere of mystery in which the confabulation of the two emperors is still wrapped, the obvious reluctance of Lamsdorf and Nelidov to mention the subject, and all we know of William II's subterranean intrigues against us at the Tsar's court.

"It is a matter of great concern, positively *vital* concern, to us that Russia shall gradually get on to a footing of collaboration with England. Otherwise, the bonds of Russo-German friendship will draw closer and closer—which will mean the end of the Franco-Russian alliance."

Rouvier remained unconvinced for a long time; his main argument is that Russia would accuse us of deserting her for England, and would therefore be all the more likely to lean on Germany. I then suggested an excellent argument with which to meet such an accusation from the Russian Government:

"You have only to invoke the opinion of your predecessor. M. Delcassé regarded a friendly understanding between Russia and England as an indispensable supplement to the Anglo-French *entente* and Franco-Russian solidarity. He frequently said so to the Emperor, Muraviev, Urussov, Lamsdorf and Nelidov. It was actually one of his first ambitions, one of the first secrets he entrusted to me, away in 1898, just after Fashoda."

Rouvier's face suddenly beamed; I could almost hear him making up his mind:

"Thank you; I'll take that course. . . . But, before taking action in St. Petersburg, I must have a friendly talk with Nelidov."

Thursday, September 28th, 1905.

After three months of acrimonious controversy on the pettiest points, Rouvier and Radolin have today signed an agreement covering the principles and programme of the future conference.

In this agreement, the essence of our rights in Morocco is safeguarded. We have a fine game to play before the areopagus of European powers.

Monday, October 16th, 1905.

Are we going to have some light on the mystery of Björko at last?

After much beating about the bush, Nelidov has asked Rouvier if he was prepared to consider a fresh grouping of the European powers, a triple alliance, for instance, between Russia, France and—Germany.

Rouvier, as if he regarded the question as purely academic, replied in the most natural tone:

"I can't see either the value or the possibility of such a grouping. You know the lines of our foreign policy; it is based on alliance with Russia and friendship with England. These are all we require. . . . And can you see public opinion in France accepting the idea of a German alliance? Can you see William II received in Paris?"

The ambassador immediately changed the subject.

Nelidov is a fervent partisan of the Franco-Russian alliance, and I assume that he hated carrying out his formal instructions and must have been exceedingly pleased with Rouvier's categorical answer.[1]

---

[1] The Björko mystery has now been cleared up; the documents published by the Soviet Government have made the whole story quite plain.

The moment the Kaiser found himself alone with 'his beloved brother,' he thrust under his nose a draft scheme for a diplomatic and military alliance between Germany and Russia. This compact, directed specifically against 'perfidious Albion,' stipulated that France should be summoned to join in; the Russian Government was to take the necessary steps to overcome her resistance; from William himself we have the story of the incredible scene which followed: "The Tsar read the draft once, twice, thrice, whilst I was making a short fervent prayer to God. . . . Nicholas suddenly said: *It's splendid! I agree!* My heart beat so wildly that I could hear it. I continued, as casually as possible: *Will you sign?* He glanced through the document again and then took a pen and signed 'Nicholas' in a firm hand. I signed in turn. When I got up, he put his arm round me with the words: *Thank God and thank you: our alliance will have the happiest results for our two countries!* . . . I wept with joy . . . I thought of Frederick-William III, Queen Louise, grandpapa and Nicholas I looking down on us from heaven. . . . So, thanks to divine protection, July 24th, 1905 marks a turning-point in European history. And my dear country is at last out of the terrible Franco-Russian vice!"

On his return to Tsarskoei-Selo a few days later, Nicholas II communicated the treaty to Count Lamsdorf, who at first could hardly believe his eyes. Then, with the necessary deference, the minister made the Emperor realize the appalling mistake he had made and his betrayal of the solemn obligations binding Russia to France. The Tsar thus found himself under the humiliating necessity of going back on his

Wednesday, October 18th, 1905.

Paris and Berlin have definitely come to terms over the agenda of the international conference which is to undertake the task of solving the Moroccan problem. All that is now required is the participation of Sultan Abd-el-Aziz; the French and German ministers at Fez are visiting him to secure it.

The Spanish Government has put the town of Algeciras at the disposal of the powers for the meetings of the conference.

Monday, October 23rd, 1905.

The Sultan of Morocco has accepted the programme of the international conference "at which the reforms His Majesty proposes to effect in his states (if God wills), will be discussed. . . ." The draftsmen in musulman government departments are past-masters at high-sounding phrases.

It is thought that the conference will commence its work on January 10th in the town of Algeciras.

Tuesday, October 24th, 1905.

We no longer have any doubt that, at the mysterious Björko interview, the Emperor William used all his wiles and graces and his long practice in the arts of wheedling, insinuation and deceit to drag the feeble "Nicky" into a coalition of Russia, Germany and France against England.

But during the last few days—and especially since Rouvier's emphatic reply[1] to Nelidov—we are under the impression that Nicholas II has recovered his balance.

---

signature and having William informed that his government regarded the treaty of July 25th as invalid, in view of the fact that one of its essential terms—the adhesion of France—was known to be beyond the bounds of possibility. William lost his temper completely when he saw his dream fading, but, in hopes of recovering his hold on his weak-minded cousin, he telegraphed to him: *We signed before God, who heard our oath. . . . What was signed is still signed. . . . God is our witness!* . . . Nicholas did not continue the dialogue and the Björko compact was immediately buried in the most secret drawer in the Russian archives.

It is difficult to judge the part played by the Tsar in this incident. Was he guilty of treachery towards France in signing the Björko agreement? No. The sequel to the incident is sufficient to exonerate him; but, through inadvertence and ignorance, he certainly went much too far.

[1] We know now that this categorical answer encouraged Count Lamsdorf to address the Tsar in language equally plain: "Sire," he said, "the Treaty of Björko is a flagrant breach of the promise made by the Emperor Alexander III to support France with his forces in the event of a war with Germany. If the French heard of

What is more, he is said to welcome the idea of co-operating with England over the great Asiatic problems, the Persian question in particular: if this is so, he agrees with the views expressed by Lord Lansdowne to Cambon, and on which Rouvier laid stress in his conversation with Nelidov. Sir Charles Hardinge, the British Ambassador in St. Petersburg, has just had a long talk with the Emperor on the subject and the latter was extremely friendly.

Sunday, October 29th, 1905.

Once again William II has been blowing Bellona's trumpet.

Last Thursday, he paid an official visit to Dresden where the King of Saxony, Frederick Augustus, gave him a most impressive reception.

At the banquet on the first evening, the Emperor proposed a toast in these terms: "If the German Empire develops as it should, with lowered visor and courage befitting men of our race, we can look in the face anyone who tries to stand in our way or dispute with us the legitimate expansion of our interests."

The next day he made another speech. After unveiling a statue to General von Moltke, he addressed the officers of the Saxon Guard: "First let us thank Providence which gave us the great Emperor and his paladins at a critical moment in our history. Then think of the future, gentlemen. You have seen the position in which we were in, only a few months ago, in the eyes of the world. *Three cheers for dry powder and a well-sharpened sword!*"

The whole of the German Press, with the exception of the socialist papers, have greeted these imperial harangues with obsequious flattery. Lest we should fail to realize their significance, the official *Post* reminds us that "every word the Emperor utters is the fruit of long meditation."

Saturday, November 4th, 1905.

I met Prince von Radolin this evening at dinner with the Dowager Marquise de Castellane; as only some twenty guests were

---

this arrangement, they would have every right to say that we had betrayed them. Personally, I have no particular enthusiasm for the French, but I believe in our alliance with them, as a counterpoise against Germany. As soon as the Germans were sure of their alliance with Russia, they would be only too pleased to tell France all about it, suggesting that we were faithless allies. The Emperor William is far more concerned to make mischief betwen ourselves and France than to have the help of our army, which is tied up in the Far East, or our navy, which is at the bottom of the sea."

present, the ambassador had no difficulty in finding a quiet corner
for a talk with me. He began by telling me that he is going to
Germany very shortly:

"I need a holiday very badly."

His haggard face and bad colour were sufficient proof of the
truth of his words.

"I'm going to spend a month, a good month, at my place at
Jarotschin, in Posen; I shan't be back in Paris before the end of
December, unless . . ."

He stopped short.

"Unless what?" I asked.

He looked very grave as he finished his sentence:

"Unless something serious occurs to bring me back unexpectedly."

"Something serious? At the moment I don't anticipate anything.
The issues which still divide us will soon be settled by the Algeciras
conference. . . . Don't forget that it was you yourselves who insisted on this conference!"

After a pause, he continued in weary tones:

"We must see things as they are; we are not getting on. I don't
know what the end will be. All the hopes I based on the sagacity
and practical common sense of M. Rouvier have faded away one
by one. May I tell you what is really in my mind? The situation
today seems to me as dangerous as it was six months ago."

I interrupted him:

"But do you think that His Majesty's latest speeches are calculated to improve this situation?"

"His Majesty would never talk in that way if public opinion in
France honestly tried to realize Germany's place in the world, and
her right to it. Our quarrel over Morocco is only a detail and the
Algeciras conference will soon have settled it. I'm not worried on
that score any longer. But there's a much greater issue between
our two countries, an issue which may result in many sorrows; you
know what it is. All I can tell you is that when I try to approach
it, there's no one to talk to; I am met with silence, evasion or a
refusal to discuss general policy; no one wants to collaborate or
even talk with us; in a word, we are treated as enemies—as if
thirty-five years had not passed since 1870! That is what worries
me, irritates the Emperor and justifies his speeches."

"Yes, it is all decidedly worrying. But between ourselves, Ambassador, how can you expect France to forget her defeats in 1870 when the Emperor is always reminding her of them?"

"Then fate must take its course!"

He sighed deeply. Then he noticed that we were being watched. To show that our conversation had not concluded with some unpleasant topic, he immediately described with gusto the pleasures of open-air life, no work, sport and good company, which he will soon be enjoying on his ancestral demesne at Jarotschin.

When I left the ambassador, one of the guests, a great critic and novelist, took me aside:

"What have you just been plotting with that sham German, a dirty little Polish renegade? What have you been giving him now? Luxemburg, Hainaut, Brabant, the Ardennes, Champagne or Franche-Comté? Surely we shall be allowed to keep the ancient frontiers of Lorraine? We've so humbled ourselves before Germany that, even if it pleased William to confine France to the frontiers of the Treaty of Verdun, we'd agree.[1] Anyhow, we shall soon be involved in the Russian revolution and the same flood will sweep away the social systems of both. All the better! I prefer sudden extinction to our ignoble death-struggle."

Monday, November 6th, 1905.

I have had a talk with General Brun; we discussed the inevitability of a Franco-German war and, more particularly, the mortal peril in which France finds herself as the result of the "Avenger's" revelations.

"I'm very much afraid," he said, "that, at the outset of hostilities, we shall find ourselves under the necessity of bringing our armies a very long way back—perhaps even to the Seine and Aube. . . ."

Our Chief of Staff then expounded Clausewitz's doctrine of *the limit of the offensive*, i.e., the point at which the victor is compelled to stop, exhausted by the excessive speed of his advance and the toll of his victories. It is then that *the redistribution of force* takes place. Provided that the loser has preserved his morale and freedom of manœuvre, the chances in the struggle suddenly swing round in his favour. It is the great lesson which emerges from the

[1] The Treaty of Verdun, concluded in 843 by Louis the Debonair's sons, completed the dismemberment of the Empire of Charlemagne. In accordance with this partition treaty, the Kingdom of France had the Scheldt, the Sambre, the Meuse, the Saône and the Rhone for its frontiers on the German side.

Napoleonic wars, the real explanation of their final stages. . . .

General Brun concluded in these words:

"In drawing up our strategic plans, I have always kept our 1870 mistakes before my eyes, in particular, the march on Sedan—the worst and most serious of all. Anyone who had the most elementary notions of war, or had not lost his head, would never have dreamed of marching the Army of Châlons to the Ardennes and the Meuse. The operation was impossible, particularly with a general as slow, timorous, vacillating and *borné* as MacMahon. To bring it off would have called for nothing less than the impetuous audacity and lightning speed of Frederick the Great or Napoleon I. Mac-Mahon's original idea, which he was compelled to abandon by the Empress's orders,[1] was the only sound one, the only plan which could then have stopped our mad rush to disaster. It would have involved a retirement, stage by stage, to the very walls of Paris. There, supported by the defensive works of the capital but retaining all its freedom of manœuvre, the army would have given battle. If defeated, it would have continued its retreat, still stage by stage, to the Loire or the Somme—if necessary even into Touraine or Morvan. The siege of Paris would then have become an impossibility; there would have been time to organize national resistance and revive public spirit. The whole face of the war would have completely changed and, when the time for peace arrived, we should not have been delivered up to Germany, bound hand and foot."

I wound up with a question:

"I gather that, if Germany attacked us tomorrow, you anticipate our being compelled to withdraw by stages to the Seine and Aube?"

"Yes, worse luck! Until Russia has reorganized her military power, we shall have all we can do to withstand the initial onslaught of the German Armies through Belgium. . . . But don't forget what I've just told you about the *redistribution of force*."

Thursday, November 9th, 1905.

This morning, Rouvier remarked to Georges Louis:

"I've had quite enough of German recrimination and chicanery! If the Berlin gentry think they can intimidate me, they'll find they are mistaken. I won't give way another inch—come what may!"

[1] For the Empress's personal responsibility for this decision, see *Les Entretiens de l'Impératrice Eugénie*, p. 187 *et seq.*

He punctuated this outburst with a frightful oath.

The Director then quoted a phrase from a letter which Nisard wrote me a few days ago; it is a picturesque but very accurate description of the state of Franco-German relations: "At the present time, diplomatic relations between France and Germany are neither more nor less than the relations between outposts."

I presided this afternoon at a four hours' sitting of the secret *Instructions de Guerre* committee.

With Captain Malo-Lefebvre (Deputy Director at the Naval General Staff), Major Brissé (representative of Intelligence at the War Ministry), Captain Gander (A.D.C. to the Chief of Staff) and my colleague Piccioni (Director of the Cypher Department) I thoroughly overhauled all the arrangements we have made for the eventuality of a great European war, viz.:

(1) Watching the German frontiers at those points where preparations for general mobilization could not be concealed;

(2) Noting the concentration of the German Army, particularly in the vicinity of Cologne, Aix-la-Chapelle, Malmédy, Trèves, Sarrelouis, Château-Salins, Mulhausen and Altkirch;

(3) Organizing an intelligence service on enemy territory via Denmark, Holland, Belgium, Luxemburg and Switzerland;

(4) Telegraphic communication between France and Russia via Denmark (Esbjerg), Sweden (Haparanda), the United States and trans-Pacific cable, Malta, Aden, Bombay and Persia;

(5) Arrangements with regard to the neutralized zone in Savoy;

(6) Telegraphic communications with the commanders of our naval forces in the Mediterranean, Atlantic, Pacific and China Seas;

(7) Intelligence service at Gibraltar, Port Mahon, Messina, Spezzia, Corfu and the Dardanelles.

At the conclusion of the meeting, Captain Gander, speaking for General Brun, asked me to consider a scheme for our future relations with the British General Staff and the Admiralty, even assuming that England does not openly make an alliance with us.

Sunday, December 17th, 1905.

I called on Delcassé; he looked thinner, there was a curious glow in his eyes and his movements were nervous and abrupt.

He talked about the Yellow Book on Morocco, copies of which have just been issued to senators and deputies. He pointed to his own copy:

"I've hardly looked at it."

But the rapid and detailed criticism which he immediately proceeded to offer showed me that he already knew it by heart. It was wonderful to hear him castigating all the errors, illusions and miscalculations of the 'great financier-diplomat' who had driven him from office so shamefully:

"And to what end? . . . Simply to find himself compelled to revert to my policy and admit that no understanding with Germany is possible and that our only chance of salvation is to reinforce our alliances. I imagine that M. Rouvier is no longer prepared to guarantee that William is generous, peace-loving and 'straight'—as he did six months ago; I'm not making up his silly words—I can still hear them!"

Having thus given vent to his bitterness, he continued more sedately:

"Yesterday's sitting of the Chamber was mighty odd! Except on the Extreme Left benches, everyone did me justice. The deputies were always looking towards me. If I had made a speech, I should have been cheered."

He then told me of a very interesting talk he has recently had 'with a friend of Edward VII'; I could thus see that he was very well informed about the state of Franco-British relations:

" 'The Liberal Cabinet,' said this friend, 'will hesitate long before it sides openly with France. It will promise us its sympathy and goodwill; it may even go so far as to inform us that it will come to our aid if Germany attacks us. But I doubt whether it will go further; I don't believe it will agree to commit itself to writing. If Campbell-Bannerman and Grey take the course I anticipate, they will make a very grave mistake; Germany, with no England to worry about, will think she can do what she likes to France and her insolence will know no bounds.' King Edward, who is so far-sighted, said to this friend, whom I saw not long ago: *It's not enough to promise an alliance; we must make one and advertise the fact. An alliance should be preventive and not merely defensive. You can only discourage aggression by showing your strength.* . . . That's what I call real statesmanship!"

Just as I was getting up to go, Delcassé assumed a mysterious air and said:

"I've been invited to spend a fortnight in England. I've accepted. I'm going at the end of the month. Don't say a word to anyone!"

Then he suddenly opened out (it always costs him a great effort) and whispered:

"You've probably guessed that the invitation comes from Lord Northcliffe. I can always talk freely with him. There will be no difficulty at all because I'm not going to London but to his country place—Sutton Court, near Guildford, isn't it? Don't breathe a word to anyone!"[1]

Monday, December 18th, 1905.

In the course of a recent audience, the King of Spain said to our military attaché, Lieutenant-Colonel de Cornulier-Lucinière:

"I am very worried about William II's behaviour towards France. Many indications make me apprehensive that Germany is only watching for an excuse in the very near future to attack France: I need only mention the reports that have reached me during the last few months about the German Army, several letters I've had from Berlin drawing my attention to inflammatory speeches made by the Emperor in officers' clubs, and other warnings of the same kind which my relations in Bavaria have given me. I say *in the very near future* because I shouldn't be surprised if it were towards the end of February. . . ."

Becoming still more confidential, Alfonso XIII continued:

"During my last visit to Berlin,[2] William II strongly pressed me, in view of a Franco-German war, to concentrate 200,000 men on the frontier of the Pyrenees in order to tie up two of your army corps between Bayonne and Perpignan. I replied that, if I was obliged to carry out such a concentration, I would never order my troops to cross the frontier. . . ."

Rouvier sent for me to give him my views on this report from Lieutenant-Colonel de Cornulier-Lucinière; he seemed very worried by it.

[1] Lord Northcliffe, Viscount St. Peter, a great friend of Balfour. Edward VII had a high opinion of him. He was an active advocate of the *Entente Cordiale* and exercised a great deal of influence through the circulation of the *Daily Mail*, a newspaper of which he was the sole proprietor.

[2] November 6th to 12th, 1905.

"Why," he asked, "does the King of Spain anticipate being compelled by circumstances to mass 200,000 men on the frontier of the Pyrenees while we are at war with Germany?"

I told him that we had secret information which led us to believe in the existence of a compact made between Alfonso XII and the old Emperor William I, at the instigation of Bismarck; I was not therefore surprised that young Alfonso XIII was extremely alarmed at the prospect of a Franco-German war; he was proud and chivalrous and would not dare to go back on his father's signature. He had told us in order that we could help him to get out of his difficulty.

I suggested to the Minister that he should immediately inform the British Government. Georges Louis and I co-operated in drafting the necessary instructions to our ambassador in London.

Tuesday, December 19th, 1905.

Informing Paul Cambon of Alfonso XIII's odd communication to our military attaché at Madrid, Rouvier wound up as follows:

Even if we must assume that William II revealed bellicose intentions solely with the object of intimidating the young King and detaching Spain from our cause, we are not justified in neglecting this warning. If the real designs of the Emperor seem to us uncertain and, no doubt, subject to fluctuations, no one can be positive that he is not trying to create some pretext for falling upon us. . . . This dangerous state of affairs does not allow us to keep Alfonso XIII's secret to ourselves. The King of England, who has given us such strong proof of his friendship, must be informed at once: please be good enough to ask for an audience and tell him the facts which have just come to your knowledge. A talk with Edward VII seems to me both necessary and urgent—but I think it would be premature to mention the matter to the British Government.

Thursday, December 21st, 1905.

Paul Cambon was received in audience by the King of England yesterday and read him *in extenso* the report from our military attaché in Madrid. Edward VII showed the greatest interest, and occasionally 'signs of something approaching stupefaction,' during this recital: he immediately asked our ambassador:

"Have you mentioned this report to Sir Edward Grey?"

"No, and I shall not do so. This communication was not intended for the British Government. Royal confidences are not to be noised abroad and we cannot give the King of Spain away."

"But we must find some means of letting Grey know, and Campbell-Bannerman too.[1] I'll speak personally to Lascelles,[2] who is still here, and instruct him to clear this business up. . . . With a temperament like the Emperor William's I know that one can never be certain of anything; but I can't bring myself to believe in his intention of making war on you and I stick to my original opinion: it's probably only bluff."

It is none the less true that Alfonso XIII's words show that

(1) the Emperor William envisages the possibility of a war;
(2) he has asked the King of Spain to promise him something more than benevolent neutrality;
(3) Alfonso XIII is apprehensive that public opinon in his country will compel him to enter the fray.

Edward VII has thought it advisable to have instructions sent to his ambassador in Spain, Sir Arthur Nicolson, to support the young King in his resistance to the Emperor William's efforts.

As the audience was ending, Paul Cambon discreetly broached the topic of a military alliance:

"Your Majesty may remember that, at the beginning of last June, this serious question was the subject of secret discussions between Lord Lansdowne and myself. They were interrupted by M. Delcassé's fall: I don't know whether the new Cabinet would be disposed to resume them, and I am wondering whether I should ask my government for appropriate instructions."

"By all means do so. I know your government will authorize you to discuss all that with Grey. It would be very useful."

Friday, December 22, 1905.

While Paul Cambon was having his audience with Edward VII the day before yesterday, Major Huguet, our military attaché, was officially engaged with General Grierson, Director of Military

---

[1] A Liberal Cabinet had just succeeded the Conservative Cabinet. Sir Henry Campbell-Bannerman had taken Balfour's place and Sir Edward Grey that of Lord Lansdowne.

[2] British Ambassador in Berlin.

Operations at the War Office, in working out a scheme for Anglo-French co-operation against Germany.

The following is a summary of General Grierson's statements:

"We have got out a scheme for landing 115,000 men (three army corps and four cavalry brigades) at Antwerp. This army could cover Brussels between the twelfth and twenty-first days of mobilization. . . . We have also provided that two divisions, drawn from Gibraltar, Malta and Egypt, could land at Marseilles on the eighteenth day of mobilization. The British Army would join up with the Belgian, close to Brussels, and from there advance against the right flank of the German Armies. If the Belgian Government would not allow us to land at Antwerp the British Army would land in the Channel ports and proceed to join up with the left wing of the French armies."

Saturday, December 23rd, 1905.

This morning, Rouvier asked me to remind him in detail of all we know of Germany's aggressive designs and strategic plans against France. I complied with his request. While he still had in his hand the memorandum in which I had recorded the revelations of the *Avenger*, he suddenly said:

"It's obvious that the English alliance is indispensable; it has become a national necessity for us. I am going to authorize Paul Cambon to resume the secret *pourparlers*."

Force of circumstances has thus brought Rouvier round to the practical conclusions at which Delcassé had arrived.

After a conference with Georges Louis, he sent the following telegram to Paul Cambon:

I am of opinion that you should go ahead with the conversations, as King Edward advised you. It must of course be understood that there can be no question of concluding an immediate and binding agreement, which must be avoided, and you must make it clear that your sole object is to satisfy yourself that such an agreement could speedily be reached if the necessity arose.

The telegram, as drafted by the Political Director, stopped there. Rouvier, still worried, no doubt, by his recent apprehensions, thought it his duty to add in his own hand: *even if the present intentions of the British Government are so certain as to render such an agreement superfluous.*

Tuesday, January 2nd, 1906.

The King of Spain has, in strict confidence, just given our ambassador, Jules Cambon, some curious details about his recent visit to Berlin.

"The Emperor William," he said, "reminded me of a promise given by my father to his grandfather to mass 200,000 men on our frontier in order to tie up two French army corps in the region of the Pyrenees. He wanted me to make the same promise. I replied that the situation was very different from what it was in 1885. But, if war broke out between France and Germany, it was likely that all the powers would mobilize from fear of the conflict becoming general. In that case, Spain would do the same as other countries. But, if you see us concentrating 100,000 men in the Pyrenees, you've nothing to fear, and you can tell your government so at once. It need not leave a single man on our frontier. I give you my word of honour, the word of a King, that no Spaniard shall cross the border. . . . William II also spoke of a possible war with France. He and his officers have no doubt of a speedy success; they think they'll get to Paris *as easily as by rail. . . .*"

Thursday, January 4th, 1906.

Admiral Sir John Fisher, First Naval Lord of the Admiralty, recently received our naval attaché, Captain Mercier de Lostende, and told him that the policy of Germany was causing the greatest uneasiness in England. After pledging him to secrecy, he continued:

"I don't think war will break out this time, but I've made arrangements so that England shall be prepared for all eventualities. Germany will certainly attack without warning or any declaration of war. The Germans would no doubt like to imitate the Japanese; they will suddenly send out their destroyers against your ships and ports. I feel certain you won't be caught napping but will always be ready to repel an attack of that kind. . . . Next week I am issuing an order for the mobilization of all our available destroyers and I shall concentrate them at Dover. I shall concentrate all our submarines there too. To explain these movements to the public, I shall announce that they are there for flotilla exercises. Our Atlantic Squadron, which is off the English coast, will remain there until further orders. The Second Armoured Cruiser Squadron, which is at Gibraltar, is being recalled to the Channel; I shall give out that this is in view of the approaching election. The Channel Squadron, which has just left, is at Vigo; but Vigo is not far from Brest, and I shall not let it go further south. . . . If we must unite all our squadrons, Admiral Sir Arthur Wilson will be appointed Commander-in-Chief. With such a leader, I'll promise you that our fleet will be in good hands. . . . The first essential is to prevent the German ships from passing through the Straits of Dover."

Sir John Fisher concluded in a fine strain of British pride:

"If we have to fight Germany, she will soon have not a ship or a Colony left. . . . Our intelligence is splendid and we know from day to day and hour to hour where all the great German liners are; we'll go and cut them off. If the German squadrons leave their harbours, we'll fight them and destroy them. If they dare not come out, we'll harry them in every possible way until they do."

When telling me of this conversation, Rouvier said:

"That's a text Berlin would do well to ponder over!"

"Yes, indeed. But if the Emperor William is to preach on that text, he'll have to make some slight alteration in his resounding phrase: *Germany's future is on the water.* He had better say: *If England comes out against us, Germany's future will be in the water.*"

Friday, January 5th, 1906.

The President of the Council, the President of the Senate, the President of the Chamber and the Presidents of the Parliamentary Finance Committees have been in secret session the last few days, listening to the Minister of War who has asked for a supplementary credit of sixty million francs, to be expended on eighty additional batteries of artillery, the construction of fortified works and various supply services.

The credit was immediately granted, in a form which will not betray the purposes for which it is required.

Saturday, January 6th, 1906.

Three days ago, Sir Edward Grey was talking to Count Metternich and said in grave tones:

"I won't conceal from you that I am extremely uneasy about the state of Europe, and it is my duty to tell you plainly that *if Germany attacked France, the pressure of public opinion would be such that the British Government could only yield and make common cause with France."*

Thursday, January 11th, 1906.

Yesterday, Paul Cambon, citing the King's strong opinions as his authority, categorically asked Sir Edward Grey:

"If Germany attacked France, could the Government of the Republic count on England for aid and—to be more precise—the cooperation of the British forces?"

Sir Edward Grey did not seem surprised at this question, but said that he did not think he was in a position to reply before consulting his colleagues in the Cabinet. In any case, it would be necessary to wait until the approaching elections were over before embarking on the discussion of so grave a matter. The Government needed to know the verdict of the nation before it could decide on its line of action. The Secretary of State did not confine himself to these ambiguous statements; he continued:

"I think myself that the feelings of the English nation towards your country have become such that, if Germany attacked you, our public opinion would pronounce promptly and loudly in favour of helping France."

Reassured by the candour and vigour of such language, Cambon resumed:

"You know that the anxieties of recent months made it necessary for the General Staffs of our two countries to confer together, independently of their governments and in absolute secrecy, with a view to studying certain military and naval measures and strategic plans. Don't you think it would be a good thing if such discussions were resumed?"

"I see no objection."

Saturday, January 13th, 1906.

From three to six o'clock, I was with the Chief of Staff working out practical schemes to serve as a basis for our secret preparations for Franco-British cooperation against Germany.

General Brun gave me in broad outline his idea of the proper way of incorporating a British army in our line of battle to arrest the torrent of German invasion which may come sweeping through Belgium towards Maubeuge and the Valley of the Oise.

"I don't believe," he said, "that the British General Staff will be in a position for many years to send more than 120,000 men to the Continent. They should land at Dunkerque and Havre with a view to arriving on the banks of the Sambre at the earliest possible moment; I calculate that by the twelfth day they could be in position from Mons to Maubeuge, with their reserves round Valenciennes. . . . According to the revelations of the *Avenger*, it is probable that the Germans will already have passed Namur if they haven't yet reached Charleroi. . . . We can't have too many of our British allies to help us to withstand the fury of the first onslaught. . . ."

Then he enumerated all the measures we shall have to concert with the British War Office—landing the British troops in French ports; lines of communication; strategic unity with the French armies; relations of the allied staffs; supply and transport, hospitals, etc.

Tuesday, January 16th, 1906.

The Algeciras Conference held its inaugural session yesterday, the Duke of Almovodar, Minister of State, presiding.

In addition to Spain, whose guests the delegates are, twelve powers are represented—Germany, Austria-Hungary, Belgium, the United States, France, Great Britain, Italy, Morocco, the Netherlands, Portugal, Russia and Sweden.

The protagonists of this international tourney are as follows:

Germany: Herr von Radowitz, ambassador at Madrid.

The United States: Mr. Henry White, ambassador in Rome.

France: M. Révoil, ambassador at Berne.

Great Britain: Sir Arthur Nicolson, ambassador at Madrid.

Italy: The Marquis Visconti-Venosta, ex-President of the Council and Foreign Minister.

Russia: Count Cassini, ambassador at Madrid.

Morocco: El Hadj Mohammed Torres, delegate of the Sultan at Tangier.

Most of the plenipotentiaries had arrived by January 12th in order to get settled in their quarters in the little town. Of course they had been talking among each other. One impression clearly emerges from these first contacts—that Germany, which not only suggested the conference but actually forced it upon us, shows no sign of compromise or the slightest desire for accommodation.

Monday, January 22nd, 1906.

General Brun has spent two hours in my room, working on the Franco-Russian alliance and considering how far the convention of 1892 and the supplementary conventions remain in force. General Palitsin, General Sakharov's successor at the General Staff in St. Petersburg, is showing himself very well disposed towards us and freely offering us anything in his power to offer . . . not very much, unfortunately! But we think that, barring a revolutionary outbreak, Russia will be able within three or four years to attract a substantial proportion of the germanic forces to herself and even invade East Prussia. Further, General Palitsin assures us that, even now, our ally would not remain inactive if Germany attacked France; she would loyally do whatever she could. As for the form that would take, the Russian Chief of Staff was studying a scheme which he would put before us about April 15th.

From Russia we passed to Italy:

"I suppose," said General Brun, "that we can absolutely count on Italy's remaining neutral in a Franco-German war?"

"Oh, yes! The secret agreement of November 1st, 1902, is explicit: *In the case of France becoming the object of aggression, direct or indirect, Italy will maintain strict neutrality.*"

He then described the latest arrangements for swiftly transferring the army corps guarding the Alpine frontier to the Vosges frontier.

"But why," he added, "does Italy remain allied with Austria and Germany now that she realizes that, in a European War, her national interests would oblige her to throw in her lot with us? Obviously, her *strict neutrality* towards us would only be a prelude to the desertion of the Triple Alliance."

"I don't doubt for a moment that, in a European crisis, Italy would either have to attack Austria or renounce her national aspirations for ever. But we oughtn't to want her to come out openly on our side at the present moment; if she did, we should have to protect her against Austria. The mere fact that she is still a member of the Triple Alliance keeps her safe from the German powers. What matters to us is to know that she is determined to leave them. You may be quite certain that she will. . . ."

The Chief of Staff concluded by telling me privately that, in anticipation of a German offensive 'north of Verdun,' our zone of concentration will now extend to Vouziers. This 'variation' of *Plan XV*, which the Generalissimo has ordered, will be notified to the *Conseil Supérieur de la Guerre*, which is to meet on February 6th. Then General Brun bent over the map before us and said:

"If the revelations of the *Avenger* are true, obviously the centre of gravity of our concentration should be much further north. The extreme left of our line should extend to Vervins and Hirson. But is the *Avenger* simply setting a trap? Hasn't he merely *pretended* to betray his country? General Brugère still refuses to believe that the German General Staff has made up its mind to pass through Belgium to reach the valley of the Oise and sweep down on Paris. . . . I admit that I too am disconcerted by the amazing scale of this enveloping movement, which must necessarily develop in stages astride the Meuse."

Monday, January 29th, 1906.

The Emperor William's birthday[1] has furnished the German nation with another opportunity of showing exactly what rabid nationalism can mean in the way of haughty infatuation.

Let us see to what heights Count von Balestrem can rise at a parliamentary dinner:

"To preserve the peace of the world—for we do not go in for anything less than world politics in these days—let us be strong. Yes, we must be strong if we are to suppress all those who would like to disturb the peace. In any case, the powers will take good care not to move if they know that they will be beaten by the first army in the world and a fleet which is increasing every day. . . . The Reichstag must vigorously support the Emperor's policy and not haggle with him over the money he thinks necessary. We have a marvellous emperor whom other nations envy us; sometimes they cannot even conceal their spite and jealousy because they have not such a sovereign at their head. So we shall continue firmly to support our Emperor's policy, both to please him and for the greater good of Germany!"

Tuesday, February 13th, 1906.

The Algerciras negotiations are not taking a favourable turn for

[1] He was born on January 27th, 1859.

Germany, who has succeeded in ranging all Europe—except Austria, of course—against her.

William II is very irritated about it. He realizes that he made a fearful mistake in insisting that the Moroccan question should be submitted to an international areopagus. He thought he could break the ring of our alliances and friendships; he has only strengthened it. He believed he could frighten us with his threats and bellicose rhodomontade; he sees that we face with equanimity the prospect of a recourse to arms.

So, to conceal the humiliating failure of his policy, he has actually conceived the idea of reopening direct negotiations between Berlin and Paris, with a vague hope of getting round us by fair words! To that end, Prince von Radolin asked the minister for a special audience today. He was admitted at once.

After a series of honeyed phrases and a few pained remarks about the tone of the French press towards Germany, the ambassador tried to introduce a discussion of the problems now before the Algerciras conference, and therefore outside his competence. Rouvier absolutely declined to entertain his proposal:

"At your Government's obstinate insistence," he said, "I agreed to withdraw over the Moroccan question and submit it to a European tribunal. You know what it cost me to accept that course. Nevertheless I agreed, because it seemed to me a way out which was compatible with the honour of France while sparing the susceptibilities of your country. I have not changed my opinion. I will not consent to reopen direct negotiations between Paris and Berlin while the Algeciras conference is in progress."

The ambassador gravely pulled some papers out of his pocket:

"The Imperial Chancery has sent me three notes on the Moroccan question; I should like to read them to you."

"No, I cannot let you. Your Government wanted the Moroccan question submitted to a European conference: I won't discuss it again with you."

The startled Radolin protested:

"But I have orders to read you these notes."

"You're wasting your time. My answer is final!"

The ambassador rose with a dignified air, tried to smile by way of farewell and then went to the door, looking very haughty, disgusted and annoyed.

As the minister told me this story, he was beaming with pleasure and pride—the pleasure and pride of a boxer who has got in a beauty.

Wednesday, February 28th, 1906.

Last Thursday, our ambassador in St. Petersburg had a long conversation with Nicholas II. *Apropos* of the Moroccan question, they fell to talking about the Emperor William and his unhealthy restlessness, provocative conceit and habit of lying:

"Prince von Bülow and Prince von Radolin," said Bompard, "have given us in his name the most comforting assurances and conciliatory promises. Not one has materialized. We regard his word as worthless now."

Nicholas II replied in firm, sincere tones, as if he were anxious to ease his conscience:

"Unfortunately, I can only agree with you. William has often assured me too of his conciliatory intentions towards your country. When we met on our yachts at Björko he told me categorically that he desired nothing so much as friendly relations with France; he has frequently written to me in the same strain since; his last letter tells the same story. I must admit that I don't understand his present behaviour at all; it absolutely gives the lie to all the promises he has made me."

Talking to the Russian Ambassador yesterday evening, Rouvier told him of these remarks of Nicholas II. After a moment's thought, the sagacious Nelidov said gravely:

"I am very, very glad that His Majesty told M. Bompard what he thinks. We cannot distrust the Emperor William too much; his dangerous restlessness makes me more and more uneasy: he is leading Germany into evil ways. . . . If God grants me a few more years of life, I'm afraid I shall see terrible things."

Friday, August 3, 1906.

While the General Staff in Berlin is planning the invasion of Belgium for the purpose of annihilating France, the General Staff in Vienna is planning the invasion of Serbia for the purpose of establishing Austro-Hungarian domination in the Balkan Peninsula.

It has long been known that the Hapsburg monarchy had visions of forcing its way to Salonica some day. But it would seem that for some months—ever since Russia's misfortunes in the Far

East have condemned her to a long period of inactivity in Europe —that vision has begun to take shape. We have had frequent reports, for instance, of Austrian spies exploring the northern approaches to Macedonia, the Sandjak of Novi-Bazar, the Kopao-

MAP TO ILLUSTRATE THE AUSTRO-HUNGARIAN GENERAL STAFF'S PLANS FOR MILITARY OFFENSIVE IN THE BALKAN PENINSULA, AUGUST 3RD, 1906

nik *massif*, the upper valleys of the Ibar and Morava—in a word, the whole of the region which an Austro-Hungarian Army would have to traverse to reach Uskub, the Vardar and the Ægean Sea.

I have just been given an anonymous brochure, recently published in Vienna, with the title: *Mazedonien, Eine militär-politische Studie*. According to a reliable source, the author is an officer on the General Staff; he has been the mouthpiece of his general, von Beck.

The whole study is based on the theorem that Austria-Hungary will become the undisputed mistress of the Mediterranean the moment she is firmly installed in the Mitrovitza-Nish-Kumanovo-Uskub quadrilateral. To achieve that object, 400,000 men would be required—but how could the concentration of so large a force be effected in that region?

The bad roads across the Sandjak of Novi-Bazar would obviously be inadequate. Four divisions (about 60,000 men) at most could use them and they would not be able to take more than mountain guns and light transport with them.

To an Austrian army intended for operations in Macedonia, a passage through Serbia is thus a strategic necessity.

On reaching the confluence of the two Moravas, such an army would find four routes open to invasion:

(1) The road from Raska to Mitrovitza by the valley of the Ibar;
(2) The road from Nish to Pristina via Prokuplie;
(3) The road from Leskovatz to Gilan via Vranja;
(4) The Nish-Uskub railway via Kumanovo.

These four routes would amply suffice for the supply and transport of the troops.

The author of the brochure concludes that the invasion of Serbian territory must be the *essential preliminary* to Austro-Hungarian intervention in the Balkan Peninsula.

Wednesday, September 12th, 1906.

I called on General Brun, who has just come from the annual manœuvres of the 1st and 2nd Corps in the Senlis-Compiègne-Soissons region.

Among the foreign officers invited to these manœuvres were an English mission and a Belgian mission. The leader of the former was Lieutenant-General Sir John French, commanding Aldershot camp, and secretly selected as *generalissimo* in the event of war; he was accompanied by Major-General Grierson, Director of Military Operations at the War Office. The officer commanding the Belgian mission was Major-General Ducarne, Chief of Staff.

Between September 6th and 9th, General Brun had several talks with Generals French and Grierson, who spontaneously brought the conversation round to the future cooperation of the British and French Armies against Germany:

"We have no doubt," they told him, "that Germany will commence hostilities by a powerful offensive in the direction of Liége and Namur, with the object of reaching the valley of the Oise and marching straight on Paris. Nor do we doubt that, in that case, you could count on us to give you the most speedy and vigorous assistance. . . ."

According to General Grierson, the strength of the expeditionary force would not exceed 100,000 men, at any rate at the start. Whether they should be landed at Antwerp and Ostend, or in the French ports, must be left to the future to decide.

General Brun urged the advantages of landing these men on the French coast, from Havre to Dunkerque.

General Grierson appeared very anxious to know where the junction of the British contingent with the French Armies would take place:

"Where will our troops be? . . . On the Aisne, round Vouziers? or the Oise, near Hirson?—or the Sambre, in the vicinity of Aulnoye? . . . I will not conceal from you that public opinion at home would want us to be fighting on Belgian soil at the outset of hostilities; for if we entered the war, it would mainly be to defend Belgian neutrality, which we have guaranteed. Looking at it solely from our own point of view, I should prefer that, as soon as our troops are landed, they shall take up a position between the Meuse and the Sambre, from Mezières to Hirson, or better still—on the Sambre itself, from Maubeuge to Charleroi. From there they could advance on Namur and Dinant."

General Brun replied that our scheme of concentration provided that the British contingent should extend the left wing of our armies on the banks of the Aisne in the vicinity of Vouziers, but that, if operations in Belgium became necessary, the British contingent should be the first to enter that country.

As a matter of fact, General Ducarne has informed General Brun that, at the request of the British Government, he has just been considering the best way of railing 100,000 British troops, landing either in Belgian or French ports, so that they can concentrate north of the Sambre, between Mons and Charleroi.

Starting from that base, they would proceed to the Namur-Dinant front from which they would advance to meet the enemy side by side with the French Armies.

General Brun told me in conclusion:

"The talks I have just had seem to me full of promise for the future. If they continue in the same spirit, our strategic position *vis-à-vis* Germany will be greatly improved."

"What interests me most in these conversations," I observed, "is that I recognize the germ of an idea which Delcassé has very often mentioned. I think it is perfectly true: *If Germany invades Belgium, it is on Belgian soil that France and England will have to defend Belgian neutrality.*"

Thursday, November 29th, 1906.

Delcassé came to see me at nine o'clock this morning.

"I wanted to find out what you know of a subject about which one of my English friends, a man on whom I can implicitly rely, has just written to me in guarded terms; he says that our two General Staffs have signed, or are about to sign, a military convention, the main object of which is said to be the defence of Belgian territory against a German offensive. Such a defence would naturally involve French and British forces entering Belgium at the very outset of hostilities. That at any rate seems to me the sense of the somewhat sibylline language used by my London informant. How much truth is there in it?"

I reported the latest stage in the conversations in progress between our General Staff and the War Office, stressing the significance of the remarks of Generals French and Grierson to General Brun at the Compiègne manœuvres. *Public opinion at home would want us to be fighting on Belgian soil at the outset of hostilities, for, if we entered the war, it would mainly be to defend Belgian neutrality, which we have guaranteed.*

"That's splendid," he cried. "But I hope we shan't stop there, and that before long we shall have as specific, formal and binding an agreement as the Franco-Russian convention, and one which will provide for the simultaneous entrance of the French and British forces into Belgium the moment the enemy's advance-guard crosses the Belgian frontier."

We then discussed the great speech which Prince von Bülow recently made in the Reichstag. Delcassé said:

"This hypocritical knave (you know that in my eyes Bülow is as bad as his master) has been displaying all his arts and graces to dissipate the anxieties which German policy has roused all over Europe. But did you notice the threatening tone of his final tirade? *'The* entente cordiale *between France and England, without good relations between those powers and Germany, would be a menace to the cause of peace. A policy aiming at encircling Germany in order to isolate and paralyse her would be very dangerous. . . ."* In speaking thus, Bülow seems quite ignorant of the fact that, but for the provocations of German diplomacy and the megalomania of William II, there would have been no *entente cordiale.* From the moment when Germany tried to thwart the conclusion of an Anglo-French agreement—a limited agreement which was in no way aimed at her—she brought England and France together, so far as general foreign policy is concerned. If there's a Franco-British alliance before long, of which I have no doubt, Bülow will have forged it with his own hands. And that's what that fool William has made him a prince for!"

And then he said:

"I believe more than ever that the Kaiser's policy is leading us to a European conflagration."

He added mysteriously in a low voice:

"I know on good authority that it is Edward VII's opinion too."

"Oh! Hasn't his opinion altered since the Kronberg interview?" [1]

"No. Despite the presence of Tschirsky and Lascelles at Homburg, the only matters discussed were unimportant—the Eastern Question, the Baghdad railway, etc. As a matter of fact, Edward VII was only in Kronberg for twenty-four hours. His talks with William II were only brief, and confined to commonplaces. . . . What makes our friend Edward so anxious about the future is the opinion he has long held of the Emperor's character. Quite recently, he said to one of his close friends, who repeated his words to me in confidence: 'Through his incredible conceit, my nephew plays into the hands of the nationalist toadies around

[1] On August 15th, 1906, Edward VII and William II met at the Castle of Friedrichshof at Kronberg, near Homburg. The British Ambassador in Berlin, Sir Francis Lascelles, and Tschirsky, the Foreign Secretary, accompanied their sovereigns.

him who are never tired of telling him that he's the greatest monarch on earth and should make the world admit the supremacy of Germany, and so on. . . . But, as he's even more cowardly than conceited, he will tremble before these toadies when, under pressure from the General Staff, they summon him to draw the sword; he won't have the courage to bring them to their senses. He will feebly do what they tell him. If he starts a war, it will not be of his own volition, nor out of martial bravado, but through sheer weakness of character."

Delcassé ended by talking about Russia, whose rapid recovery he is already prophesying:

"A revolution," he said, "has been averted; the anarchist parties have obviously been reduced to impotence; all the leaders have been shot or hung; Stolypin's courage and energy have saved Tsarism. The agrarian reforms have been well received by the peasants; industry is in full swing again; public finance is on the mend. It won't be long before our ally plays a great part in European politics again."

As I tried to moderate the optimism of this prediction, he immediately continued in a serious tone:

"Pray Heaven that I am not mistaken, for it will certainly take nothing less than a close coalition of France, Russia and England to withstand the formidable onslaught which the germanic empires have in store for us."

INDEX